6
Steps
to
$1
Million

Also by Gordon Pape

6

Steps

to

$1

Million

How to Achieve Your Financial Dreams

VIKING
CANADA

To my children and grandchildren:

May all your dreams come true.

VIKING CANADA
Published by the Penguin Group
Penguin Books, a division of Pearson Canada, 10 Alcorn Avenue, Toronto, Ontario, Canada M4V 3B2
Penguin Books Ltd, 80 Strand, London WC2R 0RL, England
Penguin Putnam Inc., 375 Hudson Street, New York, New York 10014, U.S.A.
Penguin Books Australia Ltd, 250 Camberwell Road, Camberwell, Victoria 3124, Australia
Penguin Books India (P) Ltd, 11, Community Centre, Panchsheel Park, New Delhi – 110 017, India
Penguin Books (NZ) Ltd, cnr Rosedale and Airborne Roads, Albany, Auckland 1310, New Zealand
Penguin Books (South Africa) (Pty) Ltd, 24 Sturdee Avenue, Rosebank 2196, South Africa

Penguin Books Ltd, Registered Offices: 80 Strand, London WC2R 0RL, England

First published in Prentice Hall Canada hardcover by Pearson PTR Canada, a division of Pearson Canada, 2001

Published in Viking Canada paperback (by Penguin Books, a division of Pearson Canada), 2002

10 9 8 7 6 5 4 3 2 1

Copyright © Gordon Pape Enterprises Ltd., 2001

Manufactured in Canada.

NATIONAL LIBRARY OF CANADA CATALOGUING IN PUBLICATION DATA

Pape, Gordon, 1936–
    6 steps to $1 million : how to achieve your financial dreams / Gordon Pape.

Includes index.
ISBN 0-670-04351-6

    1. Finance, Personal. 2. Saving and investment. I. Title. I. Title: Six steps to one million dollars.

HG179.P376 2002   332.024'01   C2002-902671-7

ATTENTION: CORPORATIONS
Books are available at quantity discounts with bulk purchase for educational, business, or sales promotional use. For information, please email or write to: Penguin Books, 10 Alcorn Avenue, Suite 304, M4V 3B2. Email: lorraine.kelly@penguin.ca. Please supply: title of book, ISBN, quantity, how the book will be used, date needed.

Visit Penguin Books' website at **www.penguin.ca**

Contents

Preface

You bought this book because you believed it would help you to achieve financial success – specifically, to accumulate personal wealth of at least $1 million. I believe that, together, we can do exactly that. But I hope to be able to take you beyond that. I'm not talking about the second million. I'm talking about developing an approach to life that will allow you to enjoy the advantages of your wealth to the fullest.

Life is not simply a pursuit of money. If it were, why aren't all rich people happy? Why do so many wealthy people end up in failed marriages, on drugs, or by losing everything? We've all read stories about lottery winners who walked away with millions only to end up penniless a few years later. That's not what I want to happen to you.

Why do so many rich people fail at life? Because they are one-dimensional. They lack the qualities that are needed to take advantage of their good fortune. They don't know how to develop a satisfying and fulfilling lifestyle.

This book will not only show you how to become a millionaire in six steps. It will also help you to become a three-dimensional person. Your goal should be not only to achieve wealth, but also to find satisfaction and fulfillment in it.

So we have twin objectives here: material wealth and personal contentment. I don't claim to have all the answers – I don't believe anyone does. But I've learned a lot in my

65 years on this Earth. And I regard my own life as a material and spiritual success, by the standards I've set.

The key, of course, is which standards you use.

Success means different things to different people. For some, it's purely a synonym for material goods – the "I have more toys than you" approach to life. For others, success is measured in family terms – maintaining harmonious relations between husband and wife while raising decent, caring, motivated children in an increasingly difficult environment.

Some people define success in job terms. The higher you rise within your chosen field, the more successful you are. Or success may be defined in terms of the good one does for others. There are many people in the world who regard their lives as fulfilled if they alleviate suffering or improve the lot of those less fortunate.

The achieving of short-term goals is another common measuring stick for success. The goal may be financial, academic, athletic, romantic – it doesn't matter. Attaining it is regarded as success; not doing so is seen as failure.

The standard I'll be applying throughout this book is different. It is this: *Success is finding personal wealth and fulfillment through the optimum use of your talents.*

Or, to put it in simpler terms: Success is coming to the end of the road knowing you have done your absolute best.

Not a very demanding measuring stick, some might say. On the contrary, I believe it's the most difficult standard people can set for themselves.

I have seen many people living unhappy lives because they are too fearful or too lazy or too distracted to attempt to achieve the true goals of which they're capable. They don't understand their own inner genius (a concept we'll be discussing a lot in this book) or how to tap into it. The inevitable result is frustration, which leads in turn to an erosion in self-discipline, a breakdown in family relationships, and a loss of self-esteem.

To be the best you can is tough, there's no doubt about it. It requires you to explore your inner self in ways that may be uncomfortable at times, to understand your strengths and your weaknesses, and to use that knowledge to achieve focused lifetime objectives. It means nurturing and developing your talents, through education, personal experience, and overcoming challenges. It demands goal setting and self-discipline. It requires developing a support group of family, friends, and business associates – few people can achieve success in isolation.

It also requires knowing when to ease up, when to reduce the pressure, when to relax. You can never claim to have achieved success unless you are able to enjoy its fruits. "Money can't buy happiness," they say. No, it can't. But if you can blend money with a harmonious inner balance, the combination is hard to beat.

Clearly, achieving success is a lifetime occupation. But it's an immensely satisfying one, one that brings with it a sense of accomplishment and contentment.

And what's the alternative? A lifetime of wondering what might have been. That's not something I'd wish on my worst enemy. To my mind, that's the true hell!

Before I begin, some background is in order. Just who is Gordon Pape, and what gives him the credentials to write a book like this? And why should I, the reader, pay any attention to what he has to say?

Let me tell you.

I spent my early years in rural Michigan, in a historic country home that had been purchased in the 1920s by my father, Clifford Pape. He was a highly creative man who, without formal training of any kind, became an innovative research chemist. I still have in my possession some of the patents on processes he developed during the 1930s. These included special preservatives for nuts and citrus products to maintain freshness during shipment to northern markets and techniques for drying fruit, such as prunes and apricots. Dried fruit became a staple item for the military during World War II but by then my father had sold the rights for a pittance during the height of the Depression. I've never been sure whether that decision helped or hindered my personal development; would I have been as strongly motivated to achieve my lifetime goals if my family had been multi-millionaires from the outset?

Unfortunately, while he was doing all these things, my father never seemed to have much time for me. I remember him during my early years as a tall, aloof individual who travelled a lot and who left the day-to-day task of raising his only child to his wife. My rare encounters with him tended to coincide with occasions when punishment was required for some boyhood transgression.

My mother, who bore the unusual name of Lethe, was a good woman and loving parent. She was a cultured, sensitive person who played the baby grand piano in our living room and collected fine antiques. However, she had a fatal flaw – she was an alcoholic. She fought the disease as hard as she could, at times with some success. I remember as a child being taken to AA meetings in the evening because there were no babysitters anywhere near our remote country home. I didn't understand what those gatherings were about, and the people seemed somewhat rough-hewn, although kind. I do recall that they served good cookies. Some of these people would occasionally come to our home at odd hours of the night in response to what I later understood to be appeals for help from my mother.

Sadly, the fight was often more than she could handle. My father's lengthy absences and the isolation of our home were simply too much for her to bear. She was never cruel to me, never abused me in any way, even during her worst periods. But her behaviour was strange and erratic. She would become disoriented; she would get on the telephone and berate some local merchant in what, to a young child, was a most embarrassing way; she would insist on driving our ancient 1932 Studebaker to town, weaving from one side of the road to the other all the way while I cowered in the seat beside her (remember, this was long before seat belts were invented).

I believe that my father's prolonged absences and my mother's unpredictable behaviour were responsible for the development of a level of self-reliance in me far beyond what would normally be found in a young child. I had no siblings and my only boyhood friend lived about a mile away, so I spent much of my time alone. I became immersed in a world of books. My room was lined with shelves filled with standard boys' fare of the 1940s: the Hardy Boys, the Oz books, H. Rider Haggard potboilers, fairy tales, Lewis Carroll classics, and adventure stories of all descriptions. I loved comic books, from Walt Disney's Comics and Stories to Marvel Comics to the old Classic Comics, which served as my introduction to the world of serious literature.

There was no one to talk to but my dogs, but there was always the radio, and I was a voracious listener. My childhood friends included such wonderful characters as the Shadow, Jack Armstrong, Captain Midnight, Superman, Tom Mix, the Lone Ranger, Fred Allen, Jack Benny, Edgar Bergen, Charlie McCarthy, Amos and Andy, George Burns, Gracie Allen, the Detroit Tigers, and Walter Winchell (I loved his fast-paced delivery and his classic opening: "Good evening Mr. and Mrs. North America and all the ships at sea, let's go to press!"). I listened to everything and my imagination soared. Radio was a wonderful stimulus for a young mind; far more rewarding than the more confining demands of television, I believe.

Personal friendships were few. The area we lived in was farm country: fruit groves, corn, some dairy cattle. The children came from large families that often struggled to make ends meet. I was a freak; a cerebral, introverted child from somewhat mysterious, better-off-than-most parents who lived on a country estate and had no visible means of support. The kinder kids simply left me alone, unsure of what to make of me. The less kind bullied me at every opportunity.

It may sound like a miserable childhood, but it wasn't. My time alone taught me the priceless value of communication, of being able to touch and excite and influence other people's lives, whether through the printed page or the magic of radio. I have no doubt that my lifelong effort to develop my writing and speaking skills to their fullest potential was born out of those long days and nights in that lonely house in Michigan.

So, also, was my love of and fascination with nature. Much of my adult life has been spent in cities, but I have never lost my attraction to the natural world. In front of our home was a large bayou, where I observed myriad wildlife, from great blue herons to giant snapping turtles to bullfrogs as big as typewriters. It was there that I caught my first fish and captured my first aquatic creatures, water skimmers and other small insects that I kept in an old Mason jar for days until sympathy overcame me and I released them. The bayou was home to carp so big they churned the shallow water when they played. It was a place of water lilies and tangled seaweed and green algae, beneath which the bass would lurk. It was a biology lesson, a chemistry set, and a zoo, all rolled into one.

Behind the house was Lake Michigan, a nature observatory of a different kind. The wildlife wasn't as evident there; rather it was the lake that taught me respect for the forces of nature. I remember standing on the beach and watching in near terror as wind-whipped waves that seemed to reach to the sky rolled towards shore. I roamed the ice caves carved out of the bergs that formed along the shoreline in the wintertime, despite my mother's warnings to stay clear. I climbed the sand dunes, and explored the wreck of an old grain carrier destroyed in the autumn gales of the 1890s. I stood on the top of Pigeon Hill and listened in fascination as old Annie Abler, an ancient woman who lived down the road, fed me apricot pie and described how, when she was a child, the sky would be black with passenger pigeons crossing the lake. They would mass by the thousands on this, the highest point of land in the area, and the local farmers would come at night with their clubs to slaughter the resting birds for their delectable meat. "That was years ago," she said in her creaking voice. "The birds don't come any more." I still remember the puzzlement in her voice; she didn't understand why.

That love for the natural world has been a part of me ever since, and I regard it as an important ingredient in my personal success. It has provided a balance in my life, another dimension to the world of career and family. I can still sit in a boat on a lake, fly fishing for trout, and blot out the problems of the world from my mind. There is a calming, restorative effect in nature that I find nowhere else, and it has become a constant source of renewed energy for me.

As I entered my teens, the Michigan bubble burst. My father came upon hard times and underwent the heart-wrenching experience of selling off the family possessions: the baby grand, my mother's antiques, the furniture, and, finally, the home itself. He accepted a job with an aluminum fabricating company in Cap-de-la-Madeleine, Quebec, and I found myself rudely uprooted and transported into a French Canadian urban environment that was completely alien to anything I had previously experienced. For a short time, I foundered. Even though we now lived in a small city, I was more alone than ever. My books were gone, my radio stations were gone, what few friends I had were gone. We had to live in a tiny, one-bedroom apartment over a store on the main street of neighbouring Trois-Rivières, so I didn't even have the luxury of a room of my own where I could retreat. My bed was a couch in the living room; I fell asleep to the rhythm of a giant flashing neon sign directly outside the window.

I think Charles Dickens could have done wonders with this traumatic change in lifestyle – so many of his most memorable characters are young boys who fall on hard times: David Copperfield, Oliver Twist. So I find myself somewhat amazed to look back on this period and find it wasn't really as terrible as it sounds when I write about it years later. Children are resilient. They adapt. I was no different. The move to Canada undoubtedly was traumatic for my parents – my mother's struggles with the bottle became much worse. But after a short time I took it in stride. It turned out to be fortuitously timed, because I was at the stage in my life when I needed to break out of my enforced isolation and develop social skills.

My years at Three Rivers High School (to this day it defiantly retains its English name in a community that is 99 percent French-speaking) made this possible. They transformed me from a child recluse into a well-balanced teenager with the usual interests, from girls to sports. They also allowed me to start practising the communications skills I had recognized as being an essential part of my nature while in Michigan – my inner genius, as it turned out. I started writing the weekly High School Highlights column in the local English-language newspaper, I joined the debating team, and I became an accomplished public speaker, twice finishing second in a province-wide competition sponsored by the Rotary Clubs. My parents saw this as a remarkable transition from the quiet child they had known in Michigan. To me, it was nothing more than a natural maturation process, one that was perhaps more focused on specific skills because of the experiences of my younger years.

After university and a year in Europe, my goal was very simple: to find a job where I could practise these skills to earn a living. I wanted to be a writer, and the most obvious entry was through journalism. I was fortunate enough to land a position with *The Gazette* of Montreal and, after a brief period of writing obituaries and chasing fires, I was successively promoted to education writer, Quebec correspondent, Quebec bureau chief, and Ottawa correspondent. From Ottawa, I was posted to London for Southam News Services, where my responsibilities included everything from covering the rising tide of violence in Northern Ireland to writing feature stories while on safari in Africa.

The details of those years aren't important in the context of this book. What is important is that all those positions enabled me to hone my communications skills, to understand the techniques of translating complex ideas and events into comprehensible terms.

Those skills were critical to my career success. I learned that my real talent — the underlying inner genius that made all the rest possible — was communicating. But that's a broad field. There are many skilful communicators in the world who don't achieve millionaire status. The key is to go beyond simply recognizing that you have an ability. You must create a focus for that genius, just as you adjust a pair of binoculars to give you the clearest vision.

In my own case, the focusing process was a painful one. It began in the summer of 1982, when I was told I was about to lose my job. At the time, I had worked my way up the corporate ladder to the position of publisher of a national, newspaper-distributed magazine. The problem was that the magazine had become a perennial money-loser and the newspaper companies that owned it could no longer justify its existence. About 100 people were to be thrown out of work and, as the boss, I was the one who had to break the news to them. It was the most difficult day of my life, and I have been haunted by it ever since.

I delivered the bad news in June. By October, after overseeing the winding-down process, I was on the street.

Like so many other people who lost their jobs during that, and subsequent, recessions, I was shocked, hurt, and fearful. I had no idea what I would do. I was 46 years old, the sole breadwinner in the family. I had a wife, three teenaged children, a home with a $50,000 mortgage, and virtually no cash reserves (anything we'd saved along the way had gone into a retirement plan or towards paying down the mortgage principal). Given the state of the job market at the time, my prospects for finding another position were bleak.

But I did have two things going for me. One was a severance payment. The other was the insight I had gained over the years into my ability to communicate. As it turned out, they came together to open up a career I never would have envisaged.

Once the initial shock of being jobless was gone, I sat down with my wife and took stock. We discussed starting a full-scale job search, but the streets were full of out-of-work managers. I knew it would be a long, discouraging effort. There had to be an alternative.

At that point my wife reminded me of a boast I'd made during my days as a reporter: "Just give me a typewriter and I can make a living anywhere." Prove it, she said in effect. I decided to give it a try. I might not make a lot of money, but I could probably earn enough for us to live on.

That decided, the number one priority became the management of the severance money I'd received. It was not something I was particularly sanguine about. Most people are incompetent when it comes to handling their own financial affairs, and I was no exception. I've come to the conclusion that it's because we devote so much time and energy to the pursuit of our careers and family-raising that there's none left for anything else.

Certainly, I was that way. My investing record to that point was dismal. You're supposed to buy stocks low and sell high, right? I bought high and sold low. I had no clear investing philosophy, no objectives beyond making money, and no reason for choosing one particular security over another beyond the fact that my broker said it might be a good idea.

I tried giving some money to an investment counsellor to manage for me. That turned out to be a dismal failure, probably due to my own lack of understanding and my consequent inability to provide any clear guidance and direction. The result was the loss of about a third of my funds before I pulled my money out.

That's when my old reporter's instincts came to the fore. There had to be good information on money management out there. It was simply a matter of finding and using it. I started to research tax shelters but quickly found there wasn't much to research. Most of the material was either out of date, unintelligible to a layperson, misinformed, or promotional. I found little that was helpful.

That was the trigger. If I couldn't find helpful information, surely there were many thousands of other people in the same situation. I began looking into other financial topics, from stocks to mortgage management. Everywhere I turned, I was struck by the paucity of available information that was written in clear, easy-to-understand terms. There was obviously an opportunity here for someone with good communications skills. Talent and necessity began to merge. It was almost as if someone had erected a big sign in the road saying: This Way ☞.

That was how I finally got on track. In the years that followed, I built my personal wealth in two ways, both of which we will explore together in this book. The first was as an entrepreneur, using my communications skills to build a small financial communications company that publishes books, newsletters, and databases. The second was as an investor, putting my own advice into practice with gratifying success.

That's how I came to where I am today, and why I believe that the knowledge and experience I have accumulated can be helpful to others.

But there's another important dimension that needs to be mentioned before we move on: my family. I had the immense good fortune to marry a wonderful woman who turned out to be a perfect lifetime mate. We found each other in high school and have been together ever since. Without her support and love, my life would have been very different.

I'm not saying this as some kind of nice aside. I believe strong, loving support networks are absolutely essential to achieving material and personal success. Sure, there are loners who have made it to the top. But if you look behind the facade, you'll find that in almost every case they are intense, driven, unhappy people.

Your support network begins with your family. That's one of the reasons I've made it one of my primary goals in life to keep my small family as close and as harmonious as possible. When you need help or reassurance or support or love, that's where you should be able to turn first. But you can never take your family for granted. Just because you're related doesn't automatically make you friends. Family trust and affection must be earned. If it isn't, your family will gradually disintegrate and you will be left in the end with no one.

Beyond the family is a small circle of close friends. Most of us have very few of these. We have acquaintances — people with whom we can share a dinner or a golf game. But friends are different. Friends are the people with whom you can share problems and concerns and tragedies – the ones who will be around when you really need them. They are rare, and they are to be treasured.

I think that, by most objective measures, my life has been a success. But, even more important, it's been a success by my personal standards of evaluation. I have fulfilled the career goals I set for myself many years ago. I have been blessed with a fine family, who brings joy to my life every day. I have friends whom I deeply value. And, yes, I have achieved a measure of personal wealth. I have made my first million, and more, from a standing start.

That's why I feel qualified to write this book. Not because I'm super-rich (Warren Buffett or Bill Gates will never feel threatened by me). Not because I'm world-famous. Not because I consort with the powerful. Not because I have changed the course of history.

None of that. Rather, I write this book because I believe I have achieved what so many people seek – a fulfilled life and financial independence. And because I believe I can offer some advice and insight that will help you reach those same, elusive objectives.

As I said at the outset, I don't have all the answers – many have to come from within you. But if I can help point the way, then this book will have done its work.

Step 1

Stop Dreaming,
Start Acting

TV critics shook their heads in wonder. Producers warned it could sound the death knell of expensive television drama. Detractors set up spoof Regis Web sites. Audiences didn't care. They just loved the show. In fact, they couldn't get enough of it.

Week after week, month after month, *Who Wants to Be a Millionaire* topped the ratings charts in its first year on the air. ABC put it up against every blockbuster rival on the tube and it invariably walked off with the prize. Hardly a single week went by when *Millionaire* didn't occupy three of the top five slots in the Nielsen ratings. More often than not, it scored gold, silver, and bronze.

The show almost single-handedly revived the sagging fortunes of the Walt Disney Company, which owns ABC. In August 1999, when the program was launched, Disney shares were trading in the U.S.$25 range and the company was being hammered by financial analysts. Six months later, the stock was back over U.S.$40 and Disney's bottom line was looking better than it had in years!

Millionaire's ratings fell back a bit in the show's second full season as the novelty wore off, and ABC pushed the envelope by airing the show four times a week. But it still continued to draw huge audiences.

What was behind the astounding success of this prime-time game show? Certainly host Regis Philbin, an attractive TV personality, helped. So did the high-tech setting and the humorous early questions, which are designed mainly to keep the kids interested, although they occasionally catch unsuspecting contestants off guard (one man was eliminated at $100 when he said that Little Jack Horner had stuck his thumb into his Christmas pie and pulled out a – blackbird!).

Who Wants to Be a Millionaire? Everybody!

Why do so many people watch? Because at the core of the program's success lies everyone's secret dream: becoming rich. It's the same passion that drives us to buy lottery tickets and to play the slot machines. We want the big score. We want to be a millionaire!

And so there they were, squirming and agonizing under the relentless bright lights, flexing their hands for the next Fastest Finger Question. People just like us, with a chance, a real chance, to hit it big-time. Ordinary people. Housewives, college students, librarians, accountants, teachers, even the unemployed. Fat, thin, handsome, dowdy, attractive, introverted, gay, straight, moms, dads, sons, daughters – a cross-section of Middle America, all looking for lightning to strike, just once, right here.

The show itself might have been new, but the concept wasn't. Smart marketers have used the millionaire sales pitch for more than a century, for everything from selling magazine subscriptions to promoting Internet sites. They play to everyone's dream that one day we will achieve financial independence. Suddenly, we will be able to buy anything we want, go anywhere we want, do anything we want, give away anything we want. No more working at a job we hate, never again struggling to balance the cheque-book. We'd have it all.

Of course, most people believe in their heart of hearts that it will never happen. They play the lotto and hope for the best. "You can't win if you don't buy a ticket," is the rationale. But they know they won't really end up with the winning number. It's always someone else. When you wake up in the morning, it will be the same life. Nothing will have changed, except for the ripped-up ticket in the wastebasket.

Maybe that's true in your case. But maybe it isn't. I can't help you pick winning lottery numbers or get you on to a game show. But I can show you how to become a millionaire – if you're prepared to stop dreaming and start acting.

It won't happen overnight. There are very few instant millionaires in this world. But it will happen over time, if you really want to make it so. Not everyone will have the patience and the discipline to do it. I can't provide those qualities, although I believe I can give you the motivation necessary to seek them within yourself. If you can do your part, then together we can build your fortune.

As Regis would say, "Let's play!"

The Four Paths to Wealth

When you strip away all the frills, there are really only four basic ways to become a millionaire (legal ways, that is – we aren't including becoming a Mafia boss on this list). Your first priority is to decide which one is best suited to you, and then set out to make it happen.

Path #1: Win It

Become a contestant on a big-time game show. Hold the only winning ticket in the lottery. Be the 78th person to log into the Web site. Put your stickers in the right places and mail them off to the magazine folks. Collect all the letters under the soda pop tops. Play video poker all night. There are thousands of ways to do it.

Of course, the odds of ever actually winning the million, or anything more than $10, are hugely stacked against you. You're more likely to end up dead broke than you are with a million bucks. You're certainly letting yourself in for a lot of frustration and heartache. But some people can't resist the action. If that includes you, then this book will be of absolutely no use to you. Put it back on the shelf and invest the money in bingo cards.

Path #2: Inherit It

Much has been made about the "trillion-dollar generation" – the baby boomers who are in line to inherit a whopping amount of money from their parents over the next 20 years. Maybe that's your road to riches – but don't be too quick to make that assumption.

As with games of chance, there's a large element of luck involved here too. After all, you didn't choose your parents. But if there *is* wealth somewhere in your family, then you may be in line for a share of it. Don't get your hopes up too high, though. Several things can happen between now and the time the money reaches you.

For one, your wealthy parents (or other relatives) may spend most or all of it. People are living longer these days, and enjoying their later years more. I can't count the number of times I've heard someone say, as they were about to leave on an exotic trip, "We're off to spend our kids' inheritance." If they take enough of those trips, it won't be a joke any more.

Even if there's still some money left in the pot when the wealthy relative finally departs, the government may end up with more of it than you will. We don't have any estate taxes in Canada, but we might as well have. At death, any capital gains are deemed to have been realized and half of the profits will be taxed. All the money remaining in registered plans, such as RRSPs and RRIFs, will be considered as income when the last surviving spouse dies and taxed at a rate that may be close to 50 percent. The cottage up at the lake, if it's not a principal residence, may attract a large tax bill. And on and on.

After the Canada Customs and Revenue Agency finishes, anything that's left may be divided among several heirs. Your final share may be a mere pittance compared to the amount you'd been dreaming of. All in all, unless the family fortune is worth millions (in which case you wouldn't be reading this book), inherited money is probably not your ticket to great wealth.

Path #3: Create It

Now we're getting into more serious territory. Not everyone has the ability to create wealth, but if you are one of those who does, you should certainly take advantage of the opportunity.

Wealth creation in this context means the ability to earn large amounts of money with your mind and/or your talent. It encompasses everything from writing the great novel of the 21st century to starting an exciting new dot-com company and taking it public. Many people are blessed with the potential to create wealth – perhaps through a great voice, perhaps by being a masterful computer programmer, perhaps by being a top athlete – there are many possibilities.

The key to success, as everyone who has created their own wealth will tell you, is to believe in yourself. I doubt that you will find a single creative millionaire who does not have a story of adversity to tell. Other, less talented, people will simply not believe you can do it.

"You're wasting your time."

"Stop your daydreaming."

"No one can support a family doing that."

"It's about time you got serious and took some responsibility."

The litany of the naysayers is boundless. Thousands of movie plots revolve around the theme. That makes creating wealth the most difficult path of all. You not only have to make yourself believe you can do it, but you have to do so in the face of the negativism you will hear all around you. It can be a lonely road.

Path #4: Save It

That's right. It may be hard to believe, but you can save your way to a million dollars. Of course, this involves something more than throwing your spare change into a jam jar. You'll need to establish a disciplined savings plan, take advantage of every tax break available to you (and there aren't many), and invest the money wisely for steady, long-term growth.

But it can be done, even if you're starting relatively late in life. You've undoubtedly heard about how just $3,000 a year contributed to an RRSP starting at age 20 can grow into more than a million by age 65. It's actually true, and you don't need to be an investing genius to achieve that goal. An average annual return of just 7.5 percent will do the trick.

However, what if you're not 20 any more (and most of us aren't)? Have you blown this particular opportunity?

No way. But you have to save more and invest smarter. Even if you're pushing 50 and have little or nothing put away, you still have a decent crack at millionaire status by the time you retire. It's never too late (well, almost never).

Even if you never win a lottery, were born into a middle-income family, and have no particular creative or athletic genius, you can still save your way to a million – without seriously compromising your current lifestyle. In the pages that follow, you'll find all the information you need to get started on that road.

You'll also find some practical advice for those who want to create wealth through their own entrepreneurship – a route that has become more accessible in this era of the Internet and e-commerce.

But you won't find any more references to winning a million or inheriting a million. If either one of those is your preferred choice, you need a different book. It means you're not even willing to take the essential first step of this six-stage program: Stop Dreaming, Start Acting.

However, if you *are* ready to do that, and if you truly want to make a million while there's time to enjoy it, then let's move ahead.

The Value of Advice

Before we get too deeply into the millionaire quest, a word about the value (or otherwise) of advice. Lots of people will offer it. After all, it's free. The problem is that most of it is bad. The only thing worse than bad advice is paying attention to it.

The first test to apply to any advice you receive is to consider the credibility of the giver. Do you have any reason to believe that whatever this person is saying is based on a solid foundation — work experience, education, lifestyle, training, special relationships, remarkable intuition, or plain common sense?

Or are you listening to gossip, rumour, bias, off-the-cuff opinion, ignorance, fear, self-interest, or negativism? Of these, perhaps negativism is the worst because it instills doubt and promotes a loss of confidence.

"You want to be a millionaire! Why not something simple, like grow wings! Ha, ha, ha, ha, ha." Loud guffaws over a glass of beer. Your friend can't do it. So why should you ever hope to? You go home thinking how stupid you were to ever believe such a thing might be possible. Actually, you *are* stupid — but not for that reason. You're stupid because you let a friend's negativism destroy your dream before you even gave it a chance to succeed.

So apply the credibility test when advice or comment is offered, and be tough about it. Has this person achieved anything in life? I'm not talking strictly about money here; there are many successful people who aren't rich. They're successful because they have found the secret to a fulfilling and rewarding lifestyle, one that brings contentment to them and makes them a joy to those fortunate enough to be in their circle.

If the advice-giver does not pass the credibility test, then ignore what he or she has to say. Don't consider it. Don't brood about it. Under no circumstances apply it. Advice is only as good as its source. If the source is worthless, be guided accordingly.

Having said that, and since this book is full of my advice, it would seem appropriate that I offer my own credentials.

My wife and I are millionaires — a couple of times over, in fact. (I include her in this statement because our wealth is shared.)

I did not win it.

I did not come by it illegally.

I did not inherit it – although I might have had the fates taken a different turn. In the preface, I told you about my father, an eccentric genius who, among other inventions, developed a process for drying fruit (mainly prunes and apricots) while he was working in California in the early 1930s. Unfortunately, he sold all the patent rights at the height of the Great Depression for $5,000. Perhaps it seemed like a lot of money at the time, but those rights ended up being worth millions. My father's total estate at death was valued at around $30,000. He had been virtually wiped out financially when my mother had a stroke that left her partially paralyzed and bedridden for the last three years of her life. His company health insurance didn't cover the round-the-clock nursing care she required; he spent all his savings on retaining the services of two live-in nurses who converted our dining room into their own bed-sitting area. When he passed away in 1964, he didn't even own a home. Now you understand why I say that no one should count on an inheritance to become wealthy.

I became a millionaire through a combination of Path #3 (Create It) and Path #4 (Save It), the two paths this book will focus on. I didn't set out with the specific idea of becoming a millionaire. My initial financial goals were more basic – to own a home and to provide a decent lifestyle for my family.

Relatively modest as they may sound, they were not easy to attain. The home ownership part entailed some major sacrifices. Many young people have experienced first-hand the phenomenon of being house-poor. You give up almost every little luxury – even ordering takeout pizza becomes a budgetary challenge – in order to keep up with the mortgage payments. It's not easy, but like everything else in life, the rewards are there for those who persevere. Over time, however, we were able to achieve those initial goals and begin to dream new dreams.

At that point, the millionaire idea, while distant, began to look attainable – just as it can for you.

Dreams Are Not Enough

What do you dream about? We all have our personal fantasies – the kind of person we'd like to be, things we'd like to own, accomplishments we aspire towards, including that million dollars that is the goal of this book. Sometimes these wishes are unattainable – a 70-year-old who yearns to be 20 again isn't going to make it happen, no matter what he does. But often, dreams can come true. Not with wishing upon a star or fairy godmothers, but through planning, perseverance, and a large dose of hard work.

It happened to me. Here's how.

Ever since I was a kid, I wanted to write a novel. My mother was a member of the Book-of-the-Month Club. When the monthly promotion mailings came in, I'd read them with fascination, even though I couldn't have been more than 10 years old at the time. I was mesmerized by the exciting topics and the great literary names on offer.

One publishing house that caught my attention was The Viking Press. It was their logo that did it: a long ship with a set sail that conjured up images of adventure and romance in my impressionable young mind. Someday, I thought, I would write a book that would bear that same logo.

The years passed and my journalism career flourished. I travelled Canada and the world, writing about election campaigns, wars, great economic upheavals, and colourful personalities. But that childhood dream of writing a book with the Viking ship on the spine always lurked in the background, unfulfilled.

In my late 30s, I experienced a mid-life crisis. I know the idea is pooh-poohed by many people, but it happened to me. I went through the classic symptoms of questioning what my life was all about, where it was going, and what I hoped to accomplish with what remained of it. I remember spending most of one night staring at the fireplace and ruminating on the transitory nature of journalism. Yes, it was an exciting occupation. Yes, even after more than a decade it gave me a thrill to see my byline on the front page. But yesterday's papers are only good for the recycling box. What have you done for us today?

It was at that point that the dream of writing a novel resurfaced, along with the realization that if I didn't do something about it soon, it would never happen. I would go through life telling people about the great book I would write someday – and never actually do it.

It was the late 1970s and Quebec was much in the news. The Parti Québécois under René Lévesque has just been elected for the first time. The rest of Canada was suddenly seized with the separatist option and the United States, which normally regards Canada as a place where cold fronts originate, began to take notice of what was happening. Even *The Wall Street Journal* started writing about it.

I knew Quebec well, having spent several years as a correspondent for *The Gazette* in Quebec City. I spoke French, having lived in Quebec since age 13, I understood the politics of separatism, and I had interviewed all the key players, from Lévesque on down. Why not write a novel, using Quebec separation as the theme?

But I was holding down a full-time job as a magazine publisher. Actually, more than full time; the days were long, and by the time I got home I barely had enough energy to have dinner and read a bedtime story to the children. Where would I find the time?

If you want something in life badly enough, you must *make* the time. How often have you heard someone say, "I really would like to do thus and so, if only I could find the time." It's an excuse. If you can't make the time, then it isn't that important to you. It's only talk.

I *wanted* to write that novel. Since at the end of the day I was in a state of exhaustion, working on it at night was out of the question. The only other alternative was to get up at six in the morning and put in an hour or two of work before heading to the office.

So that's what I did. Progress was painfully slow for a while – maybe only four or five pages a day. But, gradually, the file folder holding the manuscript got fatter.

I realized early on in the process that I couldn't do it alone. While I had a good sense of plot and structure, my characterization and dialogue were weak – typical failings of a journalist whose responsibility is to report facts. I needed a partner who could bring to the table the skills that I lacked.

I found him in Tony Aspler, a novelist and wine connoisseur I had met during a stint in London as a foreign correspondent. Tony had returned to Canada as a CBC producer in Toronto. I invited him for a fishing weekend at a club in the Ottawa Valley, where I was a member. The weather was miserable, teeming with rain, but we went out on the lake anyway. As we sat in slickers, the rain running in rivulets down our bodies, I explained the plot idea and asked if he'd be interested in working with me. He was just as enthusiastic about the idea as I was, and our collaboration began.

Tony brought more than his great talent to the table. As a published novelist, he had a New York literary agent, to whom he sent a copy of the outline for *Chain Reaction*, our working title. I was in the midst of a heavy business meeting at the magazine one afternoon when I was told I had an urgent telephone call. It was Tony. He'd just heard from the agent. We'd been offered an advance of $40,000 for the novel. The publisher: The Viking Press!

Yes, it sounds made-up. Things like that don't happen in real life: a little boy's fantasies coming true. Yet dreams can come true, if they're founded in some kind of reality and you have the work ethic to make it real.

Those are the two keys. Obviously, your dream must be at least remotely within the realm of possibility. If you aren't blessed with natural speed, it's unlikely you'll become the world record holder for the hundred-metre dash. But even if you have all the talent required, it still won't happen unless you're prepared to work at it. And work hard.

Consider the world of athletics. There are many talented people in sports, but only a few make it to the top. Frequently we read stories about promising ball players who never made it to the majors. Often you'll find the explanation when a former manager is quoted as saying something like, "He just didn't have a good work ethic."

Making the Dream Come True

Sometimes, the more talent we have, the less we think we have to work. Things come easy; why strain?

The fact is that the greater your ability, the *harder* you should be working, because you have the potential to achieve so much more. Underperformance because of poor self-discipline is a waste of your natural ability.

Hard work isn't easy. It's tough to slog it out, day after day. But if you're going to reach that dream, you've got to do it. Here are a few tips that may make it easier. A reminder before you read them: Your dream must be within your power to attain. If your heart's desire is to win the Lotto 649, there's nothing I can do to help. That's pure chance.

1. *Believe it can happen.* As long as you think of your dream as an unattainable wish, it will never come true because you won't do anything to make it come true. The first step is to change your mind-set. You *must* believe that this desire can indeed become reality.

2. *Set a realistic goal.* Your dream can't be vague or open-ended. It must be defined in attainable terms. Mine was to write a novel. It wasn't to write a best-selling novel or to make a million dollars doing it, although that would have been nice. It was simply to prove to myself that I could actually do something that I'd always believed I could attain — but never attempted.

   Whatever your dream, begin by defining it in terms of a realistic, attainable goal. You want to run your own company? Decide what kind of company it is and what skills are needed to be successful at it. You want to spend a year sailing the Caribbean? Begin by learning how to sail on your local lake and finding out how much your project will cost. You want to own your own home? Figure out how much of a downpayment you can scrape together and find out what kind of house that will buy, and where. And to return to the main theme of this book: Your dream is to have a million dollars? Decide how you are going to achieve that goal. Then create a plan that will make it happen.

3. *Set a target date.* Dreams need a time frame, if you genuinely hope to attain them. So your next step in making it happen is to set a target date. Again, realism is essential. You will not be a millionaire by this time next year. Probably not in 5 years. But perhaps in 10, depending on where you're starting from. If it looks like a long-term proposition, then break it down into shorter segments. If your come-true date is too far in the future, you'll lose all motivation. Better to measure your progress in stages. That way, you'll be encouraged as the ultimate objective draws closer. So, for example, set a target date for when you want your net worth to have surpassed $50,000. Then $100,000. Then $250,000, and so on. That way you'll have a measurable success timetable. You'll know at a glance if you're on schedule, running ahead, or falling behind. That allows you to make adjustments along the way.

4. *Set aside a specific amount of time each day.* Treat the dream as your most important project. Set aside some time each day (a minimum of half an hour) to be used in making it happen. If you aren't prepared to commit time, you aren't serious about it. If you're devoting a lot of time to the project each week, as I was doing when I was working on my novel, take a holiday on weekends. You'll come back on Monday with a fresh mind and new enthusiasm.

5. *Get started.* Most dreams don't come true because people never make a start on them. They procrastinate. I'll get to it tomorrow ... tomorrow ... tomorrow.... Of course, tomorrows eventually run out. If you genuinely want that dream to happen, get started on it now.

6. *Be patient.* This is one of the most important things in your life. Don't expect it to happen overnight. If it did, you wouldn't value it. Put the pieces into place step by step, watch and record the progress, and keep moving forward. You'll get there.

7. *Don't be defeated by setbacks.* It probably won't always go smoothly. It rarely does. When a setback occurs, take the time to analyze why it happened and decide how to avoid the problem in future. Then go forward from there.

8. *Enjoy the anticipation.* One of the problems with dreams is that, once attained, they often lose their lustre. You've climbed to the top of the mountain, so now what? I see this all the time. A good friend of mine recently finished building the home he'd always wanted: a chateau-like house atop a Vancouver Island hill with magnificent vistas over arbutus tree forests, mountains, and a lake. Deer came to graze on the lawn at dawn, to the delight of his young children. By any measure, it's a spectacular home. But once it was done, there was a void that could be filled only by the creation of a new dream.

   The same thing happened to other friends in Florida. They'd retired from their New Jersey business and moved to Fort Myers Beach. They bought a run-down home and turned it into a magnificent bungalow, doing most of the work themselves. They built an addition to the house, added a swimming pool and lanai, redecorated the interior, landscaped the property, and ended up with a charming home. As if that weren't enough, they bought a ramshackle motel a few blocks away, fixed it up, and turned it into a thriving business. Great accomplishments for a retired couple. Dreams fulfilled. So what are they doing now? They sold the house and the motel, pulled up stakes, and moved west to Arizona. They plan to spend part of each year in Baja California, where they've bought a property and plan to build. A new dream.

   The point is that the anticipation of the dream and the moment of its fulfillment are likely to provide your greatest satisfaction. Once you've attained it, you'll likely start thinking about moving on, searching for the next mountaintop.

   "Nonsense," you may say. "If I can become a millionaire, that will be it. I won't need to dream any more. I'll have made it!"

   You think so? Has Bill Gates stopped dreaming? Has Steven Spielberg? I don't know a single millionaire in good health who is content to do nothing but vegetate on a yacht or play an occasional game of golf. There *will* be another mountain. That's the excitement of it!

It's the way we humans are made. As a poem I learned in school puts it, *"Clay lies still, but blood's a rover...."*

Now it's time to move ahead to Step Two: Get Rid of Unwanted Baggage. This is where you put the past behind and begin to position yourself for a completely new future. Let's get to it.

Step 2

Get Rid of
Unwanted Baggage

We all carry baggage. You can't go through life without acquiring it. Mental baggage, physical baggage, financial baggage, emotional baggage – it's all part of who we are. Some of the baggage is useful and valuable – your education, your work experience, your achievements to date, your positive relationships with family and friends, your social and business networks. But some of it is hurtful and potentially damaging to your future – mental scars from past traumas, events that shook your self-confidence, financial burdens, worries about the future, interpersonal conflicts, and bad working relationships, just to name a few.

Back in the days before jet planes, when travel between the continents was the exclusive realm of the great ocean liners, embarking passengers were asked to place tags on their luggage. One set of tags read "Wanted for the Voyage." Pieces with these tags were placed in the cabins. The other set read "Not Wanted on the Voyage." Luggage with this tag went into the ship's hold and was not seen again until arrival at the port of disembarkation.

Step Two of your Six Steps is sorting your baggage. It's deciding what you want to take with you on the voyage as we go forward, and what you want to eliminate.

Make no mistake about it: This is a critical step. If you allow unwanted baggage to slow you down, the chances of you achieving the goals that you establish will be greatly diminished. Just as the passengers on the great liners had to make hard decisions about what they really needed on the journey (because cabin space was cramped and luggage room was limited), so you have to make hard decisions about what you'll take with you and what you'll store away in the hold, perhaps not to be seen again for many years, if ever.

It's a process that may be somewhat painful and will almost certainly take some time. But once we've completed it, you'll be in the strongest position of your life and ready to tackle just about anything – including the challenge of becoming a millionaire!

Get Rid of Negative Thinking

Perhaps the most damaging piece of baggage you can carry with you is negativism. If you believe you cannot achieve something, believe me, you won't. Read the story of any successful person you choose, or watch the excellent *Biography* series on A&E. You'll find the same theme repeating again and again: These people believed in themselves, believed they could do it, and eventually they did. That doesn't mean they didn't have setbacks along the way or that it was all clear sailing. Of course it wasn't. They all had their stumbles, they all had their doubts. Many struggled for years without recognition or wealth or success, but they refused to believe that the goal would never be reached. Eventually, of course, it was.

The problem is that it takes great strength of mind to maintain a positive outlook when everything around you is going wrong. It's much easier to slip into a negative mindset, to tell yourself it was all a hopeless dream and you might as well forget it and get on with your life. But if you allow that to happen, you're lost. You will doom yourself and your family to a life of mediocrity and you will infect those around you with the same kind of negative thinking. As you grow older, you will discourage your children and grandchildren from reaching for their dreams and tell them instead to be realistic and accept their lot in life. You abandoned hope, after all, so why should you encourage others to embrace it?

Let me put this in the context of my own experience. In the preface, I told you about how I lost my job in 1982. What I didn't tell you was the mental anguish I went through.

I didn't know it was happening at the time, but in retrospect I realize I allowed myself to sink into a state of depression. For a year and a half, I went through the motions of earning a living by writing and continuing to raise my family. But inside, I was a wasteland. I was without a goal, without hope, without ambition. On numerous occasions, I allowed my mind to dwell on the possibility that my family would be better off without me, because of the life insurance policies I carried. I did not actually attempt suicide or even really come close to doing so. But the fact that I would not only think such negative thoughts but allow them such a prominent place in my psyche says much for my state of mind during that dark period. My wife found me to be increasingly remote, and I know I was not the father I should have been. But I was lost in a negative world and could see no way out.

Of course, I should have been getting professional help. But at the time, I wasn't aware that anything was seriously wrong with me. I thought I was simply going through what so many other displaced middle-class executives were going through at that time.

That was true, up to a point. But we all respond to adversity in different ways. This was the first time I had really been forced to confront it and my response was to sink into depression and negativism. There was no way out of this mess. My career was over before I was 50. My family would be better off with me ... dead!

Had I remained in that mindset, my life would have been very different and who knows how the story would have ended. Fortunately, I snapped out of it. I gradually came to the realization that I was in a downward spiral that was only going to get worse unless I did something about it. That awareness didn't come overnight; it was a process that took several months. But in the end I came to the conclusion that I was not a burnt-out case. I realized my communications skills were as good as ever. I decided I didn't want to jump off a bridge and leave my wife and children to fend for themselves as best they could. Most important, I came to the awareness that there were still things I wanted to do. I wanted to write. I wanted to see my children grow into fine adults. I wanted to be wealthy.

I didn't think of it as a specific dollar amount – a million or 10 million. Rather, I thought of it in terms of financial independence. I wanted to be in a position where losing a job would never again create a life crisis for me. I wanted to know we were secure and that I could work at what I most loved.

I decided to go out and find a new job and I was not going to settle for anything dull or mediocre. I found what I was looking for at Hume Publishing, where I was hired by the president, Hugh Furneaux (who has since become a lifelong friend), and given the title of publisher. My responsibilities included overseeing the company's highly successful financial newsletter, *The MoneyLetter*, which at the time was anchored by the irascible and indomitable Dr. Morton Shulman.

Morty, as we all called him, was one of those larger-than-life characters who strides across the landscape leaving his footprints everywhere (he died in 2000 after a long battle with Parkinson's disease). During his life he was a successful physician, a best-selling author , a TV talk show host, an elected politician, the inspiration for a television drama series, a multi-millionaire investor, a dedicated art collector, and a devoted oenophile. Above all, Morty was the embodiment of positive thinking. There was nothing he could not do if he set his mind to it. He even believed he could beat Parkinson's, and for years he held it at bay, at one point even importing a new drug from Europe that alleviated the symptoms and setting up a company to distribute it in Canada.

My exposure to Morty and to many of the other financial giants of the day through the advisory board of *The MoneyLetter* taught me much about the importance of positive thinking – not only for wealth building but for life. These people changed my way of looking at the world and opened up the door to a career that I never would have envisaged as possible.

You've probably heard the old saying, "As one door closes, another one opens." That's what happened to me here, and that's what happens so often in life.

A few years later, Hume decided to downsize its Canadian operation and concentrate the company's energies on expansion in the United States. I was laid off for the second time in five years. But this time when I went home, it was with a sense of elation, not depression. I saw this development as an opportunity, not a disaster. Why? Because now I had two advantages I didn't have before: the power of a positive mindset and two clear-cut goals. I was going to create my own financial communications empire and I was going to make myself very wealthy in the process.

I've dwelt on my own story at length because I believe it is essential that you understand the importance of getting rid of the baggage of negative thinking.

I will say it one more time. If you allow negativism to dominate your thinking, you will not succeed in this particular quest or in any other.

Many years ago, the New York Mets rode to a World Series title on the strength of Tug McGraw's memorable slogan, "You gotta believe." Let that be your slogan too. Because without belief, none of what follows will be of help.

Get Rid of Bad Habits

We all have our own way of doing things, our habits. We're comfortable with them and they establish a routine in our lives that for many people is very important. Your habits can be as simple as the time you get up in the morning, the way you organize your desk, or the programs you watch on television. Or they can be as complex as how you deal with conflict resolution, your method of interacting with your children, or your approach to budgeting.

Sometimes bad habits can get in the way of achieving a difficult goal. When the objective is to accumulate a million dollars, just one critical bad habit can delay or derail the whole process.

So let's spend a little time reviewing the bad habits that can create the greatest obstacles to this venture. At first glance, some of them may appear to have nothing to do with money or wealth. But believe me, they do.

Bad Habit #1: Procrastinating

Are you the sort of person who puts things off? Is your unofficial motto "Never do today what you can do tomorrow"? Do you wait until the last minute (or even later) to complete a project? Are you chronically late for meetings? Do you think that people who rush to get things done have allowed their lives to be ruled by clocks? If so, then you're a procrastinator first class. You're the type of person who will read this book (slowly), then put it down and say to yourself, "I must do something about that." You won't. Procrastinators rarely do. They talk a lot about what they are going to achieve. But they never manage to get there because to achieve, you first have to act. Procrastinators are not incapable of action, but they tend to act only when they are forced to do so. No one is going to force you to try to become a millionaire. So the chances are that you won't, unless you stow this piece of unwanted baggage in the hold.

How do you break this particular bad habit? Like all habits, it won't be easy. Procrastination has become a way of life for you. It's the way you operate. Asking you to change it is akin to insisting that a smoker quit cold turkey. The failure rate is high.

So let's try to make things a little easier. Don't set out to change everything overnight. You won't succeed. Instead, take it in small, bite-size doses. Start with something very simple. For example, make a promise to yourself to return all phone messages today, not tomorrow. That's all — at least to begin. It doesn't matter if the last message is returned after the business day has ended and all you can expect to get is an answering machine. Do it anyway. Leave the message to say you were very busy but did call back, and that you'll be available in the morning. The other person will know you made an effort. It counts for a lot.

If you can manage that first simple habit change, others will start to fall into place. It may take some time, but gradually you'll find yourself doing more things promptly – with results that will reinforce this change in your behaviour.

Along the way, make one of the changes a resolution to act on the plan you develop after reading this book. That could end up providing the greatest reward of all.

Bad Habit #2: Wasting Time

Time is the most precious commodity we have because it is finite. Once your sands have run out, it's over. So it's essential to make the best possible use of the time we have at our disposal. That does not mean working hard 24 hours a day, seven days a week. Life is a balance, and the proper use of time recognizes the need for the harmonious integration of the elements that make up that balance. Spending too much time on work is just as much a bad habit as spending too much time watching football or figure skating. Dying people never wish they had spent more time at the office. Quite the contrary.

So learning to apportion your time is essential. But apportion it to what? Of course, you must make time for work, for family, for recreation, for sleep. But to achieve the specific goal that we are addressing here, you also need to allocate some time to learning and planning.

That may appear to be stating the obvious, but this is exactly where many would-be millionaires fall by the way. "I just don't have the time," they say. The excuses are myriad. There are the demands of the job, the home, the family. They all have to take priority, after all.

Nothing is said, of course, about the demands of watching television between seven and eleven every night. Or about going to the bridge club or the bowling league once a week. Or about the need to spend hours with *People* magazine or *Sports Illustrated* or *Gourmet*. And how could anyone expect me to give up my computer games, or my weekly visit to the mall, or my fishing, or my … (fill in the blank).

Certainly, these things are important to each of us. But the fact is that we all set our time priorities. If you can't find the time to learn the basics that will help you to become a millionaire, it's probably not really because you don't have that time available. It's because you're not prepared to give up something, even temporarily, in order to free up that time.

If that's the case, ask yourself this question. How many hours a week do you spend watching TV shows that you don't really care about – you just tune in because they're on and there's nothing else to do? If the answer is more than two hours a week, then you have the time available to start working on this project. It's simply a matter of re-allocation.

Bad Habit #3: Allowing Distractions to Sidetrack You

I receive a lot of e-mail. It's a great way to communicate. It can also be a distraction of the first order if not managed and controlled.

For several months after I first opened an e-mail account, my morning ritual began with logging on and getting my messages. Perhaps part of it was the kid-with-the-new-toy phenomenon, but I couldn't wait to see who had been in contact with me since the end of the previous working day. Of course, once I started going through the mail, several messages required immediate responses. Before I knew it, half the morning had passed and I had not even started on my task list for the day. Since I'm at my peak in the morning hours and gradually decline in mental acuity over the afternoon, I was losing some of my most productive time. I had allowed my e-mail to become a distraction, albeit an interesting one. Now, I wait until after lunch to get my new messages. My mornings are focused on creative writing and business decisions. The result is a far more efficient day.

Most of us allow ourselves to be distracted from our primary goals, sometimes temporarily, often on a systematic basis. The corporate world, especially, is replete with potential distractions. Someone drops by your work space or office and wants to chat. A phone call interrupts you in the middle of a major project. Coffee break extends from 10 minutes to 20.

Meetings are perhaps the worst distractions of all. It was only after I left the corporate world that I became aware of the incredible amount of time that is wasted in meetings. Occasionally, they're necessary. More often they're called because someone with a responsibility is unsure of what to do and wants to obtain a consensus before making a decision. It's a cover-your-ass kind of thing: "Well, we all agreed that it seemed like the best course of action."

I could vent on about the futility of meetings for three pages, but I'll spare you. I do suggest this, however: Look at the number of people around the table and calculate how many person-hours are being expended. Then ask yourself whether the meeting is truly necessary. If it is, do all these people have to be there? Or is this just one more distraction for them?

I've used the context of the workplace here because it will be familiar to many readers. But where I want you to really apply the distraction test is in your pursuit of the objectives we are discussing in this book. I am not suggesting that you should become obsessed with the idea of becoming a millionaire. But you need to adopt a dedicated approach and not allow yourself to be carried off in other directions by the potential distractions that will inevitably arise. Clarity of purpose is essential.

Bad Habit #4: Overdependence on Others

No one else is going to make you a millionaire. This is your project. That's not to say you shouldn't expect help and support from others. Your family should certainly be a source of strength and encouragement. A spouse who constantly tells you that you're crazy is hardly going to act as a confidence-builder! If that happens, ask him or her to read this book and see if it makes a difference.

You may also need the support of those outside your immediate circle, especially if your chosen path is to create your wealth. We'll explore this theme in more detail at a later stage.

But when all is said and done, the burden of success is on you. This is your project, your dream. You have to do what is necessary to make it happen.

There will be plenty of temptations to let others take over the lead role. One of the most common involves investing. If you're not knowledgeable about the securities markets, you may be only too ready to put your trust in a professional advisor and let him or her make the decisions for you. Now, I don't wish for a moment to denigrate the skills of brokers and money managers. However, the reality is that some are better at their work than others – just as in any other profession. I have dealt with all types over my life and, while I've met some who are very good, I have never yet encountered an advisor who is perfect. At last check, God doesn't play the stock market!

If you abdicate this important responsibility to someone else, however good that person's credentials may be, you are entrusting the ultimate success of your project to an outsider. And no matter how diligent that advisor may be, the fact is that he or she has many other clients to service besides you. The bottom line is that the time available to analyze your specific needs and objectives is severely limited.

This is not to say that professional advice cannot be valuable. Quite the contrary; properly used, it may speed up the entire process. But that advice needs to be weighed and considered in the context of your situation. That's up to you. Two heads are better than one, but your head is the one that must make the final choice.

Bad Habit #5: Overspending

Keep this thought in mind: No one ever became a millionaire by spending more money than they took in. Charles Dickens said it all through the words of Mr. Micawber in David Copperfield: "Annual income twenty pounds, annual expenditure nineteen and six, result happiness. Annual income twenty pounds, annual expenditure twenty and six, result misery."

We live in a material age. Credit is easy, marketing is intense, pressure to consume is enormous. No wonder the national savings rate in the United States recently dropped below zero percent by some measures, suggesting that Americans are spending more than they're earning. The personal savings rate in Canada is only marginally better – 0.7 percent in 1998 (expressed as a percentage of GDP), down from 8.9 percent in the 1980s.

The result is that we have more, sooner. Bigger cars. Better clothes. New furniture. Cruises. Electronic gizmos. Unfortunately, all too often we pay for these goodies out of future income.

I'll have much more to say about this problem shortly. For the moment, let me just ask you to take a close look at your own spending habits. If there's more going out than is coming in, you're going to have to make some changes. Quickly!

Get Rid of Sour Relationships

There is nothing more draining, more exhausting, and more demoralizing than a close relationship gone sour. It eats away at you night and day. It robs you of motivation and increases stress levels. It distracts you from more important goals, including this one. It is aggravating, worrisome, and debilitating. Get rid of it.

How you do that is your business. Sometimes sour relationships can be repaired through talk, therapy, counselling, and determined effort. Sometimes they cannot be fixed, in which case some hard choices have to be made. This book is not about repairing relationships. There are many other sources of information on that subject. The point I'm making here is that if you allow a bad relationship to fester and continue, the chances of achieving the goals we are pursuing together will be significantly diminished.

Sour relationships outside your immediate family also need to be dealt with, although they should be somewhat easier to manage. These can range from an intolerable boss to a nosy neighbour. A workplace situation can obviously create difficulties, and you may even have to consider changing jobs if it gets too bad. But it's a matter over which you at least have some control.

During my career as a journalist, I did a stint as a foreign correspondent based in London. Part of my assignment was to provide coverage of the conflict in Northern Ireland, which at the time was escalating into an all-out war between Catholics and Protestants, fought by their illegal surrogate armies: the Irish Republican Army or IRA (Catholic) and the Ulster Volunteer Force or UVF (Protestant).

It was a dangerous time to be a journalist in Belfast. Hotels were routinely targeted with IRA bombs. The streets would erupt in gunfire without warning – the bathtub became one of the safest places of refuge when bullets starting flying in the middle of the night. The IRA established "no-go" zones in cities like Londonderry, where the rule of law was in the hands of the gunmen. Riots were common, and if you were caught up in one no one cared that you were a foreign journalist. A car in which I was riding was almost overturned and burned by a crazed Protestant mob in Portadown for no other reason than we turned the wrong corner at the wrong time. Only the fortunate appearance of a British army patrol saved the lives of my driver and myself.

I relate all this because my boss at that time, sitting comfortably back in Canada, was obsessed about cost controls. The foreign bureaus were too expensive, so he had made it one of his priorities to slice budgets wherever possible. Safety of the correspondents never seemed to be an issue in his mind. What they reported on their expense accounts was.

The only way to get around Northern Ireland with any degree of safety at that time was to hire a car with a knowledgeable local driver – one who knew the danger zones and how to stay out of harm's way most of the time. (Even so, he was at the wheel when we ran into the Portadown riot and when a sniper pumped a bullet into the car on Belfast's Springfield Road just about a foot behind where I was sitting.) But of course hiring a car and driver for several days wasn't cheap. My boss back in Ottawa at Southam Inc. exploded when he received my expense reports.

Why, he demanded angrily, couldn't I just take a taxi to wherever I was going, or better still, a bus? Why did I need to spend this kind of money? He wanted the stories of course, and the headlines back home were terrific: "Southam Man Ambushed in Belfast" screamed one newspaper across the top of its front page. He just didn't want the expense that came with it.

Needless to say, my work situation continued to deteriorate. I had originally signed on for a three-year stint. As the third anniversary approached, I was asked to stay on for another year or two. I refused to do so, and refused to accept any other job within the organization that involved working for this person. The sour relationship was undermining my ability to work effectively and I was tired of spending so much time defending what any right-minded employer would have seen as perfectly justifiable actions. On the day the three years finished, I flew home. I didn't even have another job firmly lined up. I just knew that I had to get out of this relationship for the sake of my sanity and my future career.

Yes, it was a tough decision. In retrospect, it was absolutely the right one and I would change nothing. Sour relationships will throw you off course and cause you to lose focus. Take a look at your own situation. If you have any such relationships in your life that are serious enough to have that kind of impact, resolve to do something about them. It may take some time, but they need to be fixed or eliminated.

Get Rid of Destructive Debt

Debt is the number one enemy of the wealth builder. It compromises your ability to save. It erodes your asset base. In extreme circumstances, it can even destroy you financially.

Debt is the number one ally of the wealth builder. It allows you to become wealthy using other people's money. It accelerates the wealth-building process. In extreme circumstances, it can even make you a millionaire years before you ever dreamed possible.

How's that for two totally conflicting views of debt? Now I'll confuse you even more. Both of them can be true, depending on your circumstances.

I don't think there's any concept in the wealth-building process that's more misunderstood than the use of debt. Perhaps that's because most people don't really understand what debt is all about. They tend to relate it to consumption – the debts incurred by purchasing a car or new furniture, or by taking a vacation. They don't generally understand debt's relationship to the process of building wealth and accumulating that first million.

There's both good debt and bad debt. I'll address good debt at a later time. Right now, we're at the stage of getting rid of unwanted baggage, and bad debt certainly falls into that category. I call it Destructive Debt. It can surface at any point in life, but its highest incidence is among people under age 40. Destructive Debt has four main characteristics:

1. It is incurred for consumption purposes. The money is borrowed to purchase goods or services, not for business or investing purposes.

2. It carries a high interest rate. This is because younger people usually start in lower-paying jobs and have few assets, thus making them higher risks. A large proportion of this debt may be credit card related.

3. Servicing the debt requires a disproportionate share of the household income. In other words, it costs you more each month to meet the financing payments than you can comfortably pay.

4. Interest on the debt is not tax deductible.

It's extremely easy to fall deeply into Destructive Debt and, as I've pointed out, our society actively encourages people to do so. Financial institutions and retail outlets make credit available to almost anyone, literally for the asking. Our newspapers and television screens are cluttered with ads offering easy terms for big-ticket items, such as appliances, electronic equipment, furniture, and cars. Some retailers have scored huge successes with campaigns promising you won't have to pay a cent for six months or more. It's all part of the "Why-Wait-When-You-Can-Have-It-Now?" syndrome. It's easy; it's seductive. No wonder millions of people fall for it.

And what happens? The easy-money debts pile up. Repaying them becomes an increasing financial drain on the household. There's no money left once the debts have been serviced and the necessities looked after. There's not even enough to go out to a movie occasionally; how in blazes are we supposed to start a savings program?

Debt like that is to be avoided at all costs. It undermines the wealth-building process and takes control of your financial destiny out of your hands. Stay away from it!

I know that's far easier said than done, especially if you're just starting to build a family household. I'm aware that I'm suggesting you make personal sacrifices – that you live with your old car or buy second-hand furniture or pass up a trip south next winter. And I know forgoing those comforts isn't pleasant. But if you seriously want to start the process of building that million dollars, if you truly want to create an independent lifestyle for yourself, then this is a sacrifice you *have* to make. There are no compromises on this one. If you load yourself down with Destructive Debt, you'll face years and years of struggle just to get out from under.

So the primary rule is very simple: *Don't take on consumer debt under any circumstances.*

But what if you've already accumulated a heavy debt load? Then you've acquired some more unwanted baggage that has to be disposed of. Your number one priority should be to pay it off as quickly as possible. Above all, don't add to it.

I recognize that it's not always possible to avoid Destructive Debt. A job loss, an unexpected child, a failed business. These things happen. In such circumstances, often no other choice exists. Fair enough. But most Destructive Debt doesn't originate that way. It comes from societal pressures that encourage you to want too much too soon. Call it what you will: greed, ambition, aggressiveness. It all comes down to spending money you don't have in order to acquire possessions you can't afford. That's Destructive Debt, no matter how you look at it. The committed wealth builder will avoid it at all costs.

Everyone Needs a Budget

One of the keys to avoiding or eliminating Destructive Debt is proper budgeting. This enables you to manage your money properly and ensures you won't accidentally over-spend. Every family needs a budget, no matter how well off you are. We still have one, even though our annual income is substantial and we have attained millionaire status. It's the only way I can control the outflow of cash and know how much we have available for renovations, holidays, investments, and helping the kids.

The easiest way to set up and run a family budget is on a computer. If you own one, or have access to one, I strongly recommend going that route; it makes the whole process much easier to manage. You can set up a budget by using any spreadsheet program. The more detail you put into the budget, the better. It may take a little longer to set up, but the result will be a much clearer picture of where the money is going and how much is available for savings or special purchases you want to make. If you already have a debt load that needs to be paid down, proper budgeting will enable you to start that process in a systematic way.

Any system that works for you is fine. But if you want a model, here's what I use.

The first column is a summary of the family's monthly after-tax income from all sources: salaries, part-time work, investments, and any other revenue you receive from miscellaneous sources (gifts, a tax refund, and so on). If there is any money left over from the previous month, it can be carried forward here. The total at the bottom is your budget for the current month. It can be adjusted as the month progresses if unexpected income is received.

Each subsequent column covers a separate expense item. In each case, the total budgeted for the month is shown at the top. As expenses occur during the month, they're entered below.

Depending on your personal situation, your column headings may include

- *Mortgage payment (or rent).* The amount of the monthly payment you're required to remit.

- *Property taxes.* One-twelfth of the expected annual property tax bill. In months when payments aren't required, the outstanding balance should be carried forward to the next month.

- *Maintenance and repairs.* A monthly allocation for the upkeep of your home.

- *Insurance.* A monthly allocation for all your insurance costs, including property, car, and life insurance. Add up the total annual premiums and divide by twelve to arrive at the monthly figure.

- *Food and supplies.* Your monthly budget for food and household necessities, like light bulbs and cleaning supplies.

- *Transportation.* The monthly cost of operating a car and/or taking public transit.

- *Clothing.* Your monthly clothing allocation for the family. Money not spent should be carried forward, as clothing expenses may vary significantly from month to month.

- *Utilities.* Heating, telephone, cable, electricity, water, and similar costs. These can be broken out into separate columns, if preferred.

- *Education.* Any current expenses involved in sending the children to school can be included here along with savings for future education costs.

- *Health care.* It's a good idea to build a fund to cover future costs for glasses, dental work, uninsured prescriptions, and other health-related costs.

- *Recreation.* You need to have fun, whether it's going to a movie or joining a club. Include an appropriate monthly allocation here. Money for alcohol and tobacco should also be budgeted here.

- *Special.* There will be special occasions during the year when you'll require extra money: birthdays, anniversaries, bar and bat mitzvahs, Christmas. This is the appropriate column for that.

- *Vacation.* Saving for a holiday is easier if you put a little aside each month.

- *Retirement savings.* If you budget something each month, you won't be scrambling for cash at RRSP deadline.

- *Interest and debt reduction.* If you're carrying any Destructive Debt, you obviously have to make interest payments each month. But you also need to start paying it off. Decide how much you can afford to pay against the principal each month, add it to the interest charges, and enter the total here. Obviously, this amount must be in excess of the interest charges or you'll make no progress.

- *Investment savings.* Every wealth builder should enter something in this column each month, even if the amount is small.

- *Miscellaneous.* There are always some unexpected costs, or those that don't fit into a particular category. Allow for them here.

I set up my personal program in such a way that each entry automatically adjusts the outstanding balance at the bottom of each column. That way, I know exactly how much I still have to spend in each category at any given time.

A typical monthly budget for a two-income family might look like this.

INCOME	
Carry-forward from previous month	$1,000
Husband income (after tax)	3,500
Wife income (after tax)	3,500
Interest	200
Miscellaneous	100
Total	**$8,300**

EXPENSES	
Mortgage	$2,500
Property taxes	450
Maintenance/Repairs	300
Insurance	200
Food/Supplies	1,000
Transportation	400
Clothing	300
Utilities	400
Education	250
Health care	200
Recreation	250
Special	200
Vacation savings	250

EXPENSES (CONTINUED)	
Retirement savings	400
Interest and debt reduction	500
Investment savings	400
Miscellaneous	300
Total	**$8,300**

Creating a manageable budget will take you part of the way towards getting rid of Destructive Debt. But you're only attacking the limbs. If you really want to do the job properly, you have to chop down the whole tree.

Credit Cards – Handle with Care

The main source of Destructive Debt is credit cards. They're the first experience many people have with borrowing. Unfortunately, that first experience often turns into a financial disaster which can take years to put right.

Part of the fault lies with our credit-granting institutions. Some of the gimmicks that are used in the hot pursuit of credit card market share smack of hucksterism at its worst. As a result of all this intense promotion, we tend to lose sight of the real purpose of a credit card – as a convenient substitute for cash. Card issuers entice us to sign up with every form of inducement, from frequent flyer points to free life insurance to elaborate rewards programs. Some now even offer low carrying charges, which should be the most important consideration of all if you're carrying a balance. However, you need to read the fine print carefully; in some cases the attractive promotional interest rates apply for a limited time only.

It's not just the major companies that are aggressively pursuing your business. One of my daughters worked briefly one summer for an outfit that kept dozens of people busy every day doing telephone solicitations for a department store card. The pay was poor but the bonus incentives for signing customers were good. At one point, my daughter confessed later, she pleaded with a potential customer to sign up so she could meet her quota, telling the surprised man on the line to cut up the card and flush it down the toilet after it arrived in the mail if he didn't want to use it. Real salesmanship!

In recent years, another type of credit card has made its appearance – the affinity card. If you're a university graduate, you've probably been asked to sign up for a Visa or MasterCard issued to the alumni of your alma mater. The typical affinity card is a handsome piece of plastic, perhaps bearing a picture of one of the landmark buildings of the school. You're offered a special inducement to sign up (perhaps a reduced annual fee). The school receives a small percentage of the total purchases made by its card holders. Since every college and university needs financial help these days, there's been a rush to get on the affinity card bandwagon.

Affinity cards are also available to members of recreational organizations, environmental associations, clubs, and similar groups. You can even get an affinity card that bears the logo of your favourite professional sports team.

The fact that banks, trust companies, credit unions, department stores, oil companies, universities, clubs, and a variety of other organizations are going to such lengths to persuade you to sign up should tell you something. Credit cards are a very profitable business for them. They are not, conversely, very profitable for *you* – unless you use them correctly.

If you're a normal credit card user, you can probably save yourself hundreds of dollars each year by applying some basic financial management disciplines. That's money that could be channelled toward your goal of accumulating that first million. And by handling your cards more effectively, you'll reduce the risk and inconvenience of having them lost or stolen.

How? Here's a guide to intelligent credit card use that may help.

To begin with, a suggestion: Don't carry more than two personal cards. Unless you have some unusual credit requirements, you don't need any more. This isn't just an exercise in keeping a neat purse or wallet. Many major credit cards now charge annual user fees, so you're paying a lot of money for the privilege of carrying around all that plastic, especially if you're not making regular use of it.

Which two cards should you keep? That depends on how you use them. Take out all your credit cards and spread them on a table in front of you. Pick up those you used less than four times over the past year. They have to go – any card used that infrequently isn't worth keeping.

Once you've made your decision, don't just cut up the cards you don't need and forget them. Cancel them with the issuer, otherwise you'll continue to receive replacement cards at the expiry date, with accompanying invoices. And, of course, pay off any outstanding balances that may remain. This isn't an exercise in ruining your credit rating.

When you've completed this process, you should be down to two basic cards. Now let's consider how to use them most intelligently.

Rule #1: Reduce Your User Fees to an Absolute Minimum

Ideally, aim for zero net cost. I'm reluctant to pay credit card issuers for using their product. It may be because I remember when most credit cards were free. Of course they now carry all kinds of user changes and transaction fees. Plus the merchants are paying the card companies a percentage of everything you charge, which is built into the price you pay for goods and services.

The premium cards with all their bells and whistles charge annual fees, which can add up to several hundred dollars once supplementary cards are tacked on. It may be possible to have these fees waived; I know of cases where good clients of a financial institution were able to negotiate a free gold card. Failing that, look for a free card where you pay nothing except interest on any balance you carry.

Rule #2: Use Premium Cards Wisely

If you do pay extra for a gold or platinum card, make sure you get full value. Today's premium cards offer a wide range of services and bonuses. Whether you should pay the hefty fee depends on how much use you'll make of the card's features.

Each premium card has its own smorgasbord of goodies. You'll have to do some research to determine which combination best suits your needs. Here are some of the most common:

- *Collision damage waiver.* Renting a car is expensive. If you accept the agency's collision damage waiver coverage, you can add another $10 a day or more to your bill. Many premium cards provide this protection free, when you use the card for the rental. If you rent frequently, that saving alone could be enough to justify the extra cost of the card. But be sure you really need the coverage before using this as a rationale for going gold. You may already be protected through your personal automobile insurance policy. Check with your insurance agent.

- *Travel insurance.* This is always nice to have, but only if it covers you for the most likely contingencies. Most premium cards offer some form of accidental death or dismemberment (what an awful word!) protection. But it's not likely you'll ever use it. Far more valuable is trip cancellation and trip interruption coverage. This protects you in the event illness or a family emergency forces you to cancel or cut short your trip.

- *Rewards.* Increasingly, the big selling point of many premium cards is some form of reward program. Sometimes you will have to pay extra to enrol in the plan, however. For example, American Express charges an annual fee for participating in its program. The most common rewards are credits towards air flights. But be warned. These rewards may turn out to be expensive. For example, in the fall of 2000 American Express announced a deal with Canada 3000 that allowed cardholders to redeem points for seats on charter flights. What most people weren't aware of when they phoned in to make a claim was that they would be hit with a high fee for "taxes," which generated a bill of almost $200 on a pair of seats from Toronto to Florida. The "free" reward turned out to be rather pricey!

Rule #3: Don't Use Credit Cards to Finance Purchases

If you don't pay off your balance in full every month, you're actually using the card as a means to borrow money. That is an absolute no-no. If you need to borrow money, there are far less expensive ways to do it. Even the banks, if pressed, will admit privately that carrying a credit card balance and paying interest on it makes no sense. They try not to say it too loudly, though – after all, interest on credit card balances is one of their main revenue streams from these pieces of plastic.

Almost every financial advisor agrees that carrying a credit card balance is foolish. Articles appear in newspapers and magazines all the time that repeatedly stress this point. And yet about half the credit card holders in Canada do it – that's several million people.

It's the single most common money management mistake people make, and the main source of Destructive Debt.

Why do they do it? In part because of convenience – it's much easier to use a credit card to finance your purchases than it is to negotiate a bank loan. They may also feel the amount of interest they're paying isn't enough to get excited about. That's because they haven't done their math.

The spread between the interest rate on an ordinary loan and the interest rate on your credit card may be up to 10 percent. If you carry a balance of $2,500 on your card, that means you may be paying up to $250 a year more in interest than you should be. That's too much money to be throwing away. Take out a personal loan, pay off the credit card balance, and make a solemn vow never to make the same mistake again.

Your Destructive Debt will disappear, and you'll free up valuable assets for use in pursuing your primary goal – attaining millionaire status.

Don't Be Discouraged

I hope you're not feeling discouraged at this point. This section has been something of a downer, focusing as it has on negative things. No one likes to be reminded of their weaknesses. And the prospect of having to change long-standing habits or mindsets can be daunting, as anyone who has tried to stop smoking or go on a diet knows. But it's a necessary step to complete. And the good news is that the next stage is far more interesting and inspirational. That's because you're about to discover something you may not even realize you possess: your inner genius!

Step 3

Unlock Your
Inner Genius

"Uh-oh," you may have said to yourself when you read the title of Step Three. "Now I have to be some kind of genius to be a millionaire! Thanks a lot! Why didn't you tell me that before I wasted money on this book?"

Well, hold on just one second before you slam shut the cover and go back to the store for a refund. Let me clarify a couple of points.

First, I believe that all of us have some type of inner genius. In most cases it's not the ability to develop theories in quantum physics or to unlock the secrets of clean energy. But virtually everyone has the ability to do something exceptionally well. Genius does not automatically imply greatness. You may be a genius in the kitchen, or in dealing with your family, or in your computer skills, or in charming other people, or in communicating, or in fixing things, or in your ability to work efficiently, or in your decision-making processes, or in any of hundreds of other skills, aptitudes, and talents.

Second, it has been my experience that most people either don't fully understand the extent of their unique abilities or have not developed them effectively. The genius lies latent, often for a lifetime, occasionally manifesting itself in flashes but never asserting itself in a way that can be used to maximize one's wealth-building abilities or significantly enhance lifestyle.

And what has all this to do with accumulating a million dollars? A lot. That's because the easiest route to a million is through the use of your own inner genius. Properly used, it can provide the momentum you need to propel you forward and to get you through the trouble spots along the way. If you aren't able to call on those reserves, it becomes much more difficult to advance. Not impossible, of course – but why not make the challenge as easy as possible?

That's what Step Three is all about: Identifying your inner genius and bringing it to the forefront so that it can play a key role in your million-dollar quest.

Still not convinced? Perhaps you wonder if you really have such an inner genius. Well, let's find out.

A Word to the Savers

Before we begin, a word to those of you who plan to achieve millionaire status through saving and investing. As you read the following pages, you may wonder how relevant this section is to achieving your goal. You may feel that the advice here is better suited to wealth creators than to savers.

To an extent, that's true. But many of the qualities I will stress are equally important to savers, such as motivation, self-discipline, confidence, and education. And organizing your life so as to make it possible to do those things you enjoy most, which is one of the key themes of this section, is important no matter which path you choose to building your million. Never forget: If you aren't satisfied with yourself and with your life, no amount of money is going to fix that.

So even if finding your inner genius may seem somewhat removed from the process of saving for a million, I urge you to take this step seriously. You will gain new insights into yourself, and you will almost certainly be a happier person as a result.

The Unknown You

Recently, I came across the following quotation: "'Be yourself' is the worst advice you can give to some people." Well, if you're a latent pedophile or axe murderer, I suppose that's true. But for 99 percent of the population, it's bunk.

One of the basic problems in most people's lives is that they're *not* being themselves. And they're not being themselves because they don't know who they truly are.

"Know yourself" is one of those hoary platitudes that's been passed on from parent to child since, in all probability, Neanderthal times. It's as much a part of our upbringing as being taught to say "please." Unfortunately, we hear it so often that it's lost any meaning. "Know myself? Like, I'm some kind of stranger? An alien in my own body?"

Well, maybe you are. My experience is that few people *really* understand themselves and, even when they do, they often let perceived opportunity override self-realization.

Who are you, really? What are you good at? What are you bad at? What do you enjoy most about living? Least? What kind of people do you relate to best? Worst? Unless you know the answers to those questions, you lack the fundamental personal insights necessary to taking the first steps towards success, and you will never identify and unlock that inner genius we're talking about.

Try this self-test. Take a piece of paper and divide it into two columns: *Strengths* and *Weaknesses*. Now fill in at least six items on each side. Be absolutely honest — no one but you is going to read them. To illustrate, I'll show you mine:

STRENGTHS	WEAKNESSES
Communications skills	Impatience
Self-discipline	Overly demanding
Good physical presence	Poor administration skills
Rational mind	Lack of teaching skills
Conceptual skills	No mechanical aptitude
Leadership ability	Intolerant of mistakes

Take a close look at that list. Then consider this. When I finished university, I found myself with two job offers. One was to go to work as a junior reporter for a newspaper. The other was to become a history teacher in a local high school.

I was sorely tempted by the teaching job. The pay was better, plus it provided an opportunity to live and work in the community where I'd grown up. It was my wife-to-be who talked me out of it, by making the point that I'd always told her I wanted to be a writer. Well, this was the opportunity – and it might never come again. I didn't realize it at the time, but what she was telling me, in effect, was to tap into my inner genius and bring it forward.

So I passed on the teaching job and the extra $1,000 a year it paid – good money back in the early 1960s. Thank heaven I did. Look down my list of weaknesses. Impatience. Overly demanding. Intolerant of mistakes. Lack of teaching skills. What a lousy teacher I'd have made! I would have been frustrated in the job and my students would have been miserable. To this day, they don't realize how lucky they were!

Had I taken that position, I would have wasted valuable years and perhaps never got started on the career path that was my natural direction, because it was directed by my true inner genius. I wish I could say I made the right choice because of my clear vision of where I wanted to go, but that's not so. It was my fiancée's clear vision that was the decider. Fortunately, she was around to show me the right way.

The point, I hope, is obvious. As your life unfolds, you'll be faced with periodic crossroad decisions, such as my teacher/journalist dilemma. At times, the right choice may not always be clear. That's when you go back to your Strengths/Weaknesses list. Take time to sit quietly and contemplate it in the context of the decision you're facing.

See which direction dovetails most closely with the characteristics on the Strengths side of your personal ledger. See if one of the options is more likely to accent the traits on the Weaknesses side.

My father used to be fond of saying, "Follow the line of least resistance." That's what you're looking for in this case. Which choice offers the least resistance? In other words, which is most consistent with the attributes you regard as your strengths? That's the direction in which your inner genius is pointing.

If neither option seems right once you've submitted them to the test, then pass on both.

Now make a second list. Head your two columns *Like* and *Dislike*. Here, set down the six things you most enjoy that relate in some way to your working life, and the six things you enjoy least. Again, be absolutely honest with yourself. If sleeping on the job is one of your favourite pastimes, write it down. It will tell you something important about your job, and yourself. Here's my personal list to give you an example.

LIKE	DISLIKE
Writing	Meetings
Developing new concepts	Frequent interruptions
Finishing a project	Arguing
Working quickly	Taking orders
Using my imagination	Petty details
Working on my own	Solving other people's problems

What does this list tell you about the type of work environment someone like me will thrive in? Clearly, I'm not well suited for a bureaucratic organization where decisions are made by collective consultation. When I did end up in that kind of situation, I was miserable and did not perform to my capabilities. Here's how it came about. Be wary, because the same sort of thing can happen to you.

As a reporter, my newspaper career thrived. I received a series of rapid promotions, which culminated in my appointment as publisher of *The Canadian* — a rotogravure magazine that was included with the Saturday editions of *The Toronto Star* and the Southam newspapers.

Wait a minute, you may be saying. You were a writer. What did you know about being a magazine publisher?

The simple answer is: nothing. Nor was I given any formal management training. It was a case of the Peter Principle at its finest: I was promoted up the ladder of the newspaper industry until I reached my level of incompetence.

Perhaps I'm being hard on myself. I wasn't truly incompetent in the job. I just wasn't very good at it because 1) I lacked proper preparation, and 2) my natural likes and dislikes weren't suited to that kind of role.

Imagine a senior executive who hates meetings. Who doesn't like detail. Who's uncomfortable dealing with other people's problems. Who dislikes taking orders (like from a board of directors). Then put that person in charge of a sinking ship (the roto magazines, *The Canadian* and *Weekend*, were awash in red ink when I took over), and you'll begin to understand why I hated going to work each morning.

I had accepted a position beyond my capability, and one that ran counter to my natural talents and inclinations. I had acted out of greed (a publisher earns a lot more money than a reporter) and pride (I was still relatively young and figured I could do anything). In short, I rejected my inner genius and struck out in a different direction. The result was several miserable years that culminated in a traumatic end to what, until then, had been a highly successful newspaper career.

It's a common mistake. Avoid it if at all possible. If you've already made it, and recognize the fact, take steps to rectify the situation as soon as you can.

Let's move on to a third list. This time I want you to write down the six things you like doing most in your spare time. Then write six things you dislike doing. Here's mine.

LIKE	DISLIKE
Being with family	Cocktail parties
Playing competitive games	Making small talk
Collecting and tasting fine wine	Watching TV sitcoms
Reading a good novel	Winter sports
Boating and fishing	Yardwork
Golf	Jazz

Your work-oriented likes and dislikes are important for choosing the right career path and for recognizing where your real talents lie. Your leisure-oriented likes and dislikes are the keys to helping you attain a well-balanced lifestyle.

No one can claim to be truly successful if they don't enjoy their life. Being a millionaire may seem like a great idea, but the world has seen more than its share of miserable millionaires. How you spend your off-work hours is critical to your ultimate satisfaction in your material accomplishments.

Surprisingly, many people spend much of their spare time doing things they don't enjoy at all. There are two main reasons for this.

1. Someone else dominates your activities. You may like to watch football, but your spouse hates it. So you don't see many games. Instead, you watch a lot of made-for-TV movies, which you despise. Solution: Buy a second TV.

2. Your leisure time is duty-driven. Technically you're not working, but in fact you're still on the job. You have to make an appearance at a ceremony. You have to read work-related magazines. You have to entertain a client when you'd rather veg-out at home.

In both cases, you're letting others dictate how you spend that precious and rare commodity, leisure time. The inevitable result will be tension, irritability, and worry. None of these are conducive to a fulfilling life, even with a million dollars in the bank. If you're in this situation, resolve to change it now. Go over your list of leisure Likes. Make it a priority to do at least one of them a day, regardless of what anyone else says. And when people start to tell you how much more relaxed you seem to be these days, don't be surprised.

Now for one final list. Here I want you to write down the character traits you most admire in others, and the ones you dislike. My list:

ADMIRE	DISLIKE
Integrity	Manipulativeness
Straightforwardness	Vanity
Intelligence	Dishonesty
Ability to listen	Constant talking
Humour	Foul language
Musical talent	Pettiness

This list should tell you a lot about the type of people you prefer to do business with and associate with socially. It can be especially important in the work environment, particularly when weighing a potential new employer. It is extremely important if you decide the entrepreneurial route is the best way for you to achieve your million-dollar dream, because you'll probably need some close partnerships and strategic alliances to make it happen.

Let's consider this list in the context of an interview, whether for a job or to assess a potential partner. Remember, all interviews should cut two ways. You're trying to create a good impression and to make your case, of course. But you should also be attempting to assess the personal characteristics of your prospective new boss or partner. This can be difficult, especially if you're nervous and/or desperately want the meeting to succeed. But you should make the effort — it could keep you from making a big mistake.

In the case of a job interview, if the person you're meeting is not the one you'll be reporting to (perhaps it's someone in the human resources department), make it clear that you wish to meet that individual before a final decision is made. If you're being seriously considered for the job, ask if you can also spend some time with the employees you'll be working most closely with. This will help you assess your mutual compatibility and will make you appear much more professional in the eyes of the interviewer.

If the meeting relates to a potential partnership, investment, or strategic alliance, you should be seeking at least as much input as you provide. It should not be a situation in which you make a presentation and then field questions. There must be give and take — if not at the first meeting, then at a subsequent one (or more) before anything is finalized. Partnerships can be as touchy as marriages. A good one will bring a diversity of strengths to bear. A bad one will degenerate into squabbles and acrimony, which will ultimately sabotage the project.

By now, you should have four lists in front of you. Keep them, consult them, and revise them when necessary. They are insights into your true inner genius — who you are, what you do well, what you like, what you don't like, and what kinds of people you work best with. Apply them to every major decision you face in life. Don't get sidetracked by material gain or perceived advancement. If what you're being offered runs counter to your true inner genius, it's a trap that will inevitably lead to dissatisfaction and unhappiness in the long run. Short-term gain for long-term pain, if you like.

If you fail to recognize your inner genius and instead pursue a course that runs counter to your true nature, the chances of achieving the million-dollar goal will be greatly diminished. Use those skills properly, and you'll be amazed at how the whole process will accelerate.

You Have to Love It

"I've decided to major in business administration in college. I really don't like business very much and numbers bore me, but you have to be pragmatic these days and that's where the jobs are. But I'd really rather be a sports announcer."

Does this line of thinking make any sense to you? A rather cynical approach to life, isn't it? But that's exactly how many young people are thinking today. Forget about personal interests. Ignore talent and creativity. Put aside dreams. Go for the money! And after all, isn't that what this book is about? Yes. But don't lose sight of the fact it's about a lot more than that.

I never was a hippie, but sometimes I long for a return to the days of the flower children. At least they had a strong sense of self. The pendulum has now swung completely in the other direction, as so often happens with social attitudes. Now jobs, career, salary, and wealth are the forces that drive today's youth. The only thing they get angry about these days is not being able to find a job that pays them what they think they're worth, which is usually an inflated number. I consider myself a pragmatic person, but I think this is pragmatism run amok.

The source of this sea change in young people's view of life is, I believe, the twin recessions of 1980–82 and 1990–92. For the first time since the end of the World War II, the middle class learned what hard times were all about. There had been other economic downturns in the post-war period, but none that wreaked economic and social carnage on anything approaching a comparable scale. People who had grown up in an era of job security were suddenly, cruelly cut adrift as employers from governments to corner grocery stores downsized to cope with a new financial reality.

In recessions past, the brunt of unemployment had fallen most heavily on blue collar workers, as assembly lines were shut down, shifts discontinued, or entire plants closed. But the recessions of the 1980s and 1990s were different. This time it was the white-collar worker who got hit, especially the bloated middle-management sector. Often, these were people who had spent years working their way up the corporate ladder, who were committed to the organization, and who firmly believed the organization was committed to them.

The recessions taught a harsh lesson – that the first commitment of any organization is to survive. If parts of it have to be sacrificed in the process, so be it. Better that some people keep their jobs than that everyone ends up on the street.

Many of the people who lost their jobs in those two recessions were parents of the young men and women who are making career decisions today. They carry the scars of the experiences of their fathers and mothers – economic dislocation, depression, anger, resentment, and distrust of the system. They don't want to experience a similar fate.

So, where they have a choice, they opt for careers they think will guarantee employment, a good income, and minimal exposure to the vagaries of the economy. In short, they choose security over self-fulfillment. I understand the psychology. I think it is fundamentally flawed.

I've yet to meet a happy person who is doing something he or she doesn't like. I'll go one step further. I've never met a person who was able to make a success out of a career he or she didn't like.

One of the basic secrets to achieving success in life and acquiring wealth is to *do something you like.* That will almost by definition put you in touch with your inner genius. If you select your life's work on any other basis, here's what will inevitably happen:

- *You'll wake up feeling poorly most mornings – because, deep down inside, you don't really want to go to work.*
- *You'll avoid putting in extra hours.*
- *You won't make the effort to improve your career skills.*
- *You'll become a clock-watcher.*

- *You'll be irritable with your family at the end of the day, unconsciously taking out your resentments on them.*

- *You'll put your job or your project at risk by underperforming.*

The road to a million is well signed, if you know what you're looking for. If you decide you want to try your hand at creating your wealth, then first decide what it is in life that excites, challenges, and stimulates you.

It may not be easy. You'll undoubtedly encounter frustrations along the way. But stay with it. The long-term rewards in terms of personal satisfaction and financial gain will be well worth the effort.

There are countless ways to become a millionaire. I don't care what the field is — if you enjoy doing it, the chances of prospering financially are enhanced a hundred-fold. That's because, when you enjoy a job, the following things will happen:

- *You'll be enthusiastic about your work.*

- *You'll bring all your creative juices to it.*

- *You'll work extra hours if need be.*

- *You'll take special pride in doing it right.*

- *You'll want to be the best there is in the field.*

- *You'll take courses to improve your skills.*

- *You'll work well with others.*

- *You'll be a better person to live with, because you'll feel good about yourself.*

- *Your eagerness and accomplishments will make you a natural candidate for advancement.*

Many years ago, five-year-old Berkley Bedell's parents took him fishing with them at Spirit Lake in Iowa. They walked down the shore a way to do some fly fishing, leaving young Berkley on the bank with his bamboo pole. When they came back, he had caught his first fish and, as he tells the story more than half a century later, "I was hooked for life."

Berkley grew up determined to make a career out of his passion for fishing. At age 15 he took $50 from his paper route money and set up his own fly-tying business, employing three schoolgirls to help him at the generous wage of 15¢ an hour. He used part of the money to take out a small ad in *Sports Afield* magazine and waited for the orders to pour in. None did.

Berkley didn't lose heart. He sold his flies to local fishermen. The business grew. After finishing school he decided to expand into steel leaders (which he didn't know how to make), selling them at 10 percent below the competition. He drove 3,000 miles across the U.S. Midwest seeking orders, sleeping in his car, and living on peanut butter sandwiches. On a stop in South Bend, Indiana, he learned how to make the leaders and went home to jerry-rig the needed equipment. The business grew some more.

World War II came and Berkley Bedell suspended his operations for the duration to become a flying instructor and a B-24 pilot. After it was over, he returned to Iowa to start again, and in time created the largest fishing equipment manufacturing company in the world. If you've ever cast a line, you have probably used a Berkley product. Later he served for 12 years in the U.S. House of Representatives. His son now runs the operation, and Berkley spends more time doing what he loves most: fishing.

It's just one example of someone who did what they loved and became both wealthy and happy as a result.

Of course, it's one thing to advise young people to follow their star. But what if you're older and stuck in a dead-end job? Or what if you're just not sure you're on the right career track? Then what?

Then it's harder, no question. In this case, the starting point is some self-analysis – just how serious is your situation? Try this test to see.

YOUR CAREER SATISFACTION QUOTIENT

	USUALLY	SOMETIMES	NEVER
1. I'm one of the last people to leave my place of employment each day.	○	○	○
2. I find ways to do things better.	○	○	○
3. I read books and/or take courses to improve my skills.	○	○	○
4. I like the people I work with.	○	○	○

5. I think about how lucky I am to be doing what I'm doing. ○ ○ ○

6. I read the Careers and/or Help Wanted sections of the paper. ○ ○ ○

7. I try to avoid thinking about work when I'm at home. ○ ○ ○

8. Friday afternoon comes as a relief. ○ ○ ○

9. I call in sick a lot. ○ ○ ○

10. I'm bored. ○ ○ ○

Here's how to score. For questions one to five, count three points for every *Usually,* one point for each *Sometimes,* and zero points for *Never.* For questions six to ten, reverse the scoring: zero for *Usually,* one for *Sometimes,* three for *Never.* Here's how to interpret the results:

24–30: Congratulations! You've obviously chosen a career path that you find satisfying and challenging and that is in touch with your inner genius. Keep on in that direction but start to look for ways to enhance the wealth-creation potential of your work.

15–23: You derive some pleasure from your work, but there's a measure of discontent as well. You may be in the right field but perhaps with the wrong employer. Give some careful thought to your situation and take appropriate action.

9–14: The twilight zone. You're not totally unhappy with what you're doing, but you don't derive a lot of pleasure from it either. You're in a situation where advancement beyond your current level seems unlikely. If you're older, you may want to just stick it out until retirement, but you're unlikely to attain personal wealth if you do. Forget the million! If you're under 50, a move is indicated. There's still time for you.

0–8: You're on a dead-end track. Your career is going nowhere and your home life may be suffering as a result. Whatever your age, you should make every possible effort to break out of the current situation. It will only drag you down further.

Often, breaking away is difficult. I know; I've been there. The promotion to publisher of *The Canadian* seemed like a good idea at the time. It was a major step up the journalistic ladder. It was a job that carried prestige, more money, and big responsibilities (I didn't realize how big at the time). I got a large office, membership in a top-level golf club, a company car, and other assorted perks. I controlled a multi-million-dollar budget. I was responsible for the career destinies of almost one hundred people.

It was the worst time of my life!

The rotogravure magazines were being ground down by a combination of huge costs and an advertising industry that had switched its mass-reach dollars to television. Although I didn't realize it when I was offered the job (an experienced manager would have asked questions), the hull had been breached and the ship was sinking. I had been given the job of rearranging the deck chairs on the *Titanic*. The problem was that the board of directors, composed of nominees from Southam, Torstar and, later, Thomson, didn't know it, or at least didn't accept it. So they continued to demand ever more elaborate deck chair arrangements.

Change the editorial content. Get rid of old personnel and hire new. Offer advertisers better deals. Cut costs. Cut costs. Cut costs.

As George Floyd, my canny chief financial officer, commented after one board meeting, "When will those guys realize you can't keep feeding sawdust to a donkey?"

I developed all the classic hate-work symptoms. I disliked going in each morning. I'd experience pounding headaches in the back of my skull, something I'd never had before. I read the Careers pages. I started working on other projects in my spare time (this was the period when I was getting up early to write novels).

I told myself time and again I should simply quit, but two things stopped me. I'd never failed at anything before. To walk away would be an admission of my inadequacy. In retrospect, I realize that was just false pride. I wasn't going to save the rotos and neither was anyone else. There comes a time when you must surrender to the inevitable.

The other thing binding me to the job was the golden handcuffs. I was making more money than ever before in my life. I had all kinds of perks. We also had three kids, a mortgage, and one income – mine. How could I justify quitting under those circumstances?

Again, in hindsight, the answer is simple: easily. As events later unfolded, I could have done much better financially over the long term by making the tough decision, cutting my losses, and getting out as soon as I realized what was happening. But I didn't. I was afraid. So I hung in, worked as hard as I could, and doomed myself to the worst years of my life. They only ended when the magazine was killed by its newspaper owners at the height of the 1980–82 recession.

There's no way to achieve success or wealth in that kind of situation. You may think you're fighting the good fight, but you're wrong – you're only wasting precious years.

You may worry about taking a financial hit if you quit, and you may. There's no guarantee you'll be able to quickly find a job that pays as well. But if you make a move to a field you enjoy and have a natural propensity for (there's that inner genius again), I can almost guarantee that, over time, you'll come out better from a financial point of view. Plus, you'll have a lot more fun.

When you consider the alternative – years of frustration and discontent – it's a pretty good trade-off.

Be the Best

Michael Jordan will be remembered as one of the greatest basketball players of all time. What has already almost been forgotten is the fact that he lost two years of his brilliant career in an unsuccessful attempt to succeed at something else – baseball. Whether through pride, or ego, or curiosity, or boredom, Jordan temporarily abandoned his inner genius, with disastrous results.

His return to the Chicago Bulls after almost two years of chasing rainbows was one of the most ballyhooed sports events in recent years. The media coverage was lavish. For a week prior to the formal announcement, every TV station and newspaper in the U.S. carried "Will he or won't he?" speculation. On the day of his return to the court, *USA Today* carried stories about the comeback on its front page, in the sports section, and in the money section (the impact of The Return on advertisers). Shares of companies with Michael Jordan endorsement contracts jumped in price. Scalpers got up to $1,000 a seat for the big game against the Indiana Pacers. The U.S. was swept, again, with Jordan mania.

Why all the excitement? Because Michael Jordan was one of the best players of his generation; a court genius who dazzled with his ability. Yes, he was rusty on his return, and it showed. But sports fans, and even his opponents, applauded his comeback nonetheless. Jordan was still The Best.

At basketball. Not baseball. And therein lies a message for us all.

After retiring from the Bulls the first time, Michael Jordan decided he wanted to be a baseball player. He was 30 years old at that point, and had never played professional baseball. But with the confidence, some might say the arrogance, of a supremely gifted person, he decided to become a major leaguer.

The Chicago White Sox (which has the same ownership as the Bulls) saw the opportunity. If Jordan wasn't packing them in to the basketball arenas any more, maybe fans would come to the new Comiskey Park to see him play. The White Sox signed him to a minor league contract in the hope his superb athletic skills could indeed be translated to the diamond.

You know the rest of the story. Jordan was a bust as a baseball player. He drew crowds all right – for minor league teams, like Birmingham. But he couldn't deliver. He spent a season in the minors, barely managing to keep his batting average above .200. Hitting a small white ball with a slender bat clearly required a completely different set of athletic skills.

There were expressions of confidence about his progress, but by this time he was 32 and clearly heading nowhere. In March 1995, using the baseball strike as an excuse, he announced he was packing in the baseball adventure. A couple of weeks later, he was back with the Chicago Bulls.

Jordan's experience says something to us all. You may have multiple talents, but you will probably only be able to do one thing superbly well. Leonardo da Vinci types come along only once a millennium.

The point: *Determine your strongest skill and focus on doing it better than anyone else.* Don't be a jack-of-all-trades, master of none.

Finding Your Talents

Many people waste time and energy by trying to do too much. They jump from one job or project to another without purpose or focus.

Granted, it's sometimes not easy to determine what you're best at. Many students go through university with no clear sense of what truly interests them, what they do well, or where they should be heading in life.

But this isn't only a young person's problem. Many people go through mid-life traumas in their 30s and 40s, questioning their career direction and whether they've made the right choices.

If you're in that situation, here's a little test that may help you identify where your true talents lie. There are no right or wrong answers. This exercise is designed to get you thinking by zeroing in on your innate strengths and personality traits. If you want a more detailed analysis of your talents and the occupations best suited to them, see a professional career counsellor and take one of the many tests that are available.

In the meantime, this test will help you get started. Make note of all questions to which you answer *Yes*. They should provide you with insights into where your talents and interests lie, and point you, broadly, in the right direction.

1. *Do you enjoy math?* You'll notice the question is not "Are you good at math?" If you're not good at it, you probably don't enjoy it. If you do enjoy it, you're probably both good at it and have a strong orientation in that direction. You don't have to be a mathematical genius to make your million by investing, but it's a skill that won't hurt.

2. *Are you a good writer?* Here the question has been reversed. Many people like to write; few are good at it. Writing skills are important in every field (reports, letters, proposals), but only a truly talented writer can expect to make a living at it and to become The Best — which means creating wealth through this talent.

3. *Do you like people?* Some of us don't, at least not in a workplace context. I've always been a loner; I find I function more effectively that way. I become distracted when I have to take the opinions, or problems, or directions of others into account. Other people need the support structure of an organization. You must identify which type you are in order to focus your abilities in the right direction.

4. *Are you comfortable with technology?* Staying abreast of new technology is important to achieving success. But it's one thing to keep up with it; it's quite another to choose a career direction that requires intimate technological know-how for success.

5. *Are you a good teacher?* One of the greatest talents is the ability to impart knowledge to others in a way that makes the information practical and useful to their lives. If you have this special skill, you should search out a career direction that allows it full blossom. Teaching is an obvious choice, but there are many opportunities for instructors in business, the arts, and the sciences. And this doesn't have to be a full-time occupation. You may derive great satisfaction from lecturing once a week at a local college in an area in which you have special knowledge or skill.

6. *Are you imaginative?* Some people have great creative abilities – and waste them because they choose a career direction or accept a job that stifles those energies. The ability to conceptualize is one of the rarest and most prized gifts any person can possess. The key is to channel it in a direction that is personally rewarding and financially viable.

7. *Are you artistic?* If you have a special talent for painting, or dance, or music, or design, consider opportunities in that direction. Some may not be obvious at first glance – for example, a talent for drawing combined with a vivid imagination could lead to a successful career in advertising.

8. *Are you curious?* It may see odd to include this question here, but curiosity, properly applied, can be an extremely valuable talent. There has never been a great television interviewer or talk show host who wasn't driven by an intense sense of curiosity. At the other end of the spectrum, every great archaeologist must possess an inquiring mind. Curiosity is the driving force that fuels your other talents and leads you into unique and exciting directions.

9. *Are you patient?* Some jobs require infinite patience as a prime ingredient for success. Consider medical research – it can involve years of dead ends, of disappointments, of frustrations. But one major breakthrough makes it all worthwhile.

10. *Can you take risks?* Some people thrive on rolling the dice. They live for the opportunity to make the big hit, and they're prepared to take the risks necessary to achieve that. Others find the idea frightening; they want a sinecure where they can reduce their exposure to the vagaries of the world to an absolute minimum. The risk-taker is likely to do better financially (although bankruptcy is also a possibility). But, as we've already discussed, success means more than pure wealth. So if you're not a risk-taker by nature, don't choose a direction that requires you to be one. You probably shouldn't be running a business (yours or anyone else's). Don't get into fields like real estate, or brokerage, or merchandising. Stick with

low-risk professions that suit your talents, such as public service, teaching, or accounting.

11. *Are you flamboyant?* Some people are natural actors. They like centre stage and are comfortable with an audience. If you have this character trait and some natural talent to go with it, look for a path that takes advantage of it: acting, litigation law, broadcasting, lecturing.

12. *Are you a good leader?* If other people respect you and willingly follow your direction, take advantage of it. Natural leaders are rare. Their skills are needed in every occupation you can think of, from the military to fashion design. This is one talent that should not be suppressed under any circumstances. Just don't make the mistake of overdoing it and imposing yourself upon others. Of course, that advice is unnecessary for genuine leaders – they already recognize that leadership is earned, not demanded.

Putting Your Talents to Work

Identifying your strengths and character traits is a necessary step. But being The Best requires a lot more. You must mould and shape those talents – that inner genius – in such a way that they propel you to the objectives we have set: material wealth and personal satisfaction. Here's how:

- *Education.* Learn everything you can about what you're good at. If possible, earn a university degree in your area of specialization. If that isn't feasible, take selected night courses or vocational training programs. Read all you can about the subject. Know everything there is to know. The test of your knowledge is whether your peers come to you for information because you know more than they do.

- *Confidence.* You have to believe in yourself. If you have doubts, if you're unsure about the direction in which you're heading, there is no way you can make it to the top. You can only be the best if you *believe* you can be the best.

- *Motivation.* You can't become the best unless you *really* want to. No matter how great your talent, you'll never rise to the top without the drive that true motivation inspires.

- *Discipline.* You have to work at it. It won't come easily. It may, in fact, take years. You must exercise the self-discipline to stick with it and follow through.

- *Job selection.* Earlier, I stressed never accepting a job unless it's one you think you'll enjoy and that will enhance your chance of reaching our twin goals. Anything else is a waste of your time. You'll never become The Best by working at something that doesn't challenge your strengths and teach you how to use them better.

- *Training.* You can learn a lot in school, but the best teachers are those who have achieved success in their chosen field. They operate from a perspective of practicality, not theory. They know what works and what doesn't. That's why it's important to find a mentor, someone who's been through it and can short-circuit the process for you.

    Too often I hear younger people say: "I want to learn for myself. I want to make my own mistakes." For heaven's sake, why? Stop and think about the irrationality of such comments. You want to make your own mistakes? You want to waste your time, energy, and, perhaps, your financial resources when you don't have to? When, by listening to the advice of someone who has already gone that route, you can take a shortcut and move closer to your goal that much faster? People who say, "I want to make my own mistakes" are self-absorbed, unthinking, or plain stupid. One of life's most important rules is simply this: *Never make a mistake that can be avoided.* Mistakes are distracting, time-consuming, and frustrating. They will lengthen the time it takes to accumulate that first million. Bypass them whenever possible.

    Of course, a good mentor can do much more than help you avoid mistakes. He or she can show you the tricks of the business, introduce you to the right people, and encourage your development in a hundred little ways. If you have the opportunity to work closely with someone who's an acknowledged expert in your chosen field, grab it — even if you have to work for free. It will pay off many times over.

- *Staying ahead.* It's a cliché to note that the world is constantly changing. We all recognize that. Unfortunately, many people don't apply that little piece of common knowledge to their work. They settle into a groove and complacently decide they know it all. They don't keep up with the rapid changes that affect their field and the way in which work is completed and judged. You may become number one at what you do, but you won't retain the position for long if you stand still. There are always footsteps coming up behind. Become lazy, relax your guard for a moment, and you'll be overtaken — perhaps not by just one person but by a thundering herd.

Sure it's tough. But the challenge will keep you sharp, keep your creative juices active, and hone your skills. If you truly want to be the best at what you do, you'll welcome that opportunity.

The Importance of Self-Respect

The cornerstone of success is self-respect. If you do not believe in yourself and the value of your worth and beliefs, you cannot expect anyone else to either.

This is much more difficult than it sounds. We are all plagued with doubts throughout life. We all have made decisions that, in hindsight, we wish had been different. We all have known the sting of others telling us we were lacking, whether by a teacher, a boss, a sibling, a spouse, a parent, or whomever.

Each negative event leaves its mark, right from the time of childhood, and creates an impediment that has to be overcome. To do that may require a strong effort of will and, in some cases, professional assistance. But it's an effort that must be made.

This is not to counsel blind egotism. People with genuine self-respect are confident enough to draw knowledge and guidance from others, because they know they can only benefit and become stronger as a result. They are also aware that they cannot know everything or do everything on their own – and they do not hesitate to seek support when needed.

But self-respect goes beyond that. It means having a core set of values by which you live, and which you will seek to pass on to your children. Without them, you will be like a non-swimmer who has been thrown out of a boat. You'll thrash and churn and you may even stay afloat for a while. But you will have no direction and no purpose. Ultimately, you will sink.

Each of us must determine where our principles lie. Organized religion has attempted to establish rigid guidelines for us over the centuries, and some people take them very much to heart. Others find the religious canons to be too strict or not applicable to modern lifestyles. They question whether the Supreme Being or His prophets really meant we should have sex only for procreation purposes, or should not press an elevator button on the Sabbath, or should refrain from drinking a glass of wine with dinner.

These people seek a different set of guidelines to follow, sometimes drawing on other sources, sometimes from within themselves.

However, most people would agree on at least four fundamental virtues: honesty, reliability, loyalty, and sensitivity. The last, sensitivity, is often misunderstood. It simply means to consider the needs of others. Those that do so avoid the dangers of egotism and selfishness. Not only are personal relationships better, but so are business associations. Why? Because you're sensitive to the goals of the people you're working with, or would like to work with. That sensitivity will motivate you to look for ways in which the relationship can not only benefit you but also benefit them. Result: everybody wins.

There is one other basic tenet that many would add, the Golden Rule, or a variation of it. Do unto others as you would have them do unto you. Do no harm to others. Be kind to your fellow humans. However expressed, the meaning is basically the same: Do not cause either mental or physical distress to another person, through word or deed. It is a very difficult principle to live by, but those who apply it find immense satisfaction in their human relationships.

What has all this to do with becoming a millionaire, you may ask? A lot. If you have self-respect and fundamental integrity, the road will become much easier. Not totally smooth, of course. But many of the potholes will disappear.

Now you're ready for the next step. You've prepared yourself mentally and started the search for your inner genius. But what do you do with it when you find it? How do you channel those abilities towards the ultimate goal?

Read on and find out.

Step 4

Empower Yourself

Talent, self-respect, integrity. All are essential ingredients in the pursuit of your dreams. But there's another ingredient we haven't spent a lot of time on so far: empowerment. You need to be able to harness your abilities and apply them in an effective way. That requires knowledge, support, and discipline. In this section, we'll deal with the whole issue of empowerment and what you need to do to achieve it.

Harnessing Your Abilities

Empowerment is a strong word, and the concept may be somewhat intimidating at first glance. So let me put it in a more approachable context, using an example from one of the first books I ever wrote.

Let's suppose you're in the kitchen and you want to make a cake. You've spread out all the basic ingredients on the counter in front of you: flour, eggs, butter, sugar, milk, and baking powder. You have a mixing bowl, a measuring cup, a baking pan, and a large spoon. Now what?

Think of all these as your abilities. There they are, clearly identified. But what the heck are you supposed to do with them? You could throw all the ingredients into a bowl, stir madly, pour the resulting mess into the pan, turn on the oven, and pray. The odds are you wouldn't end up with a cake – more likely the final result would be chucked into the garbage. Or you could follow a recipe, carefully measuring out the appropriate quantities of each ingredient, mixing them together as indicated, and baking for the specified amount of time at the required heat. Even if you've never made a cake before, the chances of something edible emerging from the oven have been greatly enhanced.

What have you done? You have empowered yourself. You have drawn on a source of expertise to bring the various ingredients together in a logical way and in doing so succeeded in reaching your goal: baking a cake.

That's all we're talking about here, except on a larger scale. This step is about drawing on the experience and expertise of others to empower yourself so that you can attain the objective we're working towards: that first million.

So it's not all that intimidating after all. Let's start the process. We'll divide this section into two parts. The first will be devoted to the theme of creating wealth and how to empower yourself to do that. The second will delve into how to accumulate your million through saving and investing, and provide the basic knowledge you need to start down that road.

Creating Your Million

If your plan is to create wealth, we'll assume you intend to do so through some form of entrepreneurship. If you're a creative genius or a gifted athlete or a super-talented performer, your path will be somewhat different. But if you're in one of those categories, you really don't need this book. Just go out and hire a first-class agent.

The rest of us have to work a little harder.

In Step Three, I stressed the need to identify the right career path. Clearly, you have to start moving in the right direction if you are going to create your own wealth. To return to a previous example, if Michael Jordan had failed to recognize that basketball was his primary athletic skill, he would have become a failed baseball player and the demand for him to endorse athletic equipment or to star in movies would have been zero.

So let's assume you establish the right direction for yourself. What now? The first step is to deal with the learning curve. Just because you are talented in a field doesn't mean you're automatically good at it. Robert Redford appeared in many B movies and seriously contemplated leaving acting before finally hitting it big in *Barefoot in the Park*. Success takes time, patience, experience, and help.

The latter is especially important. One of the best training grounds for a wealth creator is to go to work for an organization that is highly successful in the person's targeted field. They've already shown they know how to do the job better than almost anyone else. Let them teach you what they've learned, so that you can then go the next step forward.

The potential trap is that you'll get too comfortable and lose your initiative. A regular salary and a steady job may divert you from your prime objective. Just remember: Few people get rich working for someone else. Those who do are usually the ones who got in at the beginning and who were willing to trade salary for stock options – a ploy that cash-strapped start-up companies love. It eases their cash-flow problems and creates a liability that becomes payable only if the company does well – and then at the expense of the other shareholders, through stock dilution.

You should be able to learn just about all any organization can teach you in two or three years, unless it's a huge company and you're constantly being moved into new areas. A good rule of thumb is the six-month test: if at the end of any six-month period you find you have not significantly added to the knowledge or experience you need to move ahead, it's time to look for an exit.

That may sound extreme, and it certainly isn't going to sit well with corporations that seek loyalty and commitment from their employees. But your number one commitment must be to yourself and your family. Just keep in mind that you'll be out the door in a heartbeat if hard times set in and the company has to cut costs to survive. The days of cradle-to-grave security are gone, even in their last refuge, Japan.

At some point, the wealth-creation process demands that you strike out on your own, or in partnership with one or two other like-minded people. The reason is simple: You must own the means by which the wealth is generated, either in whole or in part. If someone else owns it, you will never be properly rewarded for your talent and effort. If you develop a product or create an intellectual property or invent something that is patentable while in the employ of someone else, it belongs to them. That's the law. If you're to own it, you have to do it on your own.

If that sounds as though it involves risk-taking, yes it does. If you're not prepared to accept that kind of risk, then the wealth creation path may not be the right one for you.

There are exceptions, of course. Top athletes can become rich without giving up security. If your talent is in throwing a baseball left-handed and you're under 25, your chances of becoming a millionaire are pretty good. Senior corporate executives can also create great wealth without sacrificing security. If you think you have what it takes to become president of General Motors, fine. But most people aren't going to be in that kind of position, so they have to make a choice. It's not an easy one.

Are You an Entrepreneur?

Do you have what it takes to strike out on your own in pursuit of wealth creation? Could you set up your own business? Maybe you don't think so, but you might surprise yourself.

Perhaps we should begin by defining *entrepreneur* in the context of this book. The word conveys images of aggressiveness, ambition, drive, risk, and money. Entrepreneurship can certainly encompass all of these, but at its core it's much simpler. Entrepreneurs are people who set out to create something for themselves rather than for someone else.

I never considered myself an entrepreneur. I was a company man from the time I entered the workforce after university. Yes, I co-authored some novels in my spare time, but I never for a moment considered quitting my job to gamble everything on a fiction writing career. I was conservative by nature, I had a family and a mortgage, and we had no savings to fall back on. Plus, I was in my mid-40s. That made me about the lousiest candidate for entrepreneurship that you could find.

But sometimes decisions are forced upon us. I ended up as an entrepreneur not by choice but by circumstance. It was a case of making it on my own or watching our standard of living crumble. The goal wasn't wealth creation at that stage. It was financial survival.

Years later, my only regret is that I didn't act sooner. But it wasn't a case of having put off the decision because I was afraid. Quite simply, the idea of going it alone had never even shown up on my radar screen.

Changing from Employee to Entrepreneur

I actually became an entrepreneur in two stages. The first stage lasted from the autumn of 1982 to the spring of 1984 and was immensely frustrating. I was able to earn a living but I lacked focus and direction. Stage two began in 1987 and continues to this day. One of the reasons I succeeded the second time around was because of the lessons I had learned from my first experience. Let me share them with you.

Lesson #1: Make the Transition as Easy as Possible.

There are two ways to make the leap from employee to entrepreneur: the hard way and the easy way. The hard way involves walking in one morning, quitting your job, and going home to get started on your new life without any clear understanding of how you're going to achieve your goal or where you'll find the money to live on in the mean-time. I don't recommend it.

The easy way is to have a well-defined plan in place before you make the move, with some certain or probable sources of income. This way, you'll begin your new incarnation with a degree of confidence and the knowledge that you're not likely to starve until the world gets around to discovering your genius.

One of the best potential sources of income is your current employer, assuming you are doing a good job for the company and that you can provide a skill or a service that they will need no matter what. For example, when Hume Publishing decided to downsize its Canadian operation in 1987, there was still a need for certain tasks to be performed. The company wasn't going out of business; it just didn't want the overhead involved in carrying a large staff. I could see the handwriting on the wall months in advance, so I care-fully analysed what services the pared-down organization would need to contract out and how my abilities could fit in. Almost immediately after I received notice, I sat down and negotiated a freelance contract that involved newsletter writing and consulting work. The company was happy to get the services and the income guarantee meant that I didn't have to be concerned about our financial well-being. In fact, when the tax advantages of running my own business were taken into account, I was actually better off than when I was a Hume employee, even though my work load had been more than cut in half, thus freeing me for other projects. It was a win-win situation all around.

Lesson #2: Don't Burn Any Bridges

The Hume contract was in part made possible by the fact that I was on good terms with the company (although I never would have gotten it if they didn't think I was the best person for the job). That's why it's important never to burn any bridges. You may be itch-ing to tell your boss where to shove it before you walk out the door. Stow it. You don't know when you may need his or her goodwill, or that of some other senior person in the company. When you're on your own, you need all the allies you can find. You don't need enemies. So don't make any if you don't have to.

Lesson #3: Maximize Synergies

The first time I went out on my own, I found myself putting in incredibly long hours for minimal returns. The reason was that I failed to create any synergies in my work. Each project was autonomous and unrelated to anything else. I would spend two weeks researching and writing an article on illegal immigration for *Reader's Digest,* then another two weeks on a story about home renovations, then another two weeks on a travel piece. Nothing fit. No synergy.

The most efficient use of time is to work on a project that can be sold in various forms to different organizations. Usually, that means specialization – focusing on one area of expertise and making yourself or your fledgling company one of the leaders in the field. I made that point earlier (Be the Best), but here it is again in a more activity-related context. Decide what you're really good at, what you will specialize in, and then find ways to sell the same work (or variations thereof) again and again.

In my second incarnation as an entrepreneur, I knew I wanted to focus on investment and personal finance. The synergies all flowed from there. Research that I did for a newsletter article was also valuable for books, radio broadcasts, magazine pieces, commercial writing, and, later, Web site content. Synergy, synergy, synergy. Don't ever forget it.

Lesson #4: Innovate

You won't create wealth by following a well-worn track. You may earn a good living at it, but we're out for a million dollars here. That kind of return demands something special, perhaps something unique.

That means innovation. You cannot be satisfied with the ordinary. You have to go the next step. That does not mean you need to figure out how to build a better car or write the Great Canadian Novel. It does mean that you have to establish yourself as a leader in whatever field it is you undertake.

The first step is to look for an obvious entree. See if there is a niche that you can comfortably fill, and move quickly to occupy it.

As the 1990s began, mutual funds surged to popularity among investors. Annual sales rose astronomically and the number of funds available expanded by the month. But no one was offering advice about how to buy funds or which were the best choices. There was an information gap just waiting to be filled. I went to my publisher with the concept for a comprehensive *Buyer's Guide to Mutual Funds.* It was a risk – no one had done anything like it – but they bought it. The first edition was the *1991 Guide.* Sales were modest, but strong enough to encourage us to keep going. Within two years the book was selling tens of thousands of copies every year, and shortly thereafter competitors began appearing. By the late '90s, half a dozen mutual fund guides were vying for the public's dollars. Of course, the others cut into our sales, but entering the new century we were still firmly positioned as number one and some of the other titles had vanished.

That's innovation – looking for opportunities within your field of expertise and running with them. Think they're hard to find? That may be because you haven't studied your field closely enough. There are always opportunities available. It's a matter of sensitizing yourself to them.

Lesson #5: Be Disciplined

Let's not mince words. You cannot succeed as an entrepreneur if you don't have self-discipline. There is no one watching you through an office door. It's you watching yourself. If you don't have the discipline to work the hours needed or to see a job through to completion, the odds are hopelessly against you.

But self-discipline isn't all that's needed. Those around you need discipline as well. You may end up working from home, at least in the early stages of your entrepreneurial career. After all, a home office saves money and gives rise to some tax breaks. But you won't be working effectively if your spouse or partner or children or parents take the view that they can drop in at any time and interrupt your work.

When my children were young, we had to teach them to respect a closed home office door. I put it to them this way: "Pretend I'm not behind that door. Pretend I've gone downtown to the office like I used to and that I'll play with you when I come home."

They grasped the concept surprisingly quickly and I was able to accomplish my work in peace – usually.

Lesson #6: Prepare for Long Hours

Do you get upset when you have to work overtime on the job? If so, you'll hate being an entrepreneur. Working overtime is a way of life. Quitting at five is such a rare luxury that it almost makes you feel guilty. A full weekend off? Not likely. A two-week holiday? Even if you could afford it, you probably couldn't spare the time, at least in the early years.

When I first began to work on my own, I promised my wife I would never work past six and would always be available on the weekends. I haven't reached that stage even today. And, no, I don't consider myself to be a workaholic. I prefer fishing. It's just that there is always something more to be done.

Lesson #7: Stay Focused

One of the problems with having a creative mind is that new ideas are always intruding. When that happens, remember this: Good ideas always translate into hard work. In a sense, bad ideas are better because you don't have to commit any time to them. Good ideas may divert you from more important pursuits.

You need to set priorities from the outset and stay focused on them until they are achieved. If a new good idea does come along, assess it in the context of those already on your plate. If it is better than any that you're currently working on, fine – pursue it. But drop something else. Don't just add the new one to an ever-growing list.

Lesson #8: Sell Yourself

Being bright and innovative and hard working is all well and good. But all those good traits won't amount to anything if you can't sell the output to someone. That's the true test of your creative genius: Is someone willing to pay good money to buy what you have to offer?

This is where many entrepreneurs come up short. They have the skill to do or to make something special, but they don't know anything about marketing it. Why do you suppose almost every top athlete has an agent? Because the athlete may be able to find a receiver anywhere on the field but knows zilch about how to get a lucrative endorsement contract or how much money to demand.

If you don't have those marketing skills, then find someone who does and hire that person. Too expensive, you say? Nowhere near as expensive as investing months or years in a project and then seeing it fail because you didn't know how to sell it.

Lesson #9: Create a Network

I've made the point before but I'll repeat it: You can't do it all yourself. You need allies and alliances. You have to work hard to create them.

If appropriate, start with your former employers. If you have done a good job for them, keep them on side. Inform them about what you're doing, especially if in some way it may benefit their organization down the road. You don't have to be calling every week; an occasional e-mail or lunch can do the job very nicely.

Look for allies among your friends. They may be in occupations that have absolutely nothing to do with your business, or so you may think. But you'd be surprised how seemingly divergent paths can intersect on occasion. At one point, one of my friends in the venture capital business provided me with some extremely valuable guidance. On another occasion, a different friend put me in touch with a top-quality consultant who helped me to deal with some problems I couldn't find solutions for. Yet another good friend came to me with an attractive business opportunity.

The beauty of having friends as part of your business network is that these are people you have probably known for a long time. The result is a mutual trust that can be of tremendous value. If you know the person to be a true friend, then you know he or she is not trying to use you for selfish ends. You are able to act on the advice without the fear that there may be a hidden agenda at work.

Your network may well extend to your competitors. Yes, these people are in the same field and may be competing for the same dollars, but that doesn't necessarily make them blood enemies. Some of my most useful relationships are with people who do much the same thing as I do, because we recognize that there's room for all of us. I may not tell them what book I'm working on, but I'm certainly willing to swap ideas for improving marketing over lunch.

Your network should include professionals that can provide expertise you don't have, from accounting to legal matters to graphics design. These people will expect to be paid, of course, but they still form part of your network. And most of them won't start the clock if you call occasionally for a quick piece of information or advice.

There may be other elements to your network, but these will get you started. Make it a point to nurture and develop them. You never know when you'll need help, or what form that need will take.

Lesson #10: Compromise When Necessary

There will be times when you have to bend a bit. Things won't always flow as smoothly as you might like and compromises may be required. The key is not to compromise the essentials. Don't lose your basic direction, or you may never get back on track.

If you have to divert your attention to another project temporarily to generate some needed cash flow, fine. But once that's out of the way, get back to the main objective. If you have to modify your plan in order to make a sale, do it — as long as you're not undermining its fundamental value. If you need to take on another partner to ensure success, do it.

Life is a series of compromises. It's a matter of understanding which ones are necessary for ultimate success and which may lead to the abandonment of everything you've been working towards. Those are the compromises you must walk away from.

Let me stress that again: *Never compromise your fundamental integrity.* You may be sorely tempted to do so in order to achieve a seemingly important short-term goal or to short-circuit the route to wealth. But if you succumb, you'll begin a slide down a slippery slope from which there is no recovery.

Compensation, Not Perspiration

Thomas Edison is said to have described success as "1 percent inspiration and 99 percent perspiration." Edison was wrong. His remark is understandable in the context of his time, but nonetheless he was dead wrong. In fact, if he had been right no one would ever have heard of him.

Thomas Alva Edison was a product of the 19th century, and was therefore imbued with 19th-century thinking. It was a time in history when North America was on the rise and when even little people dreamed great dreams. Immigrants flooded to North America's shores. Most of them knew the streets weren't paved with gold. But most believed that with hard work they could succeed and build a better life for themselves and their families in this brave new world.

Edison was a product of the upper classes. His father was a shingle manufacturer who fled to the U.S. from Canada during the 1837 Rebellion. (That's how close we came to having one of history's greatest inventors as a native son.) He had only three months of formal education – he irritated teachers by asking too many questions so his mother schooled him at home.

The tradition of the work ethic was strong during this time. It served not only to keep the poor docile but also to encourage the children of the rich not to become indolent. Thus it became part of American culture – the man who is willing to work hard (for in those days few women ventured outside the home) will surely find success.

Thus "1 percent inspiration and 99 percent perspiration." Sure, you have to have a great idea, said the man who invented the electric light, the phonograph, the voting machine, and the dictating machine, and who was a pioneer in the field of talking pictures. But that's only a small part of the whole equation. The largest part, by far, is the willingness and the ability to work very, very hard – at least according to the Edison standard.

Edison had it partially right. Of course, you need to work hard, which is a point I've already made. But suppose all Edison had going for him were the two factors he named: a good idea and a powerful work ethic. Would we know his name today? Probably not.

Why? Because there is an even more important ingredient to entrepreneurial success that Edison failed to mention: Compensation. Somebody has to make some money from the idea and all the hard work. If they don't, the whole scheme will end up in the trash can of history. Even if the concept is absolutely brilliant, it will die, at least temporarily. How often have you read stories about someone else having invented the telephone before Alexander Graham Bell or wireless telegraphy (the forerunner of radio) before Marconi? Why aren't they remembered? The compensation factor. No one could figure out how to make any money from the idea — perhaps only because it was a generation ahead of its time. So it died stillborn and the original inventor passed into oblivion.

Even Edison himself recognized this after he tried unsuccessfully to sell his voting machine to the U.S. Congress. After he was turned down, he vowed, "I will never again invent anything that nobody wants." By that he meant, of course, something that no one was willing to pay for. Compensation. He himself would not work without it, yet it never became part of his proclaimed success formula.

The Internet Meltdown

You don't have to dig into the history books to find examples of the role compensation plays in entrepreneurial success. They're in the newspapers every day. The latest just unfolded before our eyes: the Internet Meltdown that shattered the dreams of many hard-working geniuses and near-geniuses.

The explosion of the Internet is the most exciting development to hit the communications industry since the birth of moving pictures at the end of the 19th century. It is even more powerful, I suggest, than television. That's because TV has evolved into a one-dimensional medium. We turn to it, by and large, to be entertained. Yes, it offers wonderful educational possibilities, but except as babysitting devices for small children who learn their numbers and letters while quietly watching *Sesame Street* as Mom grabs a coffee, the potential has been woefully underutilized. Yes, TV provides dramatic and immediate insights into the great news stories of the day, whether it is a hurricane sweeping out of the Gulf of Mexico, an earthquake in California, or a military flare-up in the Balkans. But such events are rare and hold our attention for a relatively short time.

Answer honestly: How do you spend most of your hours in front of the television set? Watching sitcoms? Regis? Sports? Movies? How often do you turn on PBS? How many televised education courses have you taken? How many historical documentaries did you watch last month? I rest my case.

The advent of moving pictures was a seminal event in the communications industry because for the first time it made people aware of how others lived and felt and reacted. It brought the world into every small town and broadened our horizons beyond anything we had ever before imagined. Television took it the next step, by bringing the world into our homes. But we had already experienced the phenomenon many times at the Roxy. We had seen World War II fought out in the newsreels. We first met Bugs Bunny and Donald Duck while munching popcorn and watching their cartoons. We knew what Jack Benny and Bob Hope and Bing Crosby looked like because we had seen them on the screen. We even saw our first filmed commercials at the local theatre. So TV was only an extension. Moving pictures – that was the seminal development.

Hollywood in those early days was like the Internet world is today. Anyone with vision knew that something incredibly important was happening – something that would make many people very rich. What they didn't know was exactly how it would all unfold and who would end up still standing once the dust had cleared. What technologies would work best? Who would be most successful in making moving pictures people would pay to see? And what exactly *did* people want to see? Where would the pictures be shown and how would they be distributed? Who could make money doing that? Ideas were born, ideas died; companies came and went. It was a time of chaos and uncertainty and mind-churning excitement. In the end, one of the most powerful industries on earth emerged, an industry that has had an influence on almost everyone around the globe. Fortunes were made. They were also lost.

And so we come to the Internet. This is the 21st-century equivalent of the birth of Hollywood. Perhaps not surprisingly, it too has a strong California connection, although by its nature the Internet is much more geographically dispersed. There is another huge difference as well. The Internet is Everyone's revolution. You don't need a truckload of money, the way you did to build a sound stage or a movie palace. Kids can create their own Web site after school, and they do. For a few bucks you can buy the software to get you going.

That's why we have seen the phenomenon of the dot-com millionaires. At the outset (which was less than a decade ago, remember), you could build a Web site, offer a lot of free stuff, pull in thousands of surfers (in the early days there wasn't a lot of competition), and convince people with money that you were on to something big. The venture capitalists moved in, a public share issue followed, and before you could turn around someone was writing a cheque for a million dollars in your name. It was soooo easy.

That was then. This is now. Yes, there will still be some new dot-com millionaires created. But the big stories these days are about cash burns and meltdowns and site closings. We've moved to stage two: Consolidation. This is where it hurts; where sites that aren't generating adequate revenue (most of them) are running out of money just as investors have become nervous and backed off. New IPOs (initial public offerings) are increasingly difficult to sell to a market where skepticism has replaced greed as the main motivating force. Even well-positioned companies with excellent prospects are feeling the crunch.

There is nothing surprising or unusual about this, and it is certainly not fatal for the industry the way some doomsayers are predicting. Hollywood went through the same thing, only few people knew about it at the time because business failures weren't something the newspapers paid much attention to and newspapers were the only means of mass communication at the turn of the last century.

The Internet industry will grow and expand and boom for the rest of our lives. The reason is very simple. It is multi-dimensional. It meets our needs on a range of levels far beyond anything imagined by motion pictures or TV.

Entertainment? Sure, there's tons of it on the Internet, from pop music to games to sports to gambling and all the way down to porn. And with coming advances in technology, it won't be long before you're watching Internet movies.

Information? What do you want to know? How to deal with baby's cough? The symptoms of gout? When is it safe in your area to plant petunias in the spring? A recipe for the bass your son just caught? The date of the next solar eclipse? A biography of Leonardo da Vinci? Rules on tax write-offs? It's out there somewhere. The trick is to find it.

Commerce? You can buy and sell just about anything you can imagine on the Internet. Visit 15 houses in the city you're moving to in two hours, with virtual tours of the interiors and the grounds. Compare cruise ships or resorts in Provence. Rent a cottage. Buy a car. Subscribe to a newsletter. Order a sweater. Take a virtual tour of a shopping mall 1,000 miles away.

Companionship? Go into a chat room and have a lively discussion about politics, the environment, the economy, your next vacation, the sex habits of gerbils, or simply pour out your heart to anyone who'll offer some sympathy.

Communications? Many people now prefer e-mail to the telephone (quicker, you don't get bogged down). They send electronic birthday and Christmas cards. They post pictures of the new baby on the family Web site. They talk to their relatives in Australia for free via Internet telephone.

The list goes on and on. The Internet is changing the way we live, work, love, and play. The evolution will continue. Don't be fooled by those who crash and burn. There are casualties in every industry, but many more in new ones.

Believe me: there is still a lot of money to be made here. We have just begun.

The Real Success Formula

This brings us back to Mr. Edison and his 1/99 formula. I said that I believe he was wrong. Now I submit that the real formula for entrepreneurial success is this: 1 percent inspiration, 40 percent perspiration, and 59 percent compensation.

Yes, you need the idea — whether it has to do with the Internet, or with an application for the budding science of nanotechnology, or with something as simple as an improved can opener.

Yes, you need to work hard. Let me repeat a quotation I cited earlier: "All good ideas translate into hard work." It's true. If you have a good idea and you want to build on it to become an entrepreneur, then of course you have to work hard. Forget about nine to five. Forget about weekends off. To make it happen, you have to be prepared to work whatever number of hours it takes, at whatever time of the day or night is required. So yes, indeed, you have to work hard — to put in the perspiration.

But that still won't do it for you. Not by a long shot. Because for the dream to succeed and for you to become wealthy, there must be compensation. And that is the ultimate key to making it all happen. Of course, there has to be compensation for you. But that isn't enough. If you're going to get rich, you're probably going to have to make someone else rich too. Maybe a lot of someone elses. And it just could happen that they'll end up even richer than you. Don't let that possibility become an impediment to your success. Keep your attention focused on the ultimate goal. If others profit, fine. It's you that we're concerned about.

The reason that compensation is such a critical part of the equation is that without it, or the reasonable expectation that it will be forthcoming, no one will lift a finger to help you and it won't be long before you become discouraged and move on to something else. A few people will bust their buns for friendship, or love, or altruism, or religion, or a cause. But most of us are driven by the prospect of material reward. You may not like what that says about our society but it is an undeniable truth.

So compensation becomes the single most important factor in my equation, with a 59 percent weighting. I didn't pull this number out of the air. I believe it counts for more than half of the entrepreneurial success formula.

In recent years, a number of organizations have made presentations to me outlining the brilliant concepts they've devised for the Internet. All of these people have worked very hard. In most cases, the ideas were innovative and potentially valuable. So nine times out of ten they satisfied Edison's inspiration/perspiration criteria.

What they lacked in almost every case was a credible compensation plan. In most cases, the revenue flow was based on nothing more than hope, dreams, and statistics. "We have identified 20 million people in North America who are potential customers. Of these, half have access to the Internet. Of that 10 million, we believe we can sign up 10 percent, or 1 million people, within five years at an annual fee of $100 each. That's $100,000,000 in annual revenue and we haven't even touched the potential in Europe and Asia!"

Wonderful! There are only a few problems. How are all these people going to learn about the site? The Web world is a labyrinth and finding your way around is a challenge. How much money will have to be spent on marketing to reach the 10 million potential customers? Is that even possible? Probably not. And once they've been reached, who knows if 10 percent or even 1 percent will sign up for $100 a year. Internet users are notoriously stingy. They want everything for free. If you don't offer it on your site, they'll go elsewhere. They're tire kickers. I know — I operate a Web site that sells books, newsletters, and data. We generate decent revenue, but nothing like you might expect given the traffic flow.

So there must be compensation, and the compensation must be projected in a realistic manner. No one is prepared to accept "if this" and "if that" anymore. There has to be a business plan, the business plan has to make sense, and at the end of the day there has to be a payoff for everyone involved. If you can't figure out how that will happen and you don't have any business-minded friends or associates who can, then perhaps you should move on to another idea. At the very least, put this one on the back burner until the compensation part of the formula can be resolved.

That may seem harsh, especially if the idea is one you have lovingly nurtured. But not every great idea can be developed into a profitable business. If you fall in love with a concept, you run the danger of becoming blind to reality. Some ideas deserve to die because they will absorb your time, your energy, your creative juices — and give you nothing in return. The successful entrepreneur knows how to identify those dead ends at an early stage — and puts them in the trash can where they belong.

Learn More

Many books have been written on entrepreneurship. This is just a jumping-off point. If, after reading all this, you believe you have what it takes to create your million, then make it a priority to find out more. Read other books on the subject. Take some courses. Join a local small-business association and talk to people who have succeeded on their own. Build a store of knowledge and experience.

Whatever you do, don't plunge off on your own until you're ready. If you take a risk and fail, you may be reluctant to try again. So make sure the odds are in your favour before setting out.

Remember, dreams alone are not enough!

Saving Your Million

For most people, the savings and investment route is probably the easiest way to a million dollars.

Easy? He says it's easy? He should try living on my budget!

If that's your immediate reaction, I understand it.

Nevertheless, I'll say it again: Saving is the easiest way to become a millionaire. It's also the most comfortable route for many people because it needn't involve taking a lot of risk or quitting your job. I'll go so far as to make this flat statement: If you have a decent income, good self-discipline, and patience, I can virtually guarantee that you can be a millionaire within 20 years — perhaps a lot less. And that's strictly by saving and investing.

Not possible, you say. Yes it is, absolutely. You just have to be willing to work at it, and to empower yourself.

Unfortunately, our education system does not equip us for this challenge — in fact, in most cases the system doesn't even properly prepare young people to deal with the most basic aspects of personal finance, such as budgeting and debt management. I find it hard to believe that a course in the fundamentals of personal finance isn't mandatory at some level in the secondary school curriculum, but that is the case in most school districts. No wonder so many people get themselves into financial difficulty in their 20s and then have to spend years trying to recover.

That's why if you've come to this part of the book feeling that you lack the knowledge needed to begin a successful savings/investing program, you're not alone. Most people are in exactly the same position.

So was I, for much of my life. Like most of us, becoming a millionaire was the furthest thing from my mind when I finished college and began my working career. My priorities were to perform well in my new job, to increase my income, and to be able to afford to get married. Once I had achieved those goals, the focus shifted to advancement, buying a home, and earning enough income to support my growing family.

Most of us go through a similar cycle. We're too preoccupied with family and career to be concerned about the serious acquisition of wealth or to devote the time required to set out on that road. By the time we get around to thinking seriously about it, we may be in our 40s and decide it's too late. Actually, it's not – but the process would be a lot easier if we had started in our 20s.

Whatever your age now, this is the time to make a commitment. In fact, it may be your only opportunity to become wealthy because if you postpone making a start now you may never again have the resolve to do so. So this is it!

Let's get going.

A Few Basic Principles

We'll begin with some basic principles. You may find some of these are pretty simple, and they are. Unfortunately, many people fail to apply them and end up in trouble as a result.

Principle #1: Establish an Objective

Actually, we've already established an objective. It's to accumulate $1 million. That's a tangible figure and an achievable target. However, it is not doable in one year and probably not in five.

So let's make it a little easier by reducing it to bite-size chunks. This will give you a realistic goal to shoot for each year and will enable you to see whether you're on track to achieving your ultimate goal.

Start by choosing a time frame. You're going to be a millionaire at the end of _____ years. You fill in the blank. Five years? Ten? Fifteen? Twenty? Let's make it 20, tops. Anything else will seem so long as to be in another eon. If you think you can do it sooner, great. Just be realistic.

Now create a little chart for yourself. Start with your net worth as it stands today. If you don't know your net worth, use the Net Worth Calculator in Appendix A at the back of the book. Your chart can look something like the table below. I've used as an illustration the case of Jean Knowles, who currently has a net worth of $50,000 and has set her

are the very remote possibility of default (virtually non-existent in a developed country), the erosion in the value of your principal through inflation (a very real risk, even with inflation at low levels), and the high taxation of the interest payments if they are received outside a registered plan. Offsetting this is the fact that savings bonds are highly liquid (some can be cashed any time, others at regular intervals depending on their terms) and are backed with all the resources and taxing power of the issuing government (federal or provincial). I've never heard of anyone losing sleep wondering if his or her Canada Savings Bonds were safe! But the price you pay is a very low return. Usually, a Canada Savings Bond (CSB) will offer a lower yield than a regular short-term Government of Canada bond or a one-year guaranteed investment certificate (GIC). That means it will take a lot longer to accumulate that first million by going the CSB route than if you decide to accept a higher degree of risk.

The other means by which you pay for lower risk is through higher fees. In recent years, there has been an increased amount of interest in "segregated" funds. These are similar to mutual funds except they are offered through life insurance companies and come with a variety of bells and whistles. (You'll find more details about seg funds later in this chapter.) One of the most popular of these features is a guarantee. If you hold the fund for at least 10 years (the maturity guarantee) or if you die (the death guarantee), the insurer promises that you or your estate will receive no less than the specified guaranteed amount. In some cases, this is at least 75 percent of the total amount you invested, but for competitive reasons many insurers have now moved to 100 percent guarantees. What this means in practice is that you can invest your money in the most risky segregated fund you can find (say, one based on the Nasdaq Composite Index) and be assured that at the end of the day you will at least get your money back – even if the market falls to zero! Of course, if Nasdaq rises you'll benefit from the full increase in the value of your investment. The guarantee is just a floor.

The guarantee concept was made even sweeter by the introduction of a "reset" feature. This allows you to lock in any profits you have made and start a new 10-year clock. So, for example, if you invested $10,000 in a Nasdaq fund and it rose 40 percent in the first year (not impossible by any means), you could use your reset option to lock in your new value of $14,000 and restart the 10-year clock.

This is the kind of deal risk-averse investors love, and they began flocking to the hitherto ignored seg funds. The cost was a little higher, in the form of somewhat more expensive annual fees. But many people felt that the additional price was worth it.

Meanwhile, some insurance companies started to come out with increasingly high-risk offerings to take advantage of the growing mania for technology stocks. That represented a significant departure from the past, when seg funds had been about the most conservative (some might say the dullest) forms of investments around. Not surprisingly, regulators took a jaundiced view of the whole situation. Insurance companies were assuming more risk, both in terms of the guarantees they were offering and in terms of the volatility of the products they were bringing to market. The last thing anyone wanted to see was a rash of insurance company failures down the road because a stock market crash had forced them to pay out massive guarantee claims.

The regulators demanded that the insurance companies establish higher reserves against such contingencies. That, in turn, significantly drove up the fees attached to segregated funds, to the point where many companies withdrew their products from sale or diluted the guarantees.

It was just one more example of the high price of low risk. It's a trade-off you will have to constantly evaluate as you assess your investing options.

Types of Risk

In order to assess risk properly, you need to understand the different types of risk you'll encounter. Here's a quick run-down.

Inflation Risk

Let's say you've got $10,000 put aside and you want to put the money somewhere safe. A small trust company is offering 6 percent interest on a five-year GIC, paid annually. That's a better rate than the banks are paying, and it represents $600 income each year, rock-firm. And, of course, the investment is protected by deposit insurance. The Canada Deposit Insurance Corporation, an agency of the federal government, will ride to your rescue if anything should happen to the trust company. It looks safe and solid. If anything is risk-free, this is it, right?

Well, not really.

Inflation was not a problem through much of the 1990s, but as we moved into the new century it began to pose some concerns again. Governments and central banks will do everything in their power to prevent runaway inflation from taking hold again, perhaps even to the point of plunging the economy into recession. But inflation in the 2 to 3 percent range over the next few years is a real possibility.

Let's suppose the inflation rate when you invest your money is 2 percent. Over the five-year period, it increases modestly, at a rate of 0.5 percent per year. How much money, in real dollars adjusted for inflation, will you actually earn over the five years?

Take a look at the table below.

THE IMPACT OF RISING INFLATION ON REAL RETURNS

END OF YEAR	GROSS INCOME	INFLATION RATE	REAL RETURN (INFLATION ADJUSTED)
1	$600	2.0%	$588.00
2	600	2.5%	573.30
3	600	3.0%	556.10
4	600	3.5%	536.64
5	600	4.0%	515.17

As you can see, even at modest rates of inflation, your before-tax real return falls from 6 percent at the time of purchase to just over 5 percent at maturity. Plus, the $10,000 you'll get back from the trust company at maturity will have a purchasing power of just under $8,600. Your safely invested capital has dropped in real value by more than 14 percent. And this during a time when inflation is low!

If someone had told you in advance that the investment you were about to make would drop 14 percent in value over five years and that the value of the income it generated would be steadily eroded, would you go ahead anyway? Probably not!

Inflation is a risk with any fixed-income investment. The longer the term, the greater the risk. At an annual inflation rate of 3 percent, a $50,000 investment will be worth only about $36,900 in terms of real purchasing power after 10 years.

You protect yourself against inflation risk by having part of your portfolio in investments that will appreciate in value: stocks, equity mutual funds, and real estate are the three used most often. These are often regarded as higher-risk investments, but not to include them will expose you to an unacceptable level risk of another kind. It's a matter of balance.

Tax Risk

Unless your securities are held in some type of tax-sheltered environment, like an RRSP, they will be subject to tax risk. And while tax rates have been coming down in recent years, they are still quite high by comparison to those in the United States.

Let's assume you have a marginal tax rate of 40 percent. Now let's go back and look at our 6 percent GIC again. We'll operate on the basis that the investment is made outside a registered plan. The table shows you what happens.

THE IMPACT OF TAXES ON REAL RETURNS

END OF YEAR	GROSS INCOME	TAX PAYABLE	AFTER-TAX INCOME	INFLATION RATE	REAL RETURN
1	$600	$240	$360	2.0%	$352.80
2	600	240	360	2.5%	343.98
3	600	240	360	3.0%	333.66
4	600	240	360	3.5%	321.98
5	600	240	360	4.0%	309.10

The result is somewhat unnerving if you're a dedicated fixed-income investor. Your nominal after-tax rate of return drops from the 6 percent you thought you were receiving to just 3.6 percent. Moreover, in terms of the buying power of the dollar in Year One, your after-tax, inflation-adjusted return on the GIC in Year Five is down to a meagre $309.10. That's a long way from the $600 annually you were calculating on when you made the investment.

In this case, we've seen how inflation risk and tax risk combine to drive down the return on a GIC. Tax risk can take other forms as well. When Liberal Finance Minister Paul

Martin tabled his first budget in February 1994, he made clear to investors just how serious tax risk can be. His decision to end the lifetime $100,000 capital gains exemption, just at the point when many middle-income Canadians were positioning themselves to take advantage of it through mutual funds, turned investment strategy upside-down. Capital gains no longer were the most tax-effective way to earn investment income; that place of honour went to dividends instead. It wasn't until the twin budgets of 2000 that Mr. Martin restored some semblance of sanity to the tax system by effectively reducing the capital gains rate to the point where such profits, which are usually associated with higher risk, attract less tax than dividends.

The best way to protect yourself against tax risk is to structure your investment portfolio to take maximum advantage of the tax advantages that are available, while being flexible enough to make changes whenever necessary.

Interest Rate Risk

Many people think that government bonds are a safe place to put their money. We're not talking about savings bonds here; these are regular bonds that are traded on the open market. Since these bonds are issued and guaranteed by a government (federal or provincial), the assumption is that they are as safe as a church. Well, even churches have been hit by tornadoes on occasion. The same thing can happen to government bonds (or any other type of bond).

The culprit is rising interest rates. We'll get into the basics of bond investing a little later, but for now you need to keep one simple equation in mind: When interest rates rise, bond prices fall.

That painful lesson was delivered most recently in 1999–2000. Fearing that an overheated economy would lead to rising inflation, the U.S. Federal Reserve Board implemented a strategy to slow down growth through a series of rate increases. Other central banks didn't follow in lock-step, but there was a general upward move in rates throughout the industrialized world over the period.

The impact on the bond market was severe. Bond prices slumped through the latter part of 1999 and into early 2000. Investors in bond mutual funds experienced losses in many cases. They were relatively small compared to, say, a stock market crash. But bond investors don't expect to lose money. Most of them think they're in a safe haven.

Usually, they're right. But when interest rates move up, most bonds will get hit, as will other types of investments that are interest-rate sensitive, such as preferred shares and high-yield common stocks, like utilities. Stripped bonds, popular in RRSPs, are especially vulnerable to interest-rate risk. In fact, if rates spike sharply, the drop in the market value of long-term strips can be breathtaking.

There is one type of bond that is not vulnerable to interest-rate risk, however. Real-return bonds have built-in inflation protection, both for interest and principal. Since rising interest rates are almost always associated with higher inflation, these bonds (and the few mutual funds that invest in them) will generally outperform the rest of the market in that kind of environment.

Stock Market Risk

We don't need to spend a lot of time on this one. Everyone knows about stock market risk. Plunging share prices hit the headlines with unnerving regularity. Take the bursting of the high-tech bubble in April 2000. In just five trading days, the Nasdaq Composite Index lost about a quarter of its value. Now that's a crash! It came just at a time when many people seemed to believe that pigs do fly and stock prices would go to the moon. The valuations of most of the high-tech companies had reached absurd levels. Investors were paying hundreds of dollars (literally!) for a single share of a company that had never made one cent of profit, in the belief that someone else would buy that share from them for fifty or a hundred dollars more. For many months the insanity went on, reminding veteran market watchers of such classic bubbles as Tulipomania in Holland back in the 17th century and prompting U.S. Federal Reserve Board Chairman Alan Greenspan to warn on several occasions of "irrational overexuberance."

In the end, the market corrected – painfully so – with a dive that continued on into 2001 after a brief rally in the summer. Investors who came late to the high-tech party were left ruefully contemplating the lesson of stock market risk that had just been administered, yet again.

Stock market risk is a constant fact of life for equity investors. Like most other forms of risk, the timing of it is unpredictable. However, the portents can usually be seen well in advance, if you're attuned to them. The Nasdaq tumble was no great surprise; what was more surprising was that the buying mania went on for as long as it did before the correction hit. That prolonged period of steady gains prompted some market watchers who should have known better to come out with "this-time-it's-different" theories. Guess what? It's never different. A mania is a mania — always has been, always will be.

If you invest in stocks and/or equity mutual funds — and I believe you must if you are going to attain your million dollar objective through the savings/investment route — then stock market risk is something you must live with. But although you cannot eliminate it, you can minimize the risk in four ways: by holding quality stocks, by having a time horizon that's long enough to enable you to ride out any temporary setbacks, by taking profits when a stock appears to be overvalued, and by diversifying your portfolio internationally. We'll discuss stock market investing in more detail later.

Default Risk

You're not likely to encounter default risk, but it can happen and you need to be aware of it. It occurs when you buy a security and the issuer become insolvent and/or declares bankruptcy, leaving investors with little or nothing.

It can happen with any type of security: bonds, common stocks, GICs, term deposits, Treasury bills, you name it. And it doesn't happen only to individuals; Canada's banks experienced their own version of default risk when the giant development firm of Olympia and York suddenly ran into a financial crisis in the 1990s recession.

Two recent examples cost investors billions of dollars, none of which was ever recovered. The first involves a name that will live in infamy: Bre-X Resources. This Calgary-based company hit the big time when it supposedly uncovered one of the richest gold strikes in the history of the world in the remote jungles of Indonesia. Share prices soared, reaching over $200 each at the peak. Fortunes were made. The market frenzy continued to be fed by press releases from the company announcing continued good results and suggesting even bigger news yet to come.

In the end, it all turned out to be a gigantic fraud. The only ones who ended up making any money were investors who sold before the news broke and some officers of the company. Everyone who still had Bre-X shares after the hoax was revealed lost everything. The stock certificates might have some value as curiosity pieces in the future, but that's about it.

Shortly after Bre-X, a second big failure rocked the stock markets. Livent Inc., a major theatrical company that had staged hits like *Phantom of the Opera, Showboat, Ragtime,* and others, suddenly and to this day inexplicably, went down. The company appeared to be on solid financial footing and owned valuable properties in New York, Chicago, and Toronto, among other locations. The president, Garth Drabinsky, was a well-established name in the North American entertainment industry.

The lawsuits over who did what to whom are still raging and it may be years before they are resolved. But for investors, it's game over. Trading in Livent shares was suspended in New York and Toronto when the news broke. It never resumed, and, as with Bre-X, investors were left with worthless paper.

The Livent debacle blindsided almost everyone. Just weeks before, the company had received a new infusion of capital and some fresh managerial talent at the top, so there was little reason to suspect everything was about to come crashing down. Being hit by the Bre-X fiasco, while not predictable, was more avoidable because the run-up in the share price should have prompted more cautious investors to sell.

Default risk can also hit bond investors. That happens when a bond issuer runs into financial difficulty and suspends interest payments or, worse, goes bankrupt. The chances of that happening are higher in an economic slowdown, which is why returns on high-yield bonds (also known as junk bonds) will shoot up in those conditions. Investors are demanding a higher return for the added risk they are assuming.

Default risk does not happen often. But when it does, the impact can be especially painful because it usually takes place quickly, with little advance warning, leaving investors no time to bail out.

There is no way to completely avoid it. Even giant corporations are occasionally vulnerable. The best you can do is to minimize the risk by diversifying your portfolio and not taking an overly large position in any one security.

Economic Risk

Economic risk can take a variety of forms: a jump in the inflation rate that causes bond prices to drop, a bumper harvest that knocks down grain prices, a slowdown in consumer spending that leads to a drop in car and house sales — all of these have negative implications for investors.

Economic risk can come in the form of mega-events, such as the Asian Crisis of 1997 that had a profound impact on stock markets and commodity prices around the world. Or it can involve a specific industry. If you happened to have money in bank stocks, you took a beating in 1999 when share prices tumbled in response to rate increases. If you were in pharmaceutical stocks when Bill Clinton came to office, you watched in horror as their values plummeted in response to his attacks on the high cost of prescription drugs. If you owned any energy stocks, you'll remember what happened to their prices when oil dived to $12 a barrel in the fall of 1998.

The only way to mitigate economic risk is to maintain a high degree of awareness as to what's going on both at home and around the world — and understand how economic news may affect your investments.

Liquidity Risk

I have a copy of the first edition of a book titled *V,* by the novelist Thomas Pynchon. One day I read in a magazine that it was worth over $300. Terrific, I thought. I'm not a collector of first editions. I didn't particularly care for the book. It was just gathering dust on a shelf. Why not convert it to cash? Fine idea. But trying to find a buyer who would pay $300 for it was impossible. I visited several rare book stores. The best offer I got was $100. I still have the book. Maybe I should try selling it on eBay.

That's liquidity risk. You may have an asset that's worth a lot of money, but it's no good unless someone is prepared to pay your price for it. If you can't sell it for what it's supposedly worth, you've got a problem.

A common investment example of liquidity risk is the popular labour-sponsored venture capital funds. You get good tax breaks when you buy them. But you're locked in for eight years. If you sell before then, you have to repay your tax credits.

GICs are another example. Normally, you're locked in until they mature. If the issuer does let you out early, it's usually with a penalty.

Or consider locked-in RRSPs. You may desperately need the money – perhaps you've lost your job and you could use the cash to tide you over. Sorry – in most provinces the rules say you can't touch it except in extraordinary circumstances. Locked in means exactly that.

Liquidity risk is reduced by ensuring that anything you invest in has a strong and ready market of potential buyers. If it doesn't, be very certain that you will not need to draw on the funds at any time in the near future.

Political Risk

We always live with the risk that the politicians will somehow undermine our investments. This can happen in a number of ways: through policy changes, campaign rhetoric (Bill Clinton and Al Gore attacking the pharmaceutical companies), and threat of radical change (Quebec separation from Canada).

Political risk can also arise from instability; in the days following the remarkable U.S. presidential election of 2000, the stock markets were rocked by the indecisive situation and the uncertainty of whether George W. Bush or Al Gore would eventually emerge as the new president.

Investors should view politicians as the wild card in their calculations. Everything about an investment can look fine – and then a government or a party or even a lone politician can find a way to mess it up. That's why it's important to keep tuned in to what's going on in Ottawa and other capitals. It's hard to protect yourself against political risk because it can be so mercurial. Even though the polls were close, no one could have dreamed up the scenario that followed the U.S. presidential vote of November 7, 2000.

As a general rule, newly elected governments are potentially the most volatile. That's because they usually feel a commitment to fulfill at least some of their campaign promises – no matter how dumb those may have been. So at election time, pay attention to what the parties are saying. If certain policies are potentially injurious to some of your investments, consider selling.

Judicial Risk

A few years ago, no one even considered judicial risk when evaluating an investment. Then U.S. juries began handing out huge damage settlements that sent companies reeling. The tobacco industry was the hardest hit, but even companies that no one would have thought were vulnerable got rocked. One example was Vancouver-based Loewen Group, a firm in the low-profile funeral business. Its shares were socked after a jury in the southern U.S. found in favour of the plaintiff in a suit against the company and awarded a huge settlement.

The defence here? Again, it's difficult. However, major legal actions against a public company do have to be acknowledged in the annual report. Check there to see if there are any outstanding.

Currency Risk

The loonie represents yet another level of risk for Canadian investors – currency risk. Our dollar was on a downward slide for most of the 1990s and that trend continued through most of 2000. It may reverse itself in future – most economists believe the loonie should be trading at upwards of U.S.$0.70. But the uncertainty creates problems for long-term investors, especially those who are thinking about spending part of their retirement in the American Sunbelt.

Fortunately, this is one type of risk for which there is a relatively easy solution. There is nothing that impedes you from investing a portion of your assets in U.S.-dollar denominated securities. Even in registered plans like RRSPs, where foreign content limits apply, there are many U.S.-dollar denominated choices available that are considered 100 percent Canadian content – U.S.-pay federal and provincial government bonds are just one example.

Emotional Risk

Finally, there is always emotional risk to contend with. Sometimes it's very hard to do the right thing with your investments, even though logic absolutely demands that a particular course of action be followed. When stock prices are surging ever upward, it's very hard to sell, as tech investors discovered during the great bull run of the late 1990s. When share prices are in the dumps, it's equally difficult to persuade yourself to buy, even though you know that great companies are available at bargain rates.

Learning to control your investment emotions is usually a function of experience. The more you observe the financial world, the more attuned you will become to its rhythms and the more confident you will be about making moves that run against the prevailing psychology of the day.

At the outset, the best piece of advice I can offer is to keep a level head. Don't panic in a market sell-off and dump quality stocks at ridiculous prices. You'll regret it, perhaps within a few days.

In the early part of 2000, a rising company in the high-tech world, Research in Motion, of Waterloo, Ontario, saw its share price shoot up as high as $260. Then came the tech wreck of spring. In the aftermath, the stock dropped all the way down to $35, if you can believe it. That means that people were selling out their positions at those low levels. Within weeks, the price rallied and by the end of the summer the stock was trading at over $150 and climbing. Imagine how you would have felt if you had been one of those who panicked and sold out at $35.

So keep your cool at all times. Remember that stock market plunges seen in retrospect are nothing more than quick downward blips on an otherwise steadily rising chart.

After reading this section, you may be saying to yourself, "This is too much. I can't deal with all these risks! There's no point even trying."

Yes there is. Millions of people handle them quite well and profit. It's all a matter of knowing the techniques and applying them, and I'll help you with that as we go forward.

Plus there is the other side of this coin: the rewards. Those who are willing to take some chances in life are the ones who come out on top. Those who choose to sit on the sidelines because they are afraid never know the satisfaction of victory.

Your rewards may be relatively small or they may be huge, depending on how hard you work at this, the degree of risk you are prepared to accept, and, to some extent, on fortune. But there will be a payoff. Let's take a look at what you can expect.

The Rewards

Here are the major benefits you can expect to achieve by embarking on a serious savings/investment program. I have listed them in ascending order, starting with the most basic.

You Add to Your Store of Useful Knowledge

Each day we enter some new fact or experience in the database of the mind. It may be nothing more than a bit of trivia you picked up while watching *Who Wants to Be a Millionaire*. (Quick, now, for a million dollars, what is the approximate distance between the Earth and the sun?) Or it may be something far more substantial, perhaps a penetrating insight into the subliminal text in the latest Margaret Atwood novel, gleaned from a lecture you attended the night before.

Unfortunately, most of these pieces of information, while interesting, have no practical application in your day-to-day life. But everything that you learn about saving, investing, and managing money will, I assure you. This stuff may seem somewhat complicated on first exposure. But whether we like it or not, it represents the foundation on which our material lives are based. The more you know about money and how it works, the more comfortable you will be in dealing with the demands it constantly places on you. Even if you never become a millionaire, the knowledge that you gain will come into use on hundreds of occasions in the years ahead.

You Develop Better Financial Self-Discipline

Some people are very good at managing their money. Others are terrible. They can't keep track of how much is coming in or where it is going. They misplace invoices, with the result that bills don't get paid – which in turn harms their credit rating. They can't find important papers at tax time, if they ever get around to completing a return (if you don't, expect to find a big bill from the government in the mail some day estimating what you owe it). In short, their financial lives are a mess and they barely make it from paycheque to paycheque.

Most of us fall somewhere in the middle. We have a reasonable idea where the money is going, but we can never seem to get ahead. (Does that sound familiar?) We aren't irresponsible; we do our best. But it's tough trying to make ends meet.

By understanding even a little more about money, savings, and investing, you'll be able to do better — probably a lot better. You'll learn easy systems for keeping track of your cash inflow and outflow and for starting a savings plan that will eventually grow into a major investment portfolio. And you'll discover that it really wasn't so tough after all.

Family Tensions Lessen

This may seem like a rather surprising benefit at first glance. But think about it. The three main causes of friction between spouses or partners are sex, children, and money. You'll have to look elsewhere for remedies for the first two. But if you can reduce or eliminate any financial quarrels, you've taken a big step towards improving domestic harmony.

You Reduce and Eventually Eliminate Your Debts

We've already discussed how crushing a heavy debt load can be. The more financial information you have, the better you'll understand how to manage debt. You'll discover ways to reduce interest costs, know which debt to concentrate on eliminating first, and create a program that will enable you to eventually become debt-free. When that happens, you'll suddenly find yourself with a big chunk of after-tax income that can be used to accelerate your whole wealth-creation process.

You Become Less Vulnerable to Financial Crises

Once you've reached the point where you have a well-managed financial plan and are debt-free, you will be much less vulnerable to the impact of a sudden and unexpected financial crisis.

Job loss is the most common emergency most people face, but other set-backs are possible as well – a serious illness that forces you or your spouse to take an extended leave from work, the birth of a child that takes a wife out of the work force for a period of time, a recession that forces an employer to implement across-the-board pay cuts – there are all kinds of possibilities.

The greater your debt load and the more dependent you are on that regular cheque, the more precarious your position in a crisis situation. Conversely, if you're debt-free and have an emergency reserve, you may have to tighten your belt but you're not going to suddenly find yourself faced with having your phone cut off or, in extreme cases, a mortgage foreclosure.

You Gain Financial Independence

The person who is truly financially independent is the one who can do whatever he or she wishes without worrying about the monetary implications. That may mean working fewer hours, or taking a job that pays less because you love the challenge it offers, or going off on a one-year sabbatical to Nepal to find your inner self.

Most of us are constrained from doing exactly as we might like because of the financial implications of the action. A 30-year-old with two children might wish to become a teacher, but can't afford to take the necessary year off work to earn the academic credentials. A woman in her late 20s might want to be a stay-at-home mom for a few years, but the financial needs of the family make it difficult, if not impossible. A 60-year-old may want to retire early and spend winters in the Sunbelt, but he hasn't enough capital to live on for the rest of his life.

Achieving true financial independence is a wonderful accomplishment because it makes all things possible. Within the parameters of your family obligations and your health, you can follow your heart's desire without being concerned about what it may cost.

There is no magic amount of money needed to gain this kind of independence. Much depends on personal circumstances. A 25-year-old with no dependants and a modest lifestyle may need only a few thousand dollars in the bank to attain financial freedom, at least temporarily. A 35-year-old with a spouse, three children, and a mortgage has a more difficult challenge.

But this is a reward level that is well worth striving for. It brings with it immense personal satisfaction and a big-time sense of accomplishment. All your effort has really achieved something. It has fundamentally changed your life!

You Become a Millionaire

The next rung up the ladder is the one upon which this book is based: You reach millionaire status. You sit down one morning, add up your assets, subtract your liabilities, and the bottom line comes out at seven figures. You've done it! Congratulations! Now start on million number two.

You Become Truly Content

Remember that I said at the outset that this book is not simply about how to accumulate that first million dollars. It's much more than that. Great wealth is only meaningful if it brings pleasure and contentment to you, to your family, and to others for whom you care. Literature is full of tales of misers who shut themselves off from the world and lead bitter, unhappy lives. One of the classic stories of this kind is one we are all familiar with: *A Christmas Carol,* by Charles Dickens. Will any of us ever forget that wonderful scene in the movie when Alastair Sim as Ebenezer Scrooge throws open the windows and asks the passing boy what day it is? On hearing the boy's reply, "Why, it's Christmas, sir," Scrooge chortles with glee, rubs his hands with delight, and sends the boy off to buy a Christmas turkey for Bob Cratchit and his family.

Melodramatic? You bet. But every year a tear comes to the eye as we watch it. We are so happy to see this man redeemed, so joyful that he has discovered that money in and of itself is sterile and dehumanizing, that we never tire of hearing or seeing the story retold.

When you reach this rung, you have finally come to the top of the ladder and you will be filled with a sense of satisfaction with life that you never dreamed could be possible.

Dispelling Some Myths

Now you know about the risks and the rewards. Next, let's dispel some of the myths that you're likely to encounter along the way.

Myth #1: You Can Get Rich Quick in the Stock Market

Getting rich quick is not impossible. It's just unlikely. To do so, you have to be prepared to take huge risks and to be very lucky. Few people are comfortable with that kind of approach.

For many years, the preferred way to try for a big kill in the markets was by trading penny stocks. Buy shares in a small company (usually a mining exploration venture) cheap and hope that it strikes oil or hits a gold vein before it runs out of money. Every once in a while the company did, which served to perpetuate the myth. More often, the company went belly-up. Worthless share certificates can still be found stashed away in old suitcases, a reminder of the days when stock promoters made fortunes feeding off the dreams of others. There are still some around, but today most gullible people just buy lottery tickets.

More recently, we witnessed the phenomenon of the dot-com millionaires – investors who were lucky enough to get in on the ground floor of Internet companies and became rich overnight when initial public offerings hit the market and the stock price soared. But that bubble has burst and those that bought the stock at inflated prices have taken a bath.

Then we had the day trading phenomenon, which saw people spending hours in front of a computer screen buying shares and selling them an hour later on an uptick. It was rather like bringing a Las Vegas casino into your own home, and just about as addictive. Some people claimed to have made big profits by day trading. Many others admitted to huge losses. The mania hit its peak in 1999 and early 2000, when the Nasdaq index was soaring and it was nothing for a volatile high-tech stock to move $25 up or down in a single day. After Nasdaq crashed in April 2000, much of the steam went out of day trading. Hopefully, it won't come back. Only professionals can hope to beat the markets in this way, and even they have a tough time doing so.

The reality is that the stock market is indeed a place to build wealth, but not overnight. It takes time, planning, and work. There will be setbacks along the way – I have yet to meet someone who has never lost money on a stock. It happens to all of us. The key is to make sure you have two strong winners for every loser.

Myth #2: You Have to Be an Insider

"Ordinary investors can't make money in the stock market," one angry woman e-mailed me. "If you don't have insider information, you'll get taken for a ride."

I understood her frustration because I shared it. I had recommended a stock in a software manufacturer, Allaire Corp., which trades on Nasdaq. The price started to sag. There was no obvious reason for this, no public announcement of any kind. But over more than a week, the share price steadily weakened. I said in my newsletter that this action made me highly suspicious, but I was not prepared to dump the stock without some tangible reason. Such things do happen; perhaps a large mutual fund was reducing its position to take profits or to raise cash to meet redemption requests. There's no problem with the company itself; it's simply a matter of sell orders temporarily outweighing buy orders, with the result that the price drops.

But then Allaire dropped the shoe. The company issued a profit warning and the stock was hammered. It had already fallen more than $10 a share, but the profit warning knocked another $10 off the price. Later, allegations were made (but not proven in court) that insiders had been steadily selling prior to the public warning. That's what prompted the outraged e-mail.

So yes, this sort of thing can happen and it taints public perception of the essential fairness of the market. Regulators engage in a constant struggle to combat it and to ensure that all investors receive relevant information in a timely fashion. But sometimes they seem to be fighting a losing battle.

But to leap from there to the assumption that small investors cannot profit from the stock market is sheer nonsense, which is disproved every day by fact. People *do* make money in the markets. Just check out the amount of tax that is paid on capital gains every year. Most of that comes from stock trading.

The fact is that if you cut yourself off from the stock markets, the odds against accumulating that first million through the savings/investment route become much greater. It's very difficult (not impossible, but difficult) to do it using interest-bearing securities only. Real estate would be your best bet in that situation – but it's a very specialized and tricky area.

So if you're hung up on the idea that the stock market isn't for you because you're not privy to inside information, forget it. You need the market – and you can do very well, even without someone whispering in your ear.

Myth #3: You Have to Be Rich to Get Rich

Sure, it's easier to make big profits from your investments if you have a lot of money to begin with. But if you were in that situation, you probably wouldn't be reading this book.

Indeed, you *can* start out small and still succeed. It just takes more time. Let me give you just one example. Suppose you are 30 years old. You have nothing saved and zero net worth. You contribute $5,400 a year to an RRSP for the next 30 years. The money in the plan generates an average annual return of 10 percent. When you reach age 60, your RRSP will be worth almost $980,000. That's just $20,000 short of the $1 million goal. Even if you never saved another cent and didn't have a penny's worth of equity in a home, you'd have virtually achieved the objective. In reality, your total net worth would probably have passed the million-dollar mark years before.

Yes, you can get rich from a standing start.

Myth #4: Stocks That Go Down Will Go Back Up

I frequently get e-mail messages from subscribers to my electronic newsletter that read something like this: "You told us to sell our shares in XYZ company six months ago. Since then it has dropped 50 percent. Is it time to buy in again?"

Maybe. It depends on why the stock has dropped. Is it a strong company, a leader in its field that has been caught in a general market downdraft? Is it the industry sector that's suffering – perhaps an energy company that's been affected by a drop in oil prices?

Or is there something seriously wrong with this particular corporation? In that case, the stock could fall all the way to zero. It happens, even to blue-chip companies.

There was a time when Royal Trust was considered to be one of the most solid financial institutions in Canada. Then, as a result of a series of bad management decisions, the company ran into serious problems. The stock declined sharply and in the end the firm was saved from bankruptcy only by selling out to Royal Bank. Shareholders lost billions.

Laidlaw was a giant of the transportation industry not many years ago. It ran a school bus empire that extended throughout North America, local bus and ambulance services, and Greyhound Bus Lines. Its shares were part of the TSE 300 and the S&P 500. The bluest of the blue. Then the stock started a downward spiral, fed by one piece of bad news after another. Almost unbelievably, by 2000 Laidlaw had been reduced to the status of a penny stock and there were suggestions that the company would have to seek bankruptcy protection. Maybe it will eventually rise, phoenix-like, from the ashes. But investors who bought when they thought the shares were cheap discovered to their horror that today's bargain may turn out to be tomorrow's white elephant.

Myth #5: Picking Good Investments Is Complicated

Investing can be complicated. It can also be deceptively easy. Sometimes the best investment tips are right under your nose. All you need is the right mindset to recognize them.

Here's an example. During the early 1990s, I visited Vancouver frequently. I was amazed to discover the addiction the people of that beautiful city had developed to a particular brand of coffee, one that at the time was unknown in the east.

Today, the company is a household name, but back then Starbucks was a regional operation based in Seattle. Unless you lived in the Pacific Northwest, you would not have been familiar with its signature logo and its aromatic blends.

On my visits, I observed first-hand how Starbucks could move into a new territory and become the dominant player in its niche market in just a couple of years. If the formula could work there, why not elsewhere? Keep in mind that to this point I had done no research into the company itself or its financial situation. I was simply observing a phenomenon at work.

In 1992, Starbucks offered shares to the public for the first time at a price of U.S.$17. At a series of seminars in Vancouver a few months later, I asked how many people had purchased the stock. Hardly anyone raised their hand.

Why not? Because while they were busy drinking gallons of the stuff every day, they hadn't given any thought to asking questions about the company itself: how fast it was growing, who owned it, how much money it was making, and, most important, whether it might be a good investment.

I bought shares myself, and I recommended them to readers of *The MoneyLetter*. As it turned out, Starbucks was a heck of an investment. The original investors tripled their money in less than two years. The company went on to become an international giant, going from strength to strength. But anyone in Seattle or Vancouver who had a bit of foresight could have seen it coming and made a killing.

It's not an isolated story. Look at Wal-Mart. Look at Home Depot. Look at The Gap. Look at Staples. Big success stories that appeared right before our eyes. Did you buy any of their shares on the way up? This sort of situation happens all the time. It's simply a case of becoming attuned to it. You probably come across at least one good investment idea a week, perhaps more. It's a matter of training yourself to recognize them.

Start with your personal spending habits. Have you recently found a new product that you really like? Perhaps you've changed the brand of toothpaste you buy or the type of beer you drink. Ask yourself why. Does the new product have some clear advantage? If so, you won't be the only person to recognize it. Find out who makes the product and see if the stock is publicly traded. If it's a relatively small company, its share price could rise dramatically if the new product really takes off.

Perhaps the difference is only in packaging – you just happen to like the container the product comes in. Even something as basic as that can tip you off to an investment opportunity.

For many years, Peter Lynch managed the Fidelity Magellen Fund, one of the most successful mutual funds in the United States. After he retired in his mid-40s (stunning the investment world in the process), he wrote one of the best books on stock market investing I have read. It's called *One Up On Wall Street* and in it Lynch sets out some very practical, down-to-earth guidelines for stock selection.

One story he tells perfectly illustrates the point I'm making here. His wife, Carolyn, comes home from an excursion to the local grocery store. She shows him a new product she's just purchased. It's pantyhose, but with a neat twist. The product is being marketed in an eye-catching oval container. The name on the front reads *L'eggs*.

Lynch writes of being immediately struck by the imaginative design and the convenience of being able to buy the product at the grocery checkout counter. His wife, meanwhile, tries the pantyhose and likes the quality. So Lynch does some research. He discovers L'eggs are produced by a company called Hanes. The stock trades on the New York Stock Exchange. Lynch immediately recommends buying the stock. It becomes one of Fidelity's big winners, increasing six times in value before the company is taken over – and all because Carolyn Lynch went grocery shopping one day.

Start with Cash

If your goal is to become a millionaire by the saving/investing route, you must learn the basics first. So let's spend some time reviewing some money fundamentals. Perhaps you already know all this, in which case you can quickly scan the next few pages. In my experience, however, many people who think they're fairly sophisticated when it comes to financial matters actually have some big holes in their knowledge. So don't automatically assume this section is too simple for you. Make sure. After all, you don't have to confess any shortcomings to anyone else.

We'll begin with the most basic concept of money: cash. We all know what that is, right? It's the government-issued paper and metal that we stuff into our wallets and purses that other people recognize as having value and allow us to use to acquire goods and services from them. Legal tender. Cold, hard cash.

Of course, all this paper and metal only has value if we all agree it does. Intrinsically, a 5-dollar bill is nothing more than a piece of paper with some pictures and numbers on it. As a pure piece of paper, it has no value – it's only worth something because the government says it is and we accept that.

A 50-dollar bill has no more intrinsic value than a 5-dollar bill. But because the pictures and the numbers are different, the government says it is worth more and the population goes along with the idea. After all, it's a lot simpler than a barter system where there's always the potential for an argument over how many eggs it should take to get a sack of flour.

In times past, cash in many countries was backed by huge stores of gold and silver, the theory being that a paper bill could always be exchanged for a piece of precious metal. That gave paper legitimacy in many people's minds. But the gold standard is long gone, and today's currencies are basically supported by government policies and public confidence.

Occasionally, however, that confidence is shaken or even destroyed, turning cold, hard cash into stacks of worthless paper. We saw that most recently in Russia, where much of the population lost faith in the ruble when inflation soared during the Yeltsin years. As a result, they turned back to an archaic barter system. The country still hasn't fully come to grips with its cash crisis.

At its most extreme, hyperinflation can completely wipe out the value of cash and the life savings of those who rely on it. During the Weimar Republic in Germany between the world wars, the currency became so debased that housewives were forced to push wheelbarrows full of paper money through the streets when they went grocery shopping. Even mailing a letter could cost a million marks!

In Canada, we've seen a different aspect of this phenomenon at work in recent years, as our currency has steadily lost value in relation to the U.S. dollar. The result has been to increase the cost of travelling abroad and to push up the prices of many of the goods we import from the States.

So always remember that hard cash may not always be so hard. It relies on public confidence and government policy for its value. If either or both are compromised, your dreams could be shattered if you haven't prepared for that possibility. All Germans were millionaires during the Weimar Republic. But hardly anybody was rich!

Cash Is More Than Money

We think of cash in terms of bills and coins, but those are simply its physical manifestations. In reality, cash is a more complicated concept. In broad terms, cash is any asset that can quickly be converted to bills and coins at its full face value. In technical terms, we say such assets are *liquid*.

It seems like an odd choice of term. Hard cash equals liquid assets! But there are many things in the world of money that don't always make perfect sense. We learn to live with them.

If you're on the savings/investment track to millionaire status, the first thing you need to realize is that cash is the least effective way of getting there. We've all read stories, some of which may indeed be true, about people hiding cash away in their mattress, at the bottom of the sock drawer, in a cookie tin, under a floorboard, or some other place they think will be safe from theft. They're kidding themselves. If a professional burglar should ever break in (much more likely if rumour of wealth hidden in the home ever gets out), he'll almost certainly locate the stash and make off with it. But even if that never happens, the money is sitting in its hole doing nothing. It's not earning interest or dividends or building wealth in any way. In fact, its value is steadily being eroded each year as cost-of-living increases eat away its purchasing power. You don't need a thief to rob you of your life savings. Inflation will do the job just as effectively if you wait long enough.

However, we all need to hold some of our assets in cash or, more precisely, cash equivalents. We need cash to pay the bills and to make investments. So let's consider the various ways you can keep your cash, and how to make the most of each.

Deposit Accounts

All of us have savings and/or chequing accounts in a financial institution. In many cases, these are simply an institutionalized form of cookie jar. Most of these accounts pay little or no interest; in fact, we probably pay for the privilege of having them in the form of service charges. But we accept this because of the convenience they offer in the form of cheque-writing, debit card use, money transfers, and other services.

How to Do Better

Don't let large amounts of money languish in a low-interest account. Keep enough in a current account to cover your immediate financial needs and find a better home for the balance. Some financial institutions offer high interest rate savings accounts. Usually, you'll find these at smaller companies or at firms trying to establish a market presence. As long as they are covered by deposit insurance, there is no reason not to take advantage of them.

Government Savings Bonds

The federal government and many of the provinces issue savings bonds that are very safe and, in some cases, highly liquid. The best known are Canada Savings Bonds (CSBs), which are as good as cash in that they can be redeemed at any time for the full face value plus accrued interest to the end of the previous month.

How to Do Better

If you're prepared to sacrifice some flexibility, you can get a higher rate of return. Canada Premium Bonds, for example, pay more than CSBs but can only be cashed once a year. Many provincial bonds operate the same way.

Treasury Bills

Treasury bills are short-term notes issued by the federal and provincial governments, typically with maturities of 90 days to one year. They're very safe and can be redeemed any time. However, there is a risk that you could suffer a small loss if short-term interest rates rise sharply and you decide to cash in early. They're sold through stockbrokers, typically with a $10,000 minimum investment.

How to Do Better

The more money you have to invest, the better the interest rate you should receive when you buy T-bills. Also, provincial notes usually pay a slightly higher return than those issued by the federal government.

Banker's Acceptances

Some people use banker's acceptances as an alternative to T-bills because of the higher interest rate they pay. Banker's acceptances are promissory notes issued by companies borrowing short-term funds from Canada's major chartered banks. Instead of holding these, the banks offer them to investors with their own guarantee of repayment. Thus, while banker's acceptances may not be quite as safe as Government of Canada securities, they're not far behind. They're a good option for people who want to squeeze a little bit more out of their cash holdings, and they'll generally pay a better return than most of the alternatives mentioned here. Like T-bills, you can usually sell them before maturity if you need the cash. They're available through brokers, with a minimum of $10,000 usually required.

How to Do Better

The returns offered on banker's acceptances reflect the current short-term interest rate climate. So you'll get a better yield at times when rates are high generally. Also, if you have a lot of money to invest you may be able to negotiate a better yield.

Money Market Mutual Funds

Money market mutual funds invest in short-term notes, such as Treasury bills, banker's acceptances, and other commercial paper. Every financial institution offers them and there are no sales commissions involved. Fund units normally have a fixed value of $10 and can be redeemed at any time at that price. Returns will usually be somewhat less than you would get by investing in Treasury bills, but the minimum investment required is much smaller.

If you're considering money market funds as an alternative for your cash assets, here are some things to watch for:

- *Current yield.* Check the money market funds section in the mutual funds quotations in the business pages of your newspaper. There you'll see two columns of figures. One, usually headed *curr,* shows the fund's current yield – the actual rate of return over the past seven days, expressed as an annualized percentage. The second column, headed *eff,* represents effective yield – a projection of the current yield over the next 12 months, assuming all interest is reinvested and compounded weekly. Neither number is a valid indicator of what you can expect to receive for your investment over the next year. Much will depend on whether interest rates are rising or falling. The current yield is the best number to work with in making value assessments, although it can be manipulated by clever fund managers. All else being equal, and assuming no sales commissions are involved, choose a fund with a high current yield since your money will probably be there only for a short time.

- *Sales commission.* Don't buy a money market fund that carries a sales commission, either front- or back-end. The return isn't high enough, and you probably won't be in it long enough to justify such a payment. In fact, it may eat up your entire profit.

- *Early redemption penalties.* Some money funds hit you for an early redemption charge (typically 2 percent) if you cash in your units within 90 days. Ask in advance and avoid any such fund because it limits your liquidity.

- *Timing.* Generally, money market funds lag the market. That means their current yields will be somewhat behind those you can receive if you invest directly in T-bills. That's because the fund portfolio contains a mixture of securities, some of which were acquired several months ago. Therefore, money market funds are not a good place to be when short-term rates are rising. You'll get a better return from T-bills or banker's acceptances. When interest rates are declining, however, these funds are a good spot for your cash since you'll continue to benefit from securities that were issued when rates were higher.

How to Do Better

If you have a lot of cash to invest, ask if the financial institution offers a premium money market fund. These carry lower administrative fees and therefore generate returns that may be as much as half a percentage point higher. Also, check out the current yield on both Canadian and U.S. dollar money funds. In recent years, the U.S. currency funds have paid better returns.

Term Deposits

All financial institutions offer term deposits (TDs) of various durations up to one year (beyond that they're usually called guaranteed investment certificates, or GICs). These TDs offer a better return than savings accounts, but your money is usually locked in until maturity. If you can get out early, a penalty may be assessed.

How to Do Better

Most bank managers have the discretion to negotiate interest rates on TDs, within limits. The more money you have to invest, the better the rate you should be able to obtain. At the very least, ask for a quarter point more than the published rate.

Fixed-Income Securities – A Primer

We're now ready to take a step up the investment ladder. The essential difference between cash-type securities and fixed-income securities is their degree of liquidity. As we've seen, cash-type securities can be redeemed for their face value (or close to it) at almost any time. Fixed-income securities usually offer a better rate of return, but at a price. Either they are locked in for a longer period or there's a risk that you could suffer a meaningful loss if you sell before maturity.

The term *fixed income* is actually somewhat loosely defined. Originally, it referred to securities that paid a fixed rate of return over a specified period of time. GICs are the best-known example; you lock in your money for, say, five years and you get an interest rate that is guaranteed by the financial institution that issues the note.

But the concept has become diluted over time. For example, preferred shares were once considered as classic fixed-income investments because they paid a set dividend on a regular basis. Now, however, many preferreds pay what is known as a *variable rate*, which fluctuates according to the movement of some other figure, like the Bank of Canada rate. In short, there is nothing "fixed" about it.

And what are we to make of index-linked GICs? These certificates base their return on the movement of some stock index, like the TSE 300 or the S&P 500 in the U.S. Technically, they are still GICs in that the principal is guaranteed. But there is certainly nothing "fixed" about the return you'll receive.

As with everything else in the world of investing, once-simple concepts have become more complex and the range of available options has widened considerably. And the process will continue, so even when you have mastered the current situation, don't feel your empowerment is over. It has to be an on-going process.

Now that you've been suitably warned, let's take a look at the various types of fixed-income securities you are most likely to encounter.

Guaranteed Investment Certificates (GICs)

You were probably well aware of GICs long before you picked up this book. Next to Canada Savings Bonds, GICs were the favourite choice of Canadian investors for many years, until the rise of mutual funds in the 1990s.

The basic idea is very simple. You hand over your money to a financial institution in exchange for a certificate that guarantees a specified rate of return until maturity. What could be easier?

Lots of things, actually. When interest rates began a long and more-or-less steady decline in the mid-1980s (with an upward blip in the early '90s), GICs started to lose their lustre. Investors who had been used to double-digit returns on their money began to balk as the five-year rates drifted down through 8 percent, 7 percent, 6 percent, and even 5 percent. Seeing their deposits fly away to other, more attractive, alternatives, the banks and trust companies scrambled to introduce new marketing gimmicks to restore interest in GICs. The result was a hodgepodge of choices that left many people totally confused. We were bombarded with extendible GICs, cashable GICs, monthly pay GICs, escalating GICs, laddered GICs, foreign currency GICs, and, most recently, a dazzling array of market-linked GICs.

The latter were the banks' ace-in-the-hole. They were designed to feed the twin emotions of all investors: greed and fear. Market-linked GICs were the answer. They dealt with the fear by guaranteeing that, no matter what happened, investors would get their principal back. And they fed the greed by promoting the sale of these securities during periods when stock markets were soaring to record highs (when markets were sagging we heard little about them). The strategy worked; index-linked GICs became huge sellers.

Of course, there is risk involved with these securities, even if the financial institutions play it down. The main risk is that your money will earn nothing over a period of several years. Yes, if markets tumble you'll get your principal back. But that's all. Even invested at a modest 5 percent, $5,000 will grow to almost $6,400 after five years. That's a total return of about 28 percent on your invested capital. That's the risk you take.

There's also the fact that some of the market-linked GICs place a limit on how much they'll pay out. The underlying index might double, but the certificate won't return more than, say, 40 percent on your money. You have to be a very careful shopper if you are going to invest in this type of security.

So GICs are no longer the simple invest-and-forget securities they once were. You need to ask a lot of pertinent questions before you put your money in any but the most basic type.

How to Do Better

As with term deposits, GIC interest rates are negotiable, even if the amount you have available to invest is relatively small (of course your clout will be increased if the amount is significant). Never accept the posted rate, and visit two or three financial institutions to get their best quotes. You can also buy GICs through brokers, who will shop the market for the best rates available. If you are investing in any but the most conventional type of GIC, make sure you fully understand all the terms and conditions associated with the security.

Bonds

If you're relatively new to investing, the first thing you think of when you hear the word *bond* is likely a Canada Savings Bond. Many of us received CSBs from adoring parents or relatives when we were children, so it's not surprising that's the impression we've been left with.

Actually CSBs are not really bonds at all, in the technical sense. They're cash-equivalent securities, as we've already seen. Genuine bonds are those issued by governments or corporations that normally carry a fixed interest rate and mature on a specified date. They cannot be redeemed at face value until maturity; however, they can be bought and sold in a manner similar to stocks on the bond market. That means their value can rise or fall depending on certain variables, the most important of which is the movement of interest rates. This is what differentiates them from GICs, which do not fluctuate in value under normal conditions (there is a secondary market for "used" GICs but it is small and we won't deal with it here).

You can make a lot of money on bonds as an investor if you're good at doing just one thing: predicting the general trend of interest rates. My first really big score came back in the early 1980s, when interest rates were at a post–World War II high as central banks fought to contain an inflationary pattern that was threatening to run wild. Economic growth was brought to a standstill as rates were pushed into the high teens and, eventually, topped 20 percent. One of the worst recessions of the century resulted, as businesses closed down and people were laid off by the hundreds of thousands (including me).

It didn't take a genius to figure out that this couldn't go on very long. Interest rates might edge a bit higher, but with unemployment figures shooting up and economic activity winding down, it was obvious that the U.S. Federal Reserve Board, the Bank of Canada, and other central banks would soon have to ease back – and do so quickly. So I sucked in my gut and aggressively bought Government of Canada bonds, which at the time were yielding about 15 percent. Within two years, I was able to sell them for a big profit. The capital gain was great. The psychological lift from having my calculated risk pay off was even greater.

Therein lies the most important single thing I can tell you about bonds: When interest rates go up, bond prices fall. Conversely, when interest rates go down, bond prices increase. Once you've grasped that, all you have to do is figure out which way interest rates are moving and then sit back and cash in.

Of course, that's overly simplistic. If it *were* that easy, everyone would be a millionaire. The trick is guessing right on which way interest rates are moving and then having the courage to take advantage of the situation.

Let me give you a simplified example. Suppose you bought a $1,000 bond when interest rates were 5 percent. You'd get $50 interest a year. Now you want to sell, but interest rates have gone up. Similar bonds are now paying 6 percent. Do you think anyone is going to buy your bond for $1,000? Not likely. They'll want a 6 percent return on their money, not 5 percent. That means in order to sell the bond, it will have to be at a price such that the $50 a year it pays in interest will give the buyer an annual return on investment (a *current yield)* of 6 percent. That means you'll have to sell the bond for around $830. You've lost money — $170 of your principal, to be precise!

Conversely, if interest rates had gone *down* to 4 percent, it would be a different story. Your bond is still paying $50 a year interest. But now, with rates at 4 percent, your buyer will have to pay $1,250 to get that return. Your bond has increased by 25 percent in value and you've got a nice capital gain.

The key to building wealth with bonds is to catch the trend once it's begun and ride it — rather like a surfer riding a wave. Of course, sooner or later the wave crashes and the surfer wipes out. But it's a great ride while it lasts. You don't want to wipe out, of course. And you don't have to if you're careful and pay attention to your bond investments.

Now let's look at some bond basics. Here are four terms you need to know:

- *Coupon.* This refers to the interest rate the bond pays, based on its face value. Bonds are normally sold to individual investors in $1,000 units. So a bond with a coupon rate of 6 percent would pay $60 a year interest, usually in semi-annual payments.

- *Maturity.* This is the date at which the bond matures and you can cash it in at face value. No interest is payable after that date. Generally, the longer the term to maturity of a bond, the more its market value will fluctuate up or down with interest rate movements.

- *Yield to maturity.* The annual rate of return you'll receive on a bond you buy today and hold until its maturity date. It includes both the interest paid on the bond and the capital gain or loss that will result if you keep the bond until it matures. The yield to maturity may be very different from the coupon rate, depending on the price of the bond, time left to maturity, and the general interest rate picture.

- *Rating.* A measure of the safety of the investment, expressed in letters. A rating of AAA (or A++) means the chances of the issuer going belly up and leaving you holding a worthless certificate are almost nil. A bond with a B rating or below, on the other hand, is a signal to run quickly in the opposite direction unless you're prepared to take big risks in hopes of a spectacular return.

As you learn more about bonds, you'll find you can use these variables to improve your returns. But the thing I most like about bonds is that you really don't have to bother with all this stuff if you don't want to.

What you *do* have to constantly remember is the relationship between time and risk. The longer time to the bond's maturity, the more risky it will be – it's as simple as that. Bonds with 20 years to maturity will move more sharply in price, up or down, than those with, say, five years left.

The thing that makes bonds so attractive to many investors is that you don't have to spend a lot of time worrying about which one to choose. That's what makes bond trading so different from the stock market. With stocks, you not only have to think about which way the broad market is moving, but you also have to look at specific industries and then at individual stocks within those industries. Bonds aren't as complicated. Most bonds with similar maturity dates and ratings will tend to move in the same direction in the market. You don't normally expect to find one 20-year Government of Canada bond moving up while another is going down.

So once you decide you want to invest in bonds, you don't have to do a lot of agonizing about which one to choose. If you're just starting out, stick with Government of Canada bonds. Don't even consider anything else until you have a clear understanding of what you're doing. Decide whether you prefer short-term bonds (those with maturity dates no longer than 5 years from now), medium-term (5 to 10 years), or long-term (over 10 years).

Short-term bonds are less risky because their maturity date is relatively close. At that time they can be cashed at face value. So if interest rates rise – causing bond prices to fall – short-term bonds won't usually suffer as great a loss as long-term bonds will.

Conversely, long-term bonds offer the potential for large profits if interest rates decline. Prices of those bonds will increase more, because the holders can collect the coupon interest rate, which is now substantially more than new bonds are paying, for a longer period of time. So if you believe interest rates are in a downward trend, and you're willing to accept a higher degree of risk, buy some long-term Government of Canada bonds. That's exactly what I did back in the early 1980s, and again when rates spiked up a decade later.

Stripped Bonds

Strips, or zero-coupon bonds as they're commonly called in the U.S., are quite different from regular bonds. They can be used as a conservative, long-term investment or as a short-term speculation, depending on your goals.

This is how they work. Let's take as an example a Government of Canada bond with a face value of $1,000, maturing in 15 years and paying 6 percent interest. If you purchase such a bond in the usual way, you receive two separate components: the bond itself, guaranteeing repayment of the principal on the maturity date, plus the right to collect 30 interest rate payments every six months until maturity (these used to be paper coupons that were clipped and cashed, hence the name, but now it's all done electronically).

When you invest in stripped bonds (or stripped coupons, as they're still called), you can invest in each of these components separately. You can choose the bond alone, without the coupons, at a discounted price and hold it until it matures. The increase in value during that period would be, in effect, the interest on your investment.

Stripped bonds offer two advantages to the investor. The first is that your yield to maturity is guaranteed. With an ordinary bond, you have to reinvest interest payments as they are received; if rates fall, you won't receive as high a return as you anticipated.

The second advantage is the ability to buy more assets because of the discounted price of a stripped bond. For example, a regular bond has a face value of $1,000, and if you were to buy it at issue that's what you'd pay (or close to it). But the price of a stripped bond is discounted, so you might be able to buy five of the same bonds as strips for, say, $200 each.

Buying stripped coupons simply means you're purchasing the other component of the bond – the semi-annual interest payments. Again, the same principle applies: You buy the coupons at their present value and cash them in at maturity. The advantage here is that, because the payments are due every six months, you can vary the maturity dates to suit your own needs.

Stripped bonds and coupons carry the magic of compound interest to its ultimate degree. Unlike GICs or CSBs, you can lock in a guaranteed interest rate for 15, 20, even 30 years into the future. That offers some intriguing possibilities. For example, when interest rates were sky-high in the early 1980s, an investor could have guaranteed an annual return of 15 percent (or more) on their money for a period that would still be continuing to this day! Such opportunities come along very rarely, however.

Real Return Bonds

There is one other type of bond that requires special mention here. Real return bonds are designed to protect investors against the impact of inflation, both in terms of principal and interest.

As we've seen, investing in bonds at a time of rising interest rates can be tricky and potentially dangerous. Real return bonds, however, offer a way to protect fixed-income assets against inflation and generate a decent return in the process.

They work like this. Semi-annual interest payments are adjusted to reflect increases in the Consumer Price Index (CPI) so that you're always getting an inflation-adjusted return equal to the original coupon of the bond (usually around 4.25 percent). As well, at maturity the bond holder receives a payment equal to the face value ($1,000) plus an inflation bonus that protects the purchasing power of the original investment.

When inflation is quiescent, as it was through most of the 1990s, these bonds sit quietly in a corner of a fixed-income portfolio, producing a steady but unspectacular return. But when the CPI starts to rise, real return bonds come into their own. They were especially strong during 1999–2000, when inflation began to resurface as a growing concern for the first time in several years. In fact, during a time when most bond prices were weakening, real return bonds were rising in value.

The federal government is the main issuer of these bonds ($1.25 billion worth came to market in fiscal 1999–2000) so there is always a decent supply. There are many issues of real return bonds available, with differing interest rate guarantees and maturities.

How to Do Better

Bonds issued by the federal government are considered the safest you can invest in. Accordingly, their yield is the lowest on the scale (the less the risk, the lower the return). You can improve your returns with very little additional risk by instead putting your money into top-grade provincial bonds (e.g., issues from Alberta and Ontario). If you're prepared to take slightly more risk, choose high-quality corporate bonds, such as those issued by any of the Big Five banks.

Preferred Shares

The easiest way to grasp the concept of preferred shares is to think of them as bonds that pay dividends instead of interest. Of course, it's not quite that simple, but it gives you the idea.

The advantage of collecting your payments in dividends is that you get a tax break. Interest is taxed as regular income. Dividends, by contrast, get the benefit of the *dividend tax credit,* which reduces the amount you pay considerably. The rationale for this credit is that corporations pay dividends to shareholders out of after-tax earnings – in other words, from money that has already been taxed once. The dividend tax credit is supposed to eliminate double taxation. It doesn't, of course – in fact, the credit has been watered down considerably over the years. But even in its present weakened state, it still provides a better deal than straight interest income when the money is received outside a registered plan.

To give you an idea of the magnitude of this tax advantage, a top-bracket Ontario taxpayer paid a rate of 47.9 percent on interest income received in 2000. If the money had come as dividends instead, the rate would have been only 32.3 percent.

The credit actually works most effectively for lower-income taxpayers. If you had taxable income of between $12,000 and $30,000 in Ontario in 2000, your effective rate on dividend income would have been only 6.1 percent. (The rate will vary depending on where you live but the principle is the same across Canada.)

Dividends are paid by common stock, which we'll discuss later, and preferred shares, or *preference shares* as they are more correctly known. Preferreds (the commonly used term) are actually something of a cross between a stock and a bond. As with bond interest, the dividend is usually (but not always) fixed. Payments are normally made quarterly. Preferreds rank ahead of common stocks in the financial pecking order, which means that a company must pay all its preferred dividends first, including any that are overdue, before owners of common stock get a cent. In the event a firm is wound up, preferred shareholders rank ahead of common stock owners but behind bond holders in terms of asset distribution. Normally, preferred shareholders have no voting rights in a company, whereas common stockholders do.

Although the price of preferreds will usually not vary as greatly as that of the common stock of the same company, these shares do carry the potential for a capital gain if interest rates decline, and will tend to fall in value when rates rise, in the same manner as bonds.

Like bonds, preferreds are rated as to safety by the national bond rating agencies, with P-1 the highest rating (safest) and P-5 the lowest (most risky). Lower-rated preferreds will usually offer a higher yield, perhaps much higher than normal, but you have to be very careful if you decide to invest in them. The low rating is a red flag; it means the company is likely in financial difficulty. If you pick up the Business section of the paper and come across a preferred share with an extraordinarily high yield, you can be sure there's a good reason for it. No one gives away something for nothing.

Investing in preferred shares can be somewhat tricky because they often come with riders attached. These aren't apparent at first glance; you need to ask a financial advisor to investigate on your behalf or do some research on your own. The most common wrinkle you'll encounter is that preferreds are often *callable*. That means the issuing company can buy them back at certain times under pre-set conditions. This condition is built in to protect the issuer, not the investor, the idea being that if interest rates have dropped since the preferred was issued, the company can get off the hook by calling it in. They save money but you lose a good deal. You may even suffer a capital loss – for example, if you paid, say, $26.50 per share and they're called in at $25. So before you buy, be sure to check what the earliest call date is on any preferred in which you're interested.

There are several types of preferreds that you should know about:

Floating Rate Preferreds

Floating rate preferreds pay a rate of interest that fluctuates according to market conditions. For example, the dividend may be calculated as a percentage of the banks' prime lending rate or the Bank of Canada rate.

Non-Cumulative Preferreds

With regular preferreds, if dividends are missed, they have to be made up later before common stock holders can receive any payment. This is not the case with non-cumulative preferreds, which are often issued by the big banks. So non-cumulative preferreds carry a higher level of risk. Holders of the non-cumulative preferreds issued by Royal Trust discovered this when the company was sold to Royal Bank back in the 1990s. Although all Royal Trust preferreds were hammered in the stock market, the non-cumulatives fared worst. However, non-cumulatives also usually offer a better yield than regular preferreds, so you are compensated for the additional risk. Since it seems unlikely that any of the Big Five banks would miss a dividend payment under current conditions, this looks like a reasonable risk to take.

U.S.-Pay Preferreds

Some Canadian preferred share issues are denominated in U.S. dollars, and pay dividends in that currency. The banks are especially active in issuing this type of stock. U.S.-pay preferreds are eligible for the dividend tax credit and offer an opportunity for currency gains at times when the Canadian dollar is falling.

Convertible Preferreds

These allow investors to convert into shares of the company's common stock according to a specific formula. This feature can produce significant capital gains if the value of the common stock rises well beyond the conversion price.

How to Do Better

Like bonds, the market price of preferred shares will fluctuate according to interest rates. Most affected will be fixed-rate preferreds, which pay exactly the same dividend at all times (as opposed to floating-rate preferreds, where the dividend fluctuates). If you expect interest rates to fall, an investment in good-quality fixed-rate preferreds could pay off handsomely, for exactly the same reason that bonds will do well in that situation.

Mortgage-Backed Securities

Many people aren't familiar with mortgage-backed securities (MBSs), but they are a useful investment for those who are looking for steady income with very little risk. They are actually much better suited for retirees than for younger people looking to accumulate their first million, but you should be aware of them whatever your age.

An MBS certificate (also referred to by brokers as NHAs, referring to the National Housing Act) represents a share in a pool of residential mortgages. These pools are put together by financial institutions, and vary in size. Each pool is self-contained, with its own coupon rate and payment schedule.

MBS units always are dated as of the 1st of the month and start paying returns on the 15th of the month following the issue. Most have 5-year terms, although terms can range from as little as six months to as long as 25 years. Minimum investment is usually

$5,000, but that can vary depending on where you buy. They're eligible for registered plans.

Here are some of their main features.

Safety

Residential first mortgages have always been low-risk investments. But these certificates are as close to no-risk as you can get. Canada Mortgage and Housing Corporation (CMHC) guarantees you'll receive full interest and principal payments on the due dates, even if there are defaults within the pool. Since CMHC is a Crown corporation, your guarantee is backed by the Government of Canada. And there's no limit on the guarantee (unlike deposit insurance, which covers only the first $60,000). So you don't have to be concerned about the financial stability of the MBS issuer or of the mortgages within the pool. The government protects you both ways.

Competitive Yield

The coupon rate in any given MBS pool is based on the mortgage holders' interest rate, and must be at least half a point less than the lowest mortgage rate in the pool. So if the lowest rate is 7 percent, the MBS coupon rate cannot exceed 6.5 percent. However, the coupon rate doesn't represent your actual return. MBSs, like bonds, are priced daily, and your yield will depend on the price you pay. According to brokers, these securities normally yield about 15 to 30 basis points (a basis point is 1/100 of a percent) more than five-year Government of Canada bonds.

Liquidity

There's an active secondary market for MBSs. You can sell them through a broker before maturity if you wish, giving them a clear advantage over locked-in investments such as GICs. Although MBS prices tend to be more stable than those of government bonds, you could suffer a capital loss if interest rates rise after your purchase. If interest rates fall, on the other hand, you'll enjoy a capital gain, albeit not a large one.

Availability

MBS issues are available through major stockbrokers. If you don't have a broker or don't wish to open an account, you can buy them through some of the chartered banks.

Monthly Pay

Very few securities offer monthly payments, especially combined with decent interest rates. That makes MBSs particularly appealing to retired people, either inside or outside an RRIF. But be aware that the monthly payment is not interest-only – it's a blend of interest and principal. And it can vary, sometimes substantially, depending on the extent to which the mortgage holders within the pool make early payments.

The blended principal and interest payments mean you won't receive the full face value of the certificate at maturity. CMHC calculates that without prepayments, you'd receive about 6 percent of your original principal over a five-year term. So at maturity you'd recover only about 94 percent of the original value of the certificate, or about $4,700 on each $5,000 certificate. Prepayments will reduce that even more. Remember to consider this in your calculations. If you don't like the uncertainty of prepayments, then consider a closed mortgage pool. The closed MBS is the ideal income security. Payments will never vary over the term. No prepayments are allowed, so you know exactly what your monthly income will be. Yields on non-prepayable MBS certificates tend to be slightly lower for a comparable term.

There are some drawbacks to MBS investments. The return they offer is very low, reflecting the high safety level. Capital gains potential is limited. And there is a 15-day period between the maturity date of a certificate and the date the final payment is due. No interest is paid during that time, which could mean a loss of several hundred dollars on very large investments.

In making an MBS investment, it doesn't matter much whether you buy a new issue or one being traded in the secondary market. The yield will be about the same in either case; the only difference is that older issues have a shorter maturity.

You might be wise to do a little shopping around, though. There may be slight variations (five to ten basis points) in the yields being offered by various brokers. A few phone calls will give you that information. If there's an edge, you might as well have it in your favour, especially if you're investing a substantial amount.

How to Do Better

While large prepayments can upset income calculations, they can also generate additional income in the form of penalties. That money is pure gravy – because penalty payments can't be anticipated, they're not included in your projected yield. So if you want to add some profit potential to an MBS investment, go into a pool in which prepayments are allowed.

Understanding the Stock Market

Finally! I can hear the sigh of relief. After all that dull stuff about bonds and preferreds, we get into something exciting. This is where the action is, where I'm going to make that million. The stock market! Let me at it!

Well, hold on just a minute. Yes, you can make a lot of money in the stock market, and I'm going to try to help you do that. But let's be realistic. You can also lose a lot too. This is not a place for anyone with a heart condition. It is quite possible to accumulate that $1 million without ever buying a stock. It's more difficult, yes, but it can be done. So before you plunge in, make sure you can handle the pressure and that there aren't more advantageous uses for your money.

Recently, for example, a friend of one of my children decided he wanted to become a stock market investor. He was in his early 30s and knew nothing about the market, but he'd been at a party and heard about a fledgling diamond mine that was trading on the Montreal Exchange for pennies a share. The party gossip was that the company had just hired an expert promoter, who was going to push the share price up to $2 or $3, perhaps even higher. Anyone who got in right away would make a killing! There was no discussion of the merits of the company itself or whether it was likely to make a big diamond strike in the Canadian North (where diamonds have been found in quantity in recent years). The story was the promoter and what he would do for the stock once he got going.

Variations on this theme have been around for years – cocktail party tips, high-powered promoters. In years past, the combination sometimes worked; junior mining companies trading on the old Vancouver Stock Exchange could be pushed to record levels on air alone. Of course, they eventually deflated, but by then anyone in the know would have exited with a profit.

This particular fellow was seduced by the 21st-century version of the ploy and invested a few hundred dollars. The stock, which was trading at around the 30¢ level when he bought, briefly got as high as 62¢ before settling back down. When he ran out of patience, he sold for about the same price he originally paid. Actually, he was lucky he didn't lose the whole stake.

I tell you this story because it's a classic example of how *not* to invest in the stock market. If this is how you expect to make your million, forget it. Believe me, it simply won't happen this way – on some enchanted evening, a stranger will *not* give you a winning stock tip across a crowded room.

If you are going to succeed in the stock market, you must have discipline, patience, commitment, sound advice, and courage. A measure of luck will also be helpful.

I'll admit that there's nothing in the investment world that matches the rush of adrenaline you get when you pick up the business pages and discover that the stock you bought last week has doubled in value overnight because of a takeover bid. But it doesn't happen very often, and if your winner is sitting on a portfolio of losers, the satisfaction won't last long.

You have to realize that it is not easy to consistently pick winning stocks. The choice is immense: you not only have to consider the Canadian market but the U.S. and international markets as well. Also, the process takes a great deal of hands-on management. You can get advice from a broker, but if you're smart you won't automatically invest in everything he or she suggests. You'll have empowered yourself with enough knowledge to ask intelligent questions and participate in a carefully thought-out decision.

I do not want to discourage you from investing in the stock market, far from it. I simply want to stress the challenges involved and impress upon you the importance of taking them seriously. If you do, your chances of reaching the $1 million goal sooner than you thought possible will be greatly enhanced.

As a starting point, never lose sight of the fact that the stock market is like an elevator: it goes both up *and* down. I emphasize this because in the late 1990s there was a growing belief that the down button on the elevator was permanently out of order. This was the era of the Internet bubble, when high-tech stocks were driving markets to record levels. Leading the way was Nasdaq, which set record after record during the period from 1998 to March 2000. Some financial experts added to the feeding frenzy by coming out with theories that the old laws governing market valuations had been rewritten. The tremendous growth potential of the Internet, fibre optics, biotech, and wireless technology had made long-standing measures like price/earnings ratios and even profits meaningless. Growth rates were what mattered.

The last time I heard something like that was in the late 1980s, when some people tried to tell us that Japan's soaring stock market could not be measured in conventional North American terms. We all know what happened there – the Nikkei Index crashed and now, more than a decade later, it is still trading at less than half its previous high.

Predictably, the latest bubble burst as well, and those who proclaimed that "This time it's different" discovered that it's never different. As 2001 began, the Nasdaq Composite Index was back below 2,500 and high-tech investors were crying the blues. The down button on the elevator was clearly functioning again.

It's a lesson you must never forget. Stock market euphoria inevitably leads to a hangover.

No matter what stock you buy, it will eventually drop in price. The decline may only be temporary, but it will happen, and when it does you may tend to become miserable, angry, frightened, or any combination of the three. You shouldn't. It's part of the process. The wise investor will have taken some profits before that happens and, assuming the company is a good one, use the opportunity to add to his or her positions at bargain prices. In other words, properly managed, a price decline should be an opportunity, not a disaster.

Remember, the long-term trend of the stock market is up. If you look at stock charts dating back to the early 19th century, you'll see a clear upward progression in prices. There are some pretty dramatic spikes along the way, of course – Toronto stock prices fell over 70 percent between 1929 and 1932. But history is clearly on the side of the patient investor.

With that thought in mind, let's look at my 12 basic principles for successful stock market investing.

Principle #1: Make Sure Time Is on Your Side

Unless you're extremely knowledgeable, I do not recommend a large stock portfolio for people over 60. The time element is too short. If you run into a major, prolonged bear market, such as prevailed in the 1930s and again in the 1970s, you may be forced to sell at a huge loss or face going into retirement with a large portion of your assets tied up in unproductive holdings. A younger person will be able to wait out the down cycle and benefit when the inevitable upturn occurs.

Principle #2: Determine Your Priorities

Before you invest in the market, have a clear idea of what you are trying to achieve. It the goal to score big capital gains? Are you interested in regular dividend income? The stocks you select will be governed by your objectives. Make sure you have a clear idea of what they are.

The goal of this book is to help you accumulate $1 million in personal wealth. Therefore, your primary purpose for investing in stocks should be to generate capital gains. They offer the greatest profit potential, plus they receive favourable tax treatment. Only half of your capital gains are taxable; the rest belong to you free and clear.

With this in mind, you should focus on stocks that offer the best potential for capital gains, consistent with risk. That means you will usually avoid shares in highly regulated industries, such as utilities and pipelines, because government agencies control the prices they are allowed to charge, thereby limiting their profit growth. Instead, you should look for companies in fast-growth sectors of the economy, or for shares in good-quality firms that are currently undervalued.

Principle #3: Diversify

Make sure your portfolio is properly balanced. This means you should not put everything in one or two stocks. You need to spread your investments across several companies and industry sectors. Some international diversification is also a good idea, especially bringing in U.S. stocks. You'll find more on diversifying in the section on asset allocation in Step 5.

Principle #4: Never Speculate

The stock market is not a casino, although some people tend to see it that way. It's serious business, and a careful, well-informed investor can do very well by sticking with good-quality companies. You don't have to speculate in penny stocks to reap big rewards. I've seen many, many blue-chip stocks double and triple in just a few short years. For example, in the *Internet Wealth Builder* newsletter, which I publish, we recommended shares in BCE Inc. in November 1997 when they were trading at $40.95. BCE is about as blue chip as a stock gets in Canada. In February 2000 we advised readers to take half-profits with the stock at $161.25. That represented a gain of 294 percent in a little over two years! We also made a profit of 60 percent on shares in the Walt Disney Company in less than a year, sold Citigroup for a 70 percent advance after about a year and a half, and took half-profits on Bombardier after about a year with a gain of 107 percent. Blue chips all! Clearly, you don't have to speculate in juniors to do well, nor do you have to spend hours in front of your computer indulging in day trading.

Principle #5: Never Buy and Hold Cyclical Stocks

Cyclical stocks, like the economy itself, go through boom and bust periods. When they're hot, they're terrific. When they're in an off period, they're dogs. Many cyclical stocks are resource-based, which means we have a lot of them in Canada. Mining companies, forestry firms, and oil and gas companies all qualify. There's nothing wrong with investing in them, as long as you do it at the right time. There are two such occasions.

One time to buy is when they're off-cycle and therefore cheap. This means the particular industry is not in favour with investors. Usually, that's because the prices for the commodities it produces (e.g., aluminum, gold, crude oil, lumber) are low, which means the profitability of the company is reduced. Typically, stocks in such companies rise and fall in tandem with the international price of the commodities in which they specialize.

The other time to buy is when the cyclical upturn appears to be in its early stages and has a while to run. The rebound in the energy sector that began in early 1999 was a good example. It soon became clear that supplies were tightening and that the profits of oil and natural gas companies would continue to strengthen for some time to come. Two years later, in the winter of 2000–2001, energy prices were still high and the stocks were doing well.

However, it's important to take profits periodically in cyclical stocks and to leave the party before they start turning out the lights. Otherwise, you'll give back all your gains when the sector again falls out of favour (which it will) and share prices go into a slump.

Principle #6: Ride the Upward Trends

It was pretty hard to lose money in the stock market in the late 1990s. Some people did, of course, through a combination of poor selection and poor timing. But many investors who held a diversified portfolio of quality stocks profited greatly during this period.

As well they should have. The tech frenzy of the late '90s produced one of the most powerful market run-ups of that century. Anyone who didn't make money under those conditions may have given up in disgust.

But hold on a minute. Even many professional money managers had trouble cashing in during that time. Why? Two reasons, mainly. Either they were focused on a sector of the market that didn't do well, such as resource shares apart from oil and gas companies, or they were using a stock selection method that was out of favour.

Look at the great Warren Buffett, the Oracle of Omaha, who is one of the world's wealthiest people. He struggled to make a buck during the late '90s because he is a classic value investor. He buys stocks of great companies when they are cheap and then waits until the market rewards his intuition. However, the market wasn't in a very rewarding mood during this period. The reason was that Buffett didn't own any technology stocks – said he didn't understand them and wasn't about to buy anything he didn't understand. Moreover, even if he did understand them, they were lousy value. Investors were grossly overpaying for the shares. He wasn't going to make that mistake. As a result, his investment company, Berkshire Hathaway Inc., once the darling of Wall Street, fell on hard times as its shares were pounded and investors lost money.

So it is possible to miss out on a rising market, even if you're the world's greatest investor.

This suggests that it never pays to be too dogmatic when it comes to money. The best investors are pragmatists who go with the flow. When a sector starts to move, up or down, it usually continues in the same direction for many months or even a few years. If you ride those updrafts, you can make some very handsome gains. But here again, you should always take some profits along the way. And don't overload your portfolio with the hot issues of the day to the exclusion of all else. Those rockets will eventually burn out and fall back to earth, and you don't want your whole portfolio to fall with them.

But what made it relatively easy in the decade of the 1990s was the fact you could ride a steady upward trend that continued almost unabated through the period except for a pause for breath in 1994 and the crash of October 1997. Some stocks performed better than others during this time, of course. But as long as you didn't pick a bunch of dogs, the tide carried you along and you made money. As they say on Bay Street, in a strong wind even the turkeys fly.

That's why it's important to have some stocks in your portfolio, whether you hold them directly or through equity funds. When the market starts to move up, you must be there if you are going to achieve the target returns I outlined at the start of this book. If you don't participate in market booms, you can't expect anything better than mediocre results.

Many Canadians were on the sidelines during the big market run-up of 1993 because they didn't follow this basic rule of investing. History shows that markets enjoy their biggest moves just as the economy is coming out of recession. It happened in 1983, when the TSE 300 gained over 35 percent, and it happened again a decade later. Of course, recessionary periods are times of general pessimism, not conducive to stock market enthusiasm. People pull out of stocks and equity mutual funds – and then shake their heads in wonder as the markets explode.

Principle #7: Be Patient

There is always a right time and a wrong time to buy a stock. One of the things I've observed is that when a broker gives you a recommendation, 7 times out of 10 the stock will drop in price before it goes up again. That's because you aren't the only one hearing about it; in fact, if it's a hot issue there will be a lot of action in the market. So don't be too quick to plunge in. If you like the look of the stock, ask your broker to send you some information on it – the analyst's research, the latest annual report, and anything else that's relevant. Look over the material carefully and see if the company fits your investment objectives.

Also, take a look at how it will fit into your portfolio; would it overweight you in bank stocks, for example? If you're an income investor, check the dividend record to see what kind of return the stock is paying and the prospects for higher dividends in the future. If on close scrutiny it seems like a stock you should own, then set a realistic target purchase level and monitor its price movements over a period of time. When it comes within buying range – and more often than not it will – make the commitment.

The patient approach is a good general strategy to use for stock purchases. But it won't work if the market is in an explosive upward move, as in the late '90s. If the stock is a good one, it may not come back to your target buy level. In that situation, you have to decide whether the prospects are good enough to pay what may be an inflated price. My general inclination is not to chase a stock except in special circumstances. The stock market has infinite variety; there's always another bargain coming along. Wait for it.

Principle #8: Set Target Points

You should always buy a stock with the idea that you will one day sell it. Even though the market may move up over the long haul, there are times when it's prudent to take profits on even your most cherished stocks with the idea of buying back when the price drops. To do this, you need to set targets – points at which you'll sell, both on the profit side and on the loss side. Your upside targets will depend on the state of the market and your personal objectives. If the market is strong and shows no signs of weakening, a profit gain of 50 to 100 percent over your purchase price is not unrealistic. If the market is moving sideways and you're looking for a fast trade, you may target a profit as low as 10 to 20 percent. Just be sure when you set a low selling target that there will be enough profit left after commissions to make the whole transaction worthwhile.

While you can be flexible on the high side, you should be quite rigid about taking losses. If the stock drops 25 percent from your purchase price, it's time to revisit it and see whether you should stick with it. The test is to ask yourself this question: Would I buy it now? If the answer is no, it's time to sell.

I've seen many cases of people holding on to a losing stock in the vain hope that it will turn around and at least come back to their purchase price. What generally happens is that the stock just keeps on sliding, and a 25 percent loss turns into a 50 or 75 percent decline. When we make a recommendation in one of our newsletters that doesn't work out, we try to get out of the stock quickly so as to minimize the damage. But I know from the e-mail I receive that some readers refuse to sell. They're reluctant to lock in the loss, so they hang around. Then, when the price has fallen another 50 percent, they write in panic to ask what they should do. The answer is that they should have cut their losses when we advised them to. When things go wrong, take your lumps and move on. Don't compound your misery by hanging on, hoping for a miracle.

As with everything else in the stock market, there are some exceptions to this general rule. You may want to keep a core holding in a solid company even though it's fallen 25 percent because the drop is mainly due to general market weakness. The company itself remains solid and will undoubtedly recover when the market rallies. This is appropriate action if you've decided to maintain a portion of your growth assets in long-term holdings and deliberately selected the stock for that purpose. In this case, you may decide to acquire additional shares at the lower price, to reduce the average per-share cost of your investment. This is called averaging down.

Another exception may arise if you've purchased a volatile low-priced stock despite my admonition not to speculate. If the prospects for the company remain good, you may decide to hold for longer. But if the price drops 50 percent, I'd be inclined to get out; something's badly wrong.

Principle #9: Remember That the Market Is Fickle

Sometimes there is no clear reason why a particular stock performs as it does. All the fundamentals may suggest it is woefully underpriced. Yet it continues to languish while other stocks of lesser pedigree flourish. At any given time, there are hundreds of these "undiscovered" stocks around. The problem is, they may never be discovered, at least not while you're holding them. That means you should be doubly cautious when it comes to buying obscure stocks with a small float (the total value of its publicly traded shares outside any control block). It may look good on paper. But if it doesn't get discovered, the price may remain low.

What's true of individual stocks is also true of industry sectors. At certain periods, almost every company in a particular sector may be out of favour. In mid-1998, oil and gas stocks were on everyone's hate list because the Asian economic crisis had dampened international demand. In that climate, even the most carefully selected stock may go nowhere. But one year later, the whole situation had turned around, proving once again that every industry group will come back into favour eventually – something that is not necessarily true of individual stocks. So buying the top-quality stocks in out-of-favour groups can be a smart strategy – provided you have the patience to wait for the turnaround.

Principle #10: Take Advantage of Buying Opportunities

One of the brokers with whom I do business has a good sense of humour and the ability to maintain his perspective, no matter what's happening. When I called him in the midst of a recent market sell-off, his first words were: "Hi. Have you heard we're having sale?"

When the markets go into a slump, that's how you should look at them – they're on sale. It may be a long time before you can pick up such valuable merchandise at knock-down prices like these.

But you must be selective about what you buy. This is a time to stay with the best companies, the industry leaders that are well-positioned to ride out the difficult period and that will re-emerge quickly when conditions improve. That's where you'll find the best opportunity to double your money with relatively little risk.

Principle #11: Keep Your Eye on the Business Cycle

Some stocks perform better at certain stages of the business cycle. If you want to maximize your profits, you should purchase these stocks when their prices are low and sell them as they reach their cyclical peak.

In the early phase of a new business cycle, when the economy is starting to pull out of a recession or a prolonged slowdown, merchandising stocks often do well. Increased consumer confidence and low interest rates lead to an upsurge in buying activity, which helps merchandisers reduce inventories and improves their profits. Financial institutions and utilities also are strong at this point. Lower interest rates mean reduced costs for utilities, which generally have a high debt load because of their expensive plant and equipment needs. Financial institutions do well because lower rates lead to increased business activity.

As the business cycle matures, profits of manufacturers start to rise. Usually, these companies have cut costs during the slowdown and are now benefiting from those savings. As well, increased business is pushing up revenues, thereby adding to profits. As quarterly earnings reports continue to improve, share prices for these companies are pushed up. Shares in brokerage houses are also strong at this point, as activity in the stock market and mutual funds picks up and earnings rise. Communications companies should also perform well, as increasing economic activity produces more advertising revenue.

The late stages of the business cycle are good for resource stocks and real estate companies. By now, inflation is starting to creep back in. High commodity prices bolster the profits of mining, forestry, and energy companies, and rising property values make real estate companies look good.

If you're an active trader and you want to maximize your profits, you must pay close attention to what the business cycle is doing at any given point in time. The buy and sell messages it generates can be extremely valuable.

Principle #12: Never Panic

The worst investment decisions are made at times of high emotional stress. People who rushed to sell after the crash of October 1997 regretted it later as prices rallied. If you are prone to overreact to stock market movements, let someone else make the decisions – an investment counsellor or a mutual fund manager. Remember, all market corrections end up looking like small blips in retrospect.

The Rise and Decline of Mutual Funds

It's hard to believe, but it wasn't very long ago that most people had only a dim understanding, at best, of what a mutual fund was. Hardly anyone had any money in them. As recently as the mid-1980s, the mutual fund industry was a fringe player in Canadian financial markets. Conservative securities like GICs and Canada Savings Bonds took the lion's share of our retail investment dollars (institutional money went into the bond markets). Most of the rest was invested in stocks.

The mutual fund phenomenon, which had been big in the U.S. for several years, suddenly took off in Canada in the late 1980s, went into a temporary hiatus during the recession of the early '90s, and then really hit its stride in the boom period from 1993 onward when North American stock markets went on one of their greatest runs in history. By 2000, some $400 billion of our savings was invested in funds and an estimated one Canadian in every three owned fund units.

This tremendous surge was fed by four main forces:

1. A revolution in fund marketing, which eliminated the onerous sales commissions that had been a major barrier to mass sales and brought in new innovations such as deferred sales charges (back-end loads) where the investor paid a fee only if units were sold within a certain time frame.

2. The rise of high-profile no-load companies, such as Altamira, which made buying mutual funds as quick and easy as picking up a telephone.

3. The phenomenal returns posted by many funds in 1993 as the markets snapped out of the recession and later as the technological revolution took hold.

4. Declining interest rates, which prompted many investors to search for alternatives to fixed-income securities. Marketing expert Dan Richards dubbed these "the GIC refugees," and the term hit the mark.

The transition added significantly to the wealth of many thousands of people. Instead of leaving their money in securities that paid modest (and declining) rates of return, they switched to mutual fund portfolios and started to realize annual gains of 10 to 15 percent — sometimes even more.

But it's never good enough, it seems. As we approached the turn of the century, disillusion began to set in. Fund sales slowed as investors complained about high fees and a bewildering array of choices. Books appeared debunking the whole idea of mutual funds, suggesting that people could get better returns more cheaply by simply building their own stock portfolios or by investing in index participation units (IPUs) that track the movement of a particular stock index.

Certainly, there is merit to both ideas. But neither is a panacea. Building and maintaining a stock portfolio is much more difficult, and requires a lot more time and attention, than choosing a few good mutual funds and letting the professional managers handle the trading decisions for you. IPUs have their place, but some are deeply flawed. The popular i60s that trade on the Toronto Stock Exchange are an example. They reflect the performance of the S&P/TSE 60 Index, a measure of the movement of 60 blue-chip stocks. However, the dominant position of Nortel Networks in the index (at one point it represented more than one-third of the total weighting before its price collapsed) skewed the returns towards the performance of that single stock. When Nortel shares went through the ceiling between mid-1999 and September 2000, investors in i60s made profits that were out of all proportion to what the rest of the index was doing. When Nortel shares collapsed in the autumn of 2000 and winter 2001, those same investors suffered disproportionate losses. That's not what index investing is supposed to be all about!

So don't get caught up in the pop theory of the day. There is definitely a place for mutual funds in your million-dollar plan. It's a matter of knowing how to use them most effectively.

Some Mutual Fund Basics

So much has been written about mutual funds that it's impossible to summarize all the knowledge here. If you want to know more after reading this section, visit your local or online bookstore and browse through the many titles. One word of warning: Many of the books are written for the U.S. market. Avoid them; the American situation is quite different from ours. Choose books that deal with the Canadian reality.

I assume you know what a mutual fund is: a pool of money from many individuals that is invested by a professional manager according to a specific mandate. The mandate defines in broad terms how the money is to be deployed: in stocks, bonds, mortgages, T-bills, or whatever. Many beginners come to mutual funds thinking they invest only in the stock market. That isn't so. You could have a large portfolio of mutual funds and not own a single share. I'm not saying that's a good idea, but it can be done.

In recent years, we've seen an explosion of highly specialized funds, investing in anything from Internet stocks to commodity futures. So perhaps the best starting point is to review the different types of funds that are available. You have to know what's out there before you can begin to make choices.

Canadian Equity Funds

Canadian equity funds invest primarily in Canadian stocks. However, many of these funds also hold U.S. and international securities, up to the foreign content limit. There are five sub-categories within this broad grouping.

Broadly Based Funds

Companies that trade publicly are divided into three types by money managers. Small-capitalization ("small-cap") firms are at the bottom of the pyramid; these are junior companies. There is no hard-and-fast rule as to what constitutes a small-cap company, and a small-cap U.S. firm might be a giant by Canadian standards. Each fund company applies its own criteria in defining a small-cap stock, but virtually everyone would agree that a company with a market capitalization (the value of all its publicly traded shares) under $50 million would fit. Mid-capitalization firms ("mid-cap") are, not surprisingly, in the middle. These are typically companies that are on the rise and historically they tend to have strong growth rates. Large-capitalization ("large-cap") firms are the giants of the industry: the big banks, Nortel, Alcan, Imperial Oil, and the like. A broadly based Canadian equity fund invests in all classes, so you're buying the full range of the market.

Large-Cap Funds

These focus only on the big firms. Again, the specific mandate is determined by the fund company, but a true large-cap fund would rarely venture beyond the stocks listed on the S&P/TSE 60 Index. Large-cap stocks are generally felt to be more stable and, therefore, less risky, so these funds will tend to appeal to more conservative investors.

Small-to-Mid-Cap Funds

Funds of this type focus on the other end of the spectrum: the smaller companies. The risk is usually higher as a result, but the theory is that the greater profit potential offsets that. It's not always the case, however; over the decade to the end of October 2000 the average Canadian large-cap fund outperformed the average small-to-mid-cap fund by a full percentage point.

Dividend Funds

In theory, the main objective of dividend funds is to deliver a regular income stream that will benefit from the dividend tax credit. In practice, many of these funds are simply blue-chip stock funds that invest heavily in bank stocks, utilities, and the like. There are a few true dividend funds around; you can identify them by taking a close look at their portfolios. If they hold a high percentage of preferred shares, they fit the classic definition of a dividend fund. Otherwise, treat them as a type of large-cap fund.

Labour-Sponsored Venture Capital Funds

The original attraction of these funds was the generous tax credits offered by the federal government and some provincial governments. These credits were given to compensate for the high-risk nature of the funds, which invest in start-up companies. The idea is to encourage the development of larger pools of venture capital in Canada, as a way of creating jobs and business expansion. Initially, returns on most of these funds were weak; however, in recent years many of them have scored big gains as a result of early-stage investments in successful technology companies. As a result, investors have enjoyed both tax deductions and profits. As well, owning units in these funds creates extra foreign content room in RRSPs.

U.S. Equity Funds

While Canadian equity funds may hold a fairly high percentage of foreign content, most U.S. equity funds are pure. In a few cases, you may find a couple of Latin American or Canadian stocks in the mix (it would not be unusual for a U.S. equity fund to own shares in Nortel, which is listed on the New York Stock Exchange as well as in Canada). But if the percentage of non-U.S. stocks is at all significant, the fund gets pushed into a different category, known as North American equity.

Our official categorization system recognizes two types of U.S. stock funds: broadly based and small-to-mid-cap funds.

Broadly Based Funds

As with broadly based Canadian funds, broadly based U.S. stock funds invest across all capitalization classes.

Small-to-Mid-Cap Funds

In the case of U.S. small-to-mid-cap funds, the companies held will usually be much larger than you'd find in a comparable Canadian stock fund. Another significant difference is that in this case, the greater profit potential of the small-cap stocks really has paid off. The average fund in this category had an annual return that was more than four percentage points higher than the average U.S. broadly based fund over the decade to October 31, 2000.

International/Global Equity Funds

This is where things can really start to get confusing. For starters, there are technically two main types of funds in this broad classification:

Global Equity Funds

Global funds can invest anywhere in the world, without exception. The confusion arises from the fact that some of these funds include the word "international" in their name — which actually means something else in the arcane language of the fund business.

International Mutual Funds

International funds can invest anywhere except in their home country. In Canada, we have extended that definition to include the U.S., so a true international fund will not hold any shares in companies resident in the U.S. or Canada. The fund may hold Mexican shares, however.

Moving beyond these two general classifications, we find more focused categories, including the following.

Regional Funds

In regional funds, the fund manager concentrates on a specific area of the world. Typical examples are European funds, Pacific Rim funds, and Latin American funds.

Country-Specific Funds

The focus sharpens to one country — at least in theory — in country-specific funds. After the U.S., Japanese equity funds are the most common. You will also find funds that focus on India, Germany, and China, although some of the China funds cheat by broadening their definition to include companies that have strong economic connections to that country but are not indigenous Chinese.

Emerging Markets Funds

The main criterion for emerging markets funds is the state of development of a nation's economy. Whether a particular country qualifies for inclusion is very much at the discretion of each fund manager. As a result, you may find that a fund will hold stocks from countries that clearly fall into the "emerging" ranks, such as Indonesia, as well as nations that we would normally think of as being relatively advanced, like Singapore, Israel, and South Korea.

Sector Equity Funds

A sector fund concentrates on one specific area of the economy, and most or all of the portfolio is invested in companies that are directly in that business or are closely related to it. A decade ago, there were very few sector equity funds in Canada. Now there are several hundred on offer. Because these funds are so tightly focused, they tend to be much more risky in nature. When the sector does well, the gains can be spectacular. But when the sector is out of favour, the losses can be heavy. As a result, many investors treat sector funds like cyclical stocks. They buy units when the prospects for the particular sector look bright and sell before the next downturn. The trick, of course, is in the timing.

Some of the most popular types of sector funds follow.

Natural Resource Funds

The emphasis of natural resource funds is on the resource sector, which includes mining, oil and gas, forest products, and the like. Some funds narrow the focus even more by honing in on a single industry, such as energy. Precious metals funds have been given a separate category of their own, but actually they belong with this broad group.

Science and Technology Funds

The tech boom of the late 1990s gave birth to dozens of science and technology (S&T) funds, many of which scored huge gains during the period when Nasdaq was running wild. There are a number of sub-sets within this broad grouping, including health sciences funds and telecommunications funds.

Financial Services Funds

As the demand for sector funds grew, the industry scrambled to find other concepts that would appeal to investors. Financial companies, such as banks, insurance firms, brokerage houses, and the like, fit the bill nicely and new funds that specialize in them have appeared in recent years. By their nature, the stocks held by these funds will tend to be interest-sensitive, which means that the general direction of rates will have an impact on their prices. So the best time to buy into a financial services fund is when it appears that interest rates are about to decline.

Real Estate Funds

There are two basic types of real estate funds. One type invests in the shares of real estate companies, and those in related industries. This makes them similar to other sector funds in their approach, and the primary objective of the manager is to produce capital gains. The second type is quite different, however. These funds actually own land and buildings, usually in the form of rental properties. In this case, the main goal is to produce tax-advantaged income. Depreciation on the properties owned by the fund can be used to shelter part of the rental revenue from taxes. As a result, when distributions are made to unitholders, a portion of the income is received on a tax-deferred basis. This type of real estate fund is not recommended if above-average capital appreciation is your goal, but it is useful for retired people who want to reduce the tax bite on their investment income.

Index Equity Funds

Index funds track the performance of a specific stock index. In Canada, the TSE 300 is the one most commonly used. The majority of U.S. index funds emulate the S&P 500 Index, although you can find funds that track Nasdaq and the Dow. There are also a number of international index funds available, which may be based on the Morgan Stanley Capital International Europe, Australia and Far East (EAFE) Index, or a combination of individual country indexes. Index funds do not have their own separate category in the current Canadian classification system.

Bond Funds

There was a time when bond funds were simple and no complex decision-making was involved in making a selection. That's no longer the case. As with equity funds, the range of bond funds offered to investors has expanded dramatically in recent years. Now you can choose amongst these classifications:

Regular Bond Funds

These are your standard meat-and-potatoes bond funds, investing in a portfolio of debt securities from different issuers with varying maturities.

Short-Term Bond Funds

Regular bond funds are vulnerable to loss during periods when interest rates are rising. Short-term bond funds are less risky because they hold only securities with a term to maturity of less than five years. If rates rise, bonds of this type will be less affected. The price you pay for this increased safety is a lower return and almost no capital gains potential.

Mortgage Funds

Mortgage funds are a variation on short-term bond funds except that they invest in residential first mortgages.

High-Yield Bond Funds

You've heard of junk bonds? This is a nicer way of saying the same thing, making the managers of these funds feel better about their work. And, truth be told, we don't have many genuine junk bonds in Canada – they're more of a U.S. phenomenon. High-yield bonds are issued by companies with a lower credit rating. As a result, the interest rate they have to pay to borrow is higher than would be charged to a blue-ribbon client like the Government of Canada or a major bank. Of course, such companies are at greater risk of going under, especially in a recession. So if you're at all risk-averse, you should steer clear of these funds during economic downturns.

Foreign Bond Funds

Foreign bond funds invest in debt securities issued by foreign governments or companies, or in Canadian bonds denominated in foreign currencies. There are a lot more of those than you think; all levels of government frequently issue U.S.-dollar bonds, and you can also find issues in Euros, Japanese yen, Swiss francs, sterling, and German marks. Funds that specialize in Canadian foreign currency issues are fully eligible for registered plans (the currency isn't what counts, it's the issuer). Those that invest offshore are considered to be foreign content for RRSP and RRIF purposes. Foreign bond funds perform best when global interest rates and the value of the Canadian dollar are falling in tandem.

Money Market Funds

As mutual funds go, this is about as simple as it gets. Money market funds invest in short-term debt securities, normally with maturity dates of less than a year. Unit values are fixed, usually at $10, and do not fluctuate. Cash distributions are made monthly. These funds are very safe and highly liquid, and are a good place to park spare cash. There are three types of these funds:

Canadian Money Market Funds

These invest in Canadian dollar securities issued by governments and corporations.

T-Bill Funds

These focus on Government of Canada Treasury bills, so are considered slightly safer than regular money market funds.

Foreign Money Market Funds

These invest in securities denominated in other currencies, usually U.S. dollars. Some of these funds are fully eligible for registered plans because they invest in foreign currency notes issued by Canadian governments and corporations.

Balanced Funds

When you buy units in a balanced fund, you're getting a mixed portfolio of stocks, bonds, and cash. The proportion of each depends on the mandate of the fund and/or the decisions of the manager. Balanced funds are designed for investors who want broad diversification without the need to purchase several different funds. Someone with limited capital who can only afford to buy units in a single fund should choose this type. Here are the main varieties.

Canadian Balanced Funds

The emphasis is on Canadian securities, although many funds also hold U.S. and international stocks up to the foreign content limit. A true balanced fund will usually operate within a ratio of 35 to 65 percent stocks, with the balance in bonds and cash.

Global Balanced Funds

Here the focus is on international securities, with little or no Canadian content in the mix. You will also find a few funds that limit themselves to U.S. securities or to those of a particular geographic region, such as Europe.

Tactical Asset Allocation Funds

Whereas a genuine balanced fund operates within specific parameters, the manager of a tactical asset allocation (TAA) fund has much more latitude. In fact, there may be times when a fund is 100-percent invested in a single type of security, usually stocks. These funds are therefore somewhat riskier than a typical balanced fund, but they also have greater capital gains potential.

High-Income Balanced Funds

This is a relatively new category. High-income balanced funds invest in securities that generate above-average income, such as royalty income trusts and real estate investment trusts. Because much of the income is tax deferred, these funds are best suited to high bracket individuals. Risk is on the high side.

Spin-Off Funds

One of the recent developments that has added greatly to the complexity of mutual fund investing is the creation of several versions of the same fund. This means an investor or an advisor not only has to decide which funds to select, but which versions of those funds as well. There are three main types of spin-off funds that you should know about.

Tax-Sheltered Funds

For those investing outside registered plans, one of the inhibiting factors in switching from one fund to another is the tax liability that arises with each transaction. The government takes the position that a switch is the same as a sale, so if the fund has increased in value since you purchased the units, you have a taxable capital gain. Even though the capital gains inclusion rate has dropped to 50 percent, that will still cause many people to hesitate before pulling the trigger, even if a switch is indicated.

Several fund companies have responded to this problem by creating "umbrella" funds. These are mega-funds that contain multiple classes of shares. Typically, under the umbrella you might expect to find a Canadian equity fund, at least one U.S. stock fund, a global fund, a fixed-income fund, and a money market fund. Usually, several more choices are offered.

Although they function in much the same way as stand-alone mutual funds, they are referred to as *classes* or, somewhat confusingly, *sector shares*. When you see either of these terms used, it indicates you are buying units in a portfolio that is actually part of an umbrella fund.

The advantage to the unitholder is that you can move your money around at will under the umbrella without triggering a taxable capital gain. You incur a tax liability only when you cash out of the umbrella fund entirely.

Often, the classes in an umbrella fund are simply a spinoff from a stand-alone parent fund, with the same manager, mandate, and much the same portfolio. However, the returns may vary because of slight differences in management expense ratio (MER) or the timing of purchases.

If there is a stand-alone option (which is not always the case), the umbrella fund version should not be used in a registered plan because there is no tax advantage in doing so and returns tend to be slightly lower than those of the parent fund. But as a tax-planning tool, this type of fund can be very useful.

Segregated Funds

For years, no one paid much attention to segregated funds, or "seg funds" as they're commonly called – not even the companies that created and marketed them. These are products of the life insurance industry. They're a means of saving for retirement (or for some other purpose) while enjoying benefits that are unique to insurance products, such as protection from creditors and capital guarantees.

It's the latter feature that shot seg funds to widespread popularity during the late 1990s. Investors discovered there was a way to participate in the torrid bull market of the period without putting their money at risk, and they rushed to take advantage of it. For years, most insurance companies had offered a maturity guarantee of 75 percent on their seg funds. This meant that after 10 years, if the value of the fund had declined, you were assured of getting at least 75 percent of your money back.

That didn't excite people very much, however, so some of the more aggressive companies bumped by the maturity guarantee to 100 percent, matching the death benefit guarantee. Now people started to take notice. The perception grew, nurtured by the industry, that you could invest in the stock markets in this way at no risk. Of course, there is risk – that at the end of 10 years you might get zero return on your money. But that didn't seem to be of much concern.

Manulife Financial took the lead in popularizing the seg fund concept by entering into arrangements with several mutual fund companies to offer their most attractive products in a seg fund wrapper. Essentially, these are spinoffs from parent mutual funds created by firms like Fidelity, AGF, Elliott & Page, and Talvest. The difference is that they offer the bells and whistles of a seg fund and, accordingly, carry a higher price tag in the form of an increased MER.

Not all seg funds are spinoffs, far from it. Many are stand-alone funds offered by insurance companies and managed independently. The MER on these seg funds tends to be somewhat lower than that of the spin-off version, so the smart investor will look at them closely before making a seg fund decision.

Some seg fund MERs have escalated recently because of new capital requirements set by the Office of the Superintendent of Financial Institutions to provide adequate reserves in the event a stock market collapse should result in large claims under the guarantee clause. So you should be aware of how much the fund will cost you on an annual basis – think of the extra fee as an insurance premium – as well as whether further escalations are likely down the road. Keep in mind that the maturity guarantee only comes into play if you have held your units for 10 years. If you sell before then, you have no protection. That makes you a prisoner to escalating MERs that are beyond your control.

The difference in MERs can be substantial. For example, at the time of writing, the MER of the Fidelity Growth America Fund was 2.48 percent. The Manulife seg fund version carried an MER of 3.15 percent, a difference of 0.67 percent. By way of comparison, the stand-alone Transamerica Growsafe U.S. Equity Fund, which at the time showed a much better record than either version of the Fidelity fund, weighed in with an MER of 2.40 percent.

As a general rule, I don't recommend paying a high MER for a seg fund version of a balanced or bond fund, and certainly not for a money market fund. The chances of any of these funds being in a loss position after a decade is negligible. Why pay a hefty premium for insurance that you will almost certainly never collect? If you're going to pay extra for a seg fund, you should choose funds with the highest degree of risk and potential return. The insurance company is taking on the risk for you, as it relates to your principal. With that concern removed, your goal should be to earn the maximum possible profit.

Clone Funds

The foreign content rules have always been a thorn in the side of investors in registered plans – RRSPs, RRIFs, and pension plans (strangely, registered education savings plans are not included in the regulations). The limit has been gradually raised over the years, from 10 percent originally to 30 percent today. However, many financial advisors believe that, for optimal balance, the foreign content in a portfolio should be between 40 and 60 percent.

In the late spring of 1999, Mackenzie Financial came to market with a spinoff version of two of its most popular foreign funds that it claimed were not subject to the foreign content rules. These "clones" were created through a complex and clever use of derivatives, with the goal of replicating the performance of an underlying parent fund. Initial sales were brisk and a few other companies tested the water. Most were cautious, however, waiting to see what position the Canada Customs and Revenue Agency (CCRA) would take on these newcomers and whether the Finance Department would attempt to shoot them down. In August, responding to a formal request from the Templeton organization, CCRA issued a ruling that gave the clones a green light with virtually no reservations. Over at Finance, nothing stirred – no rumblings of impending legislation to close the loophole. The fund companies got the message and clones flooded the market. By the time the 2000 RRSP season rolled around, there were about 100 of them and the list continued to grow.

The Canadian stock market had been in the doldrums for much of the late 1990s, so the clones were welcomed by RRSP investors as a way to get more exposure to the hot markets in the U.S. and other countries. Sales of the clones boomed, to the point that some of them actually became bigger than the original parent fund. By November 2000, the Universal RSP Select Managers Fund, one of the first to be created by Mackenzie, had almost $3.5 billion in its coffers. The original parent fund had just under $2 billion.

Clone funds can certainly boost RRSP foreign content. But they do so at a price, which many investors fail to realize. Their MERs are usually somewhat higher than those of the parent fund. And returns tend to be somewhat lower. To October 31, 2000, the Universal RSP Select Managers Fund showed a one-year gain of 5.3 percent, while the original parent fund was ahead by 5.9 percent. The AGF RSP American Growth Fund had a one-year advance of 4.2 percent, while the parent fund was ahead 6.1 percent.

In a few cases, the performance gap was so great as to raise serious questions about the structure of the clone and its ability to accurately replicate the parent fund. The AGF European Growth Class had a one-year gain of 8.7 percent to October 31, 2000, while the clone managed only 5.5 percent. That's a variation of almost 37 percent!

The message is obvious. Don't choose a clone fund for your registered plan unless you have maximized your foreign content allocation and still want to add more. Most people aren't even close to the 30 percent limit in their portfolios. Also, keep in mind that if you have any units in labour-sponsored venture capital funds in your RRSP, they will add a foreign content bonus. In fact, you can use those units to bring your allowable maximum up to 50 percent, which should be as much as you'll need.

Style Matters

If you want to be a success, you've got to have style. It's true in life. It's also true in mutual funds.

During the late 1990s when the stock markets were on the rise, I constantly received e-mail messages from investors who were moaning about the lousy returns their equity funds were producing.

"What am I doing wrong?" the typical message would say. "The TSE was up 30 percent last year, but my mutual funds did nothing. Should I sell?"

Not necessarily. What these people probably needed was better diversification – not by asset class, but by management style. It's a strategy very few fund investors have paid attention to, until now. But after what happened as the '90s wound down, there's a lot more buzz about the idea.

I'll deal with the concept of style diversification in greater detail in the next section. For now, let me summarize the basic mutual fund management styles you will encounter.

Value

Value managers seek out stocks that are cheap compared to the rest of the market, using such traditional measures as price/earnings and price/book value ratios. Value investing is a tried and true method for achieving long-term profits. It's the style used by some of the world's greatest money managers, such as Warren Buffett and Sir John Templeton. But it

Step 5

Make a Plan

We've come a long way. You now know that dreaming about being a millionaire is never going to get you there – only through action can that happen. You've begun the process of shedding your unwanted baggage, breaking down the barriers that may stand in your way in the process. You've learned more about yourself and by now should have a clear idea which route you are going to take to achieve your goal – creating it or saving it. And you're now well on the way to empowering yourself with the knowledge and skills you need to get you there.

All of this is great. But it won't come together for you unless you develop a coherent plan that focuses your ability and wisdom directly on the challenge you have undertaken. There are a lot of smart and talented people in the world who are not millionaires. Some of them are quite comfortable with that fact. You're not, or you wouldn't be reading this book. You are motivated to use your skills to gain material advantage. There is nothing wrong with that, and it is certainly nothing to be ashamed of. In fact, it is the foundation upon which our economic culture is built.

We live in a capitalist society. That means we value free enterprise and reward individual initiative. There are some who say this has led us down the wrong path, to a world that has become overly materialistic and that has lost its sense of humanity. Certainly, capitalism has been guilty of excesses, and they will continue for as long as we are around. But so far no one has devised anything better. Communism, which was supposed to be the moral antidote to capitalism, failed miserably, leaving the population of the countries that embraced it impoverished and disenfranchised. It is hardly surprising that the only major nation that still officially describes itself as communist, the People's Republic of China, has been aggressively embracing capitalist practices for several years, to the point that its leaders apparently feel no discomfort about maintaining Hong Kong as a capitalistic, free-trade window on the West.

Even socialism, a more moderate approach to collectivism, has been forced to temper its philosophy and its practices. You need look no farther than the Labour Party in Great Britain. In the years after World War II, this party was the most radical political force to be found in the Western world, dominated by militant trade unions. Industries of all types were nationalized, from steel mills to coal mines to hospitals to airlines. The welfare state philosophy reigned supreme, and capitalism was pushed back on all fronts. A predictable result of these policies was the gradual but steady decline of the U.K. as an international economic power. Eventually, things became so bad that Britain's trade unions became the butt of the world's jokes for their outrageous practices and demands, as chronicled in the classic Peter Sellers film *I'm All Right Jack*.

It took the Iron Lady, Margaret Thatcher, to break the mould and push Britain back on a road that again favoured free enterprise. But she was a Tory, and that was expected.

What is significant is that the new Labour Party, under the pragmatic Tony Blair, is a completely different creature from the trade union machine of the past. Labour has recognized that socialism can only be taken so far before it stifles initiative, destroys creativity, and gives rise to national mediocrity. Britain has come a long way in its political evolution – as have we all.

So never, not for one moment, should you believe there is something wrong or selfish about wanting to use your talents to achieve material gain. It is the way of the world. In prehistoric times, the families of the most skilful hunters ate best. The same principle applies today – the families of those who make the most effective use of their abilities will thrive. It is a much more honourable goal than depending on others for support or handouts.

Just remember two things. First, wealth is only a means to an end. A million dollars in itself is nothing – an entry on a piece of paper. It is what that money represents in terms of an enhanced lifestyle for you and your loved ones that counts. Second, no amount of money is worth a life of misery. A million dollars in your bank account will not make you happy if you have alienated your family and friends in an obsessive effort to attain it, or if you have destroyed your health in the process, or if you have compromised your fundamental principles in pursuit of it.

If ever you lose sight of these two basic truths in your quest, then you have indeed taken a wrong fork in the road. So any time you come to a decision, apply these twin tests. They should be at the core of any plan you make.

Creating Your Million

Throughout this book, we are focusing on two ways to amass your first million: creating it and saving it. Creating it can be done in a number of ways, depending on the skill sets you identify as being the most important. Unless you are a talented athlete, actor, musician, writer, or the like, this probably will mean that at some point you will need to create a business plan.

Making a Business Plan

There are many excellent books on this subject, so I am not going to try to set out all the details of a good business plan here. But, from my own experience as the president of a small company, let me offer some ideas as to what a good business plan should contain.

A Strong Concept

Of course you have to start with a good idea. You can't create a million dollars out of nothing. It may be a new product or a new service or simply a better way of doing something that people have taken for granted for years. Look at Ziploc® bags. A few years ago, they didn't even exist – we used ties to close plastic bags. Now they or similar products are in almost every kitchen, because someone came up with an idea of how to do it better.

So you begin with an idea. But you don't end there, which is the fundamental mistake made by many fledgling entrepreneurs. They think the idea is all they need. They rhapsodize about it and all that it will do. They get carried away with their creativity and lose sight of the fact that, first, the idea has to be translated into reality, and, second, people have to be persuaded to buy it.

Any business plan that is built on an idea and little more is almost doomed to fail. In fact, the idea should take up no more than a couple of pages at the front of the plan, unless it is some incredibly complex scientific concept. If the investor can't grasp the potential of the idea quickly, then it may not have any potential at all.

A Unique Selling Point

Once you've established that you have a great idea, the next step is to show why people will want it and benefit from it. You need to define at least one unique selling point – more if possible. This is what makes your idea stand out from everyone else's. The unique selling point of the first TV remote was that you didn't have to get out of your chair every time you wanted to change a channel or adjust the volume. We now take remotes for granted, but back in the early 1960s they represented a revolutionary change in the way we watched television. The unique selling point was immediately apparent. Everyone saw the benefit and wanted one. The era of the couch potato was born.

The Target Market

You will be asking people to fork out some of their hard-earned money for whatever it is you create. Who are those people going to be? Teenagers? Housewives? Business people? TV watchers? Fast-food addicts? Gadget lovers? Seniors? Babies? Everyone?

No business plan is worth anything unless it pinpoints the audience that the product or service is designed for and then goes beyond that to attempt to quantify the potential reach. Are you selling only to homeowners in your immediate neighbourhood? To automobile owners in your city? To the broad consumer market in your region of the country? Nationally? Internationally? Do you eventually expect one percent of the target market to buy the product or service? Five percent? Fifty percent?

Of course, a lot of this is blue-sky estimating at the outset. It's only when you actually begin the selling process that you'll know whether you're reasonably accurate in your initial projections or wildly off base. But you have to start somewhere. The best advice I can give is to be conservative. Terrific though your idea may be, don't expect the world to stampede to your door to buy it the moment it appears. Define your target market narrowly and keep your estimate of initial penetration low. That way, the plan will appear much more credible to any prospective investor or lender.

An Analysis of the Competition

Who else is in the same business, either offering the same thing or something similar? If you can truly say "no one," then you may really be on to something. The odds are you will be facing at least some competition – and if you're successful, there will be a lot more.

Look at your competitors objectively, from a business perspective. Find out everything you can about them. How good are they? Do they have strong customer loyalty? Or are their clients disgruntled because of high prices or poor service and looking for alternatives? How dominant is the competition in your target marketplace? A badly fragmented market offers good opportunities. One that is virtually controlled by a single company may be tough to crack, especially if that company is well managed and well financed. You need to be completely realistic with yourself on this point; underestimating the competition almost always leads to disaster.

A Production Plan

How is your product or service going to be produced? Who is going to do it, where will it happen, and what will it cost? This is where it gets really tough. You now have to move from the concept stage to the producing stage. It goes back to the principle that "all good ideas translate into hard work." Okay, so whose hard work is it and what expense will be involved? Are you planning to do it all yourself, or do you need to hire employees? If you need staff, how many, doing what? Where will they work? What equipment will they require? Will you provide it or will they? This is the kind of nitty-gritty stuff that creative people don't like to be bothered with. Unfortunately, it's also the kind of nitty-gritty stuff that bankers and investors will look at most closely.

A Marketing Plan

You know what the product or service is, you know how you are going to produce it and at what cost, and you know who you want to sell it to. Now how are you going to get your message to those folks in a way that they will pay some attention to it? That's what a marketing plan is all about – reaching the target audience and persuading them to give you a try. It can be a real challenge and very expensive.

Certain audiences are very difficult to find. I have spent many years in the investment newsletter business. These are normally marketed by direct mail, to lists of people who have previously purchased related products. In the U.S., lists containing thousands and even millions of names are available for purchase. In Canada, they are very scarce, quite expensive, and not highly productive, which is one of the reasons this particular industry has never flourished in our country. Personally, I gave up on the direct mail idea years ago and turned to different marketing approaches, focusing mainly on the Internet and electronic delivery.

You'll need to determine what method of marketing is likely to work best for you, within the limits of what you can afford. A TV commercial during prime time may be the obvious choice if you want to reach a huge number of people, but you'll need to spend big bucks to create a spot and to buy the air time. There are many much less expensive ways of marketing a new business. Your business plan should include some of these creative ideas and a realistic budget for what they will cost.

Sales Projections

Once you have identified the target audience and developed a marketing plan, you should be able to make some serious sales projections. A word of caution here: Keep your enthusiasm under control. You're probably very excited about the project and truly believe in your heart that customers will flock to your door as soon as you open for business. Take it from one who has been there and seen many other start-up operations: They probably won't. Even if you've conducted some market sampling and received positive feedback, when money is on the line the potential clients suddenly discover all kinds of reasons why they can't make a commitment. Their budget has been fully allocated for this year. The boss has just initiated a spending freeze. They want to "wait and see" (entrepreneurs hate hearing those words). It's always something.

Two recent examples in my own experience come immediately to mind. The first involved the launch of a new magazine that was targeted at a well-identified and highly affluent audience. The publication would have everything going for it: broad distribution, well-known writers, sharp graphics, solid editing, an opinionated perspective, and an attractive selling environment for a huge range of products, including cars, electronic equipment, and financial services. The entrepreneurs behind the publication had visited some of the country's key advertising agencies to brief them about the plans and received uniformly favourable reactions.

Because I was involved in the business as publisher of Canada's largest-circulation magazine at one stage in my career, I was asked for my opinion relatively late in the process. I urged the promoters to go slow. The new publication represented a significant investment. My own experience with advertisers and agencies had been one of constant frustration and disappointment. I suggested that the ad revenue projections they were formulating as a result of what they saw as a strong initial response might be overly optimistic. They decided to go ahead anyway – indeed, at that point they were probably too far along to pull back in any event.

There are times when you hate to be right. This was one of them. Advertising revenue came in well below expectations, to the point that the magazine had to go into a six-month hiatus. As of this writing, its future is uncertain, although the founders continue to be optimistic that they can make it work. I wish them well.

The second example involved the launch of a new dot-com company. Here again, the demographic target market was tightly defined (a different group from that being pursued by the magazine) and the company had already proven its ability in another medium to reach its target audience effectively and to generate good revenue and profits. The Web site had a "can't miss" feel about it.

It was the same story as with the magazine. Advertisers wanted the audience but they weren't convinced that this was an effective way to reach it. The dollars trickled in at a painfully slow rate, creating serious financial problems for the new company. Fortunately for the stakeholders, the situation began to improve as management upgraded the quality of the product, formed strategic alliances with key Internet portals, and redoubled its marketing efforts. But the slow start produced a lot of sleepless nights and churning stomachs.

I tell these stories to emphasize the importance of this point. Do not fall into the trap of overestimating your sales revenue, especially in the early stages. Take your initial estimate, cut it in half, then cut it in half again. "But if I do that the company won't be viable," you may say. Well, better you find that out now than later, I say in response. Always remember, if your revenues come in over budget you'll look like a hero. If they don't meet expectations, your reputation will suffer and the business will have to scramble to survive.

Cost Estimates

The other side of the ledger is your expense projections. Make sure they are realistic and as accurate as possible. The best strategy for a start-up is to spend as little as possible. Don't hire full-time staff if you can make do with part-time employees. Don't rent office space if you can work out of your spare room or basement. Don't upgrade the computer if the old one will do the job. In short, if you don't have to spend money, don't – at least not until you have a clearer picture of what the revenue will look like.

Investors and lenders will be impressed by a well-thought-out, carefully reasoned cost analysis. They will want to know that you are budgeting enough to do what you say you will do. But they don't want to see any fat, and neither should you. Save the convention jaunts to Las Vegas for another time!

Profit and Loss Projections

The bottom line of your revenue and cost estimates is your profit and loss (P&L) forecast. Typically, a start-up operation will lose money in the first two years, break-even in the third, and become profitable after that. If your projections accelerate that timetable, fine – just as long as they are realistic. If you can't see how you can turn a profit after the first three years, then you should ask yourself whether this is a project that is worth embarking on. Certainly potential investors will ask the same question.

Of course, profitability is relative. If you're looking at a one-person operation and you can break-even in the first year while budgeting a decent income for yourself, you'll do just fine. If you're more ambitious and require outside money to launch a bigger enterprise, then you'll have to show investors that they can get a decent return on their principal within a reasonable period. If the best you can come up with is 4 percent annually for the next five years, maybe wealthy Aunt Mary will come in, but no hard-eyed outsider will touch your project.

A Contingency Plan

What will you do if things go wrong? How will you handle a revenue shortfall, an unexpected cost escalation, or the bank calling a loan? You can't anticipate every possibility, but a contingency plan for the most likely difficulties will assure both yourself and others that you have careful considered the probable downside risks and have a program for dealing with them.

An Exit Strategy

If you are trying to attract outside investors, one critical point they should look for is an exit strategy. When are they likely to be able to get their money out, and under what conditions? If you can address this in your business plan (and it's not always possible), it will give you an added advantage.

One obvious exit strategy is a timetable to take the company public. If certain objectives are achieved within a set time frame, you commit the organization to taking the steps necessary to issue shares to the public and obtain a stock exchange listing.

If the company doesn't figure to become that big, or you just want to keep it private, you can offer investors a buyout clause under which you agree to purchase their shares at a pre-determined price (or formula) after a specific date.

There are all sorts of other possibilities as well, many of which may not be apparent at the time the first business plan is drawn up. However, by at least referring to this possibility you will make potential investors aware of your concern for their interests as well as your own and establish yourself as a person who works to achieve a win-win solution for all parties. That's a gold-plated image to have in the business world.

Some Tips for Success

Creating your million is in many ways more difficult than saving it. The savings route mainly requires discipline and knowledge. The creation route adds innovation, entrepreneurship, high energy, and leadership to the talent list. If you come up short in any of these areas, you'll have a tough slog unless you can find a partner or partners who can fill in the gaps. This is not meant to discourage you, only to stress the importance of being fully armed before you venture down that particular road.

If you decide to go that way, here are a few tips from my own experience that may ease your path.

Tip #1: Pay in Shares, Not Cash

When you're starting a new operation, cash is king. Be miserly with it. If there is another way to acquire what you need, use it. Shares in your fledgling operation may be an attractive alternative, especially if there is a high degree of confidence of success.

The dot-com bubble burst in 2000, but the stories of Internet millionaires who cashed in on their shares in start-up companies remain fresh in our minds. That should be motivation enough to encourage some of the people you need to accept at least a portion of their remuneration in the shares of your company.

It's not that the shares cost you nothing. Eventually they will, because every share that you give to someone else dilutes your own equity in your venture. If the project is a huge success, you may end up having grossly overpaid your employees for their services. But that's a risk you have to take to preserve your precious cash. And remember, the employees are taking a big risk too. The shares could end up being worthless, and they would have put in all that work for nothing!

Tip #2: Do As Much As You Can Yourself

One of the attributes of a good manager is the ability to delegate. But that assumes there is someone capable to delegate to. In the early start-up days, you want to keep overheads as low as possible, which means hiring no more people than you absolutely need. Doing more yourself means paying out less. Of course, don't get silly about it. Working to a state of perpetual exhaustion or even illness is a certain recipe for failure. We all have our limits. But a few extra hours each weekday or on a Saturday morning shouldn't be too onerous. If by putting in that time you can save some dollars, do it.

Tip #3: Avoid Full-Time Staff

If at all possible, hire outside help on a part-time, hourly pay basis. This has several advantages. You only pay for the time you actually need. You don't have to worry about severance if you have to cut staff. Your payroll taxes are dramatically reduced. You don't have to supply perks, like health insurance.

Again, much will depend on the size of the planned business and the scale of your initial operations. Full-time staff may eventually be a necessity. But don't rush the issue. There are lots of talented people out there who would be quite happy to work a few extra hours a week.

Tip #4: Seek Media Exposure

Getting your message out to the world can be very expensive. The cheapest and most effective means to do this is through media exposure. That's why book publishers spend thousands of dollars to send their top authors on tour – they know that one television interview can be worth a dozen newspaper ads. If you can present your product or service in a way that might grab the media's attention, do so. Even coverage in your local weekly newspaper can be extremely valuable. Create opportunities by identifying which media outlets are most likely to be interested and finding the name of a good contact person at each. If appropriate, send out periodic press releases. Just make sure there is genuine news value in what you have to say. Reporters have an unerring eye for self-promotion, but they will sometimes go along with it if there is a news peg on which to hang the story (which is why author tours work). But if you are blatantly self-serving and offer no news value, your press releases will quickly find their way to the wastebasket and your calls will go unreturned.

One good strategy, if appropriate, is to establish yourself as an expert in your field of business. I receive calls from national media all the time, wanting to know my views about breaking financial stories. Of course, it has taken years to establish my reputation. But you may be able to do so more quickly, depending on your background. For example, an articulate person who lectures in computer science at a college or university could probably find a receptive media audience for his or her views on related subjects.

Tip #5: Underspend Your Budget

Your business plan should contain a carefully reasoned expense budget for the first three years. If at all possible, spend less. That may seem hard, especially if you've been meticulous in your original estimates. Try anyway. Keeping a tight watch on spending and coming in under budget wherever possible is an excellent managerial discipline, especially in a start-up situation.

Tip #6: Be Quick to Adjust to Shortfalls

Keep a constant watch on your revenues and expenses. You should get monthly reports (or prepare them yourself). Be alert to any revenue shortfall or overspending and take immediate remedial action. Don't hope that things will get better next month. They probably won't. If there is a problem, you need to identify it quickly and take action to deal with it before it develops into a major crisis.

Tip #7: Insist That Your Family Co-operate

This venture represents your future. It must have every chance to succeed. That means you need the full and complete co-operation of your family. It also means there may be a period of strain while everyone adjusts to the changed situation. It's critical that this be understood and agreed to by everyone concerned, especially if you're working from home. I cannot stress this enough.

When I first went out on my own, I worked out of a home office. We set it up in a large basement area that had previously been a playroom for our three children. We divided it in half through the use of bookcases. On one side were my desk, computer, filing cabinets, and reference works. The other side was retained as a playroom, with a TV set, game station, and the like.

At that point, the kids were old enough to understand what was going on. We sat down together in a family meeting and laid out the basic ground rules. During weekdays (when the children were usually in school anyway) the room was exclusively mine. If the children were home and the door was closed, they were to respect that and not bother me for any reason other than a genuine emergency. My wife agreed to the same restrictions. In the evenings and on weekends, I relinquished my claim on the space unless something urgent was happening, and they could use the playroom area. The arrangement worked amazingly well, in large part I believe because everyone participated in the process and felt it was fair to all. As a result, I was able to work very effectively from my home and to establish the business that I run to this day.

Obviously, it's more difficult when very young children are involved. They are not amenable to reason and can't understand why daddy or mommy, who is after all just behind the door, won't come out and play with them. In situations like this, the spouses have to be in total accord. There must be a mutual agreement on work times, during which the other spouse assumes complete responsibility for the youngsters to ensure that there will be no interruptions. If both spouses work, then competent outside help must be found.

If the home environment cannot be made quiet and comfortable for work, then an alternative will have to be found. It is simply not possible to launch and maintain a start-up business in an atmosphere of chronic domestic chaos. You'll make yourself a prime candidate for a nervous breakdown.

Saving Your Million

So far in this chapter, we have focused on creating wealth. However, if you've decided that your road to a million should be the savings/investment route, it is also time to begin some serious planning.

Create a Savings Plan

You need to determine how much you can put towards the program at the outset and how much you expect to add to it over time. When added to any savings you already have, and factoring in an expected annual rate of return, this will enable you to estimate how quickly your pool of capital will grow and to put a meaningful time frame on the process. You can then decide if the plan is acceptable or, if not, what you will do to change it.

Let's take a moment to consider each component.

Current Savings

If you have not already done so, complete the Net Worth Calculator in Appendix A at the end of the book. From that, pick up the numbers from the following lines in the Assets section:

Current value of RRSPs (and/or RRIFs)   _____

Current value of all non-registered liquid assets   _____

These are the only two lines in the Net Worth Calculator that you need to be concerned about right now. Together, they represent your total liquid savings to date. We do not include the value of pension plans or deferred profit sharing plans because that money is locked in and cannot be touched by you. The equity in your home, while clearly an asset, is treated separately for this purpose.

One-Year Savings Target

Now that you know what your base is, you have to start building on it. Based on past experience and your current financial situation, decide how much you can put aside each month for the next year. Make an RRSP contribution your number one priority. If there is additional money available after the plan is topped up, it can be directed to a non-registered investment portfolio.

The best approach is to decide on a set percentage of your after-tax household income that will be devoted to this purpose and to include it as part of your budget. If possible, the minimum should not be less than 5 percent a month. A 10 percent target would be ideal.

Future Savings Targets

Make a commitment to allocate a higher percentage of any future increases in family income to your program – say 25 percent of the after-tax value of a raise. Finally, decide on a percentage of "windfall" money that will go towards your plan – I recommend 50 percent of the after-tax amount. This would include income tax refunds, bonuses, financial gifts, inheritances, and investment income (if you don't depend on it to live on).

Taking all this into account, arrive at an estimate of how much you will be able to increase your savings each year. A good target is a 10 percent annual increase.

By taking this kind of approach, you will find that the amount of money being directed into your savings program will steadily increase as the years go by.

Expected Annual Rate of Return

The figure you choose will depend on several factors, including your age, family situation, the aggressiveness of your investments, and taxes. If you're very conservative and don't like a lot of risk, choose a low figure – say, 6 percent, before tax. Just be aware that it will take much longer to reach your goal if you do. Those who are prepared to take more risk and invest a larger portion of their assets in the stock market can aim higher – say 10 percent annually. Anything beyond that is unrealistic (although not impossible) over the long term. For a middle-of-the-road investor, an average annual return of 8 percent is a good figure to use. Remember, all these projections are before tax.

Do Some Projections

Based on the figures you have decided on, you are now in a position to do some projections that will show you how much your savings/investment plan will grow over time. It's important that you do these calculations because you'll immediately get a good idea of how long it may take to achieve your goal, which in turn will help you decide if you want to speed up the whole process by either saving more or taking on additional risk.

There are software programs available that will do these calculations for you quickly and easily. Or you can do them yourself manually if you prefer.

There are two parts to this process. The first is to project the future value of your existing savings. If you are doing this manually, turn to the table in Appendix B titled Future Value of Present Investments and fill in the following lines, starting from the figures that you drew from the Net Worth Calculator and entered above. For example, if you showed the current value of your RRSPs as $15,000, you have a 25-year time horizon, and you project a 10 percent return, your number below will be $162,450 ($15,000 × 10.83).

Future value of current registered plans   _____

Future value of current non-registered liquid assets   _____

Next, you want to get some idea of what your ongoing investments will be worth over time. Here you will use the tables titled Future Value of Ongoing Investments 1 and 2. Note that this first table is based on the assumption that you will increase by 10 percent the amount of money you are putting aside each year. So if you plan to invest $3,000 in the first year, you will increase that to $3,300 in year two, $3,630 in year three, and so on. The other table assumes no annual increment. Also, the tables are structured to reflect your return based on investments made at the start of each year. If you spread out your investments over 12 months, or wait until year-end, your returns will be slightly lower. Here again, I suggest you do a separate calculation for registered and non-registered investments.

Future value of ongoing registered plan contributions   _____

Future value of ongoing non-registered investments   _____

This is the heart of your saving/investing program. As you will see if you study the table closely, the amount of money you accumulate will depend on three main factors: how much you save, how long a time horizon you have, and how well your investments perform.

Let's look at several scenarios to see how you can work with these variables.

Scenario #1: You Have a Limited Amount of Money to Invest

In this case, your budget is tight. You are motivated to start on a savings/investment program, but there isn't a lot of cash you can free up, at least at present. Fine. We all have to start somewhere. Let's work with $100 a month to begin with, which is $1,200 a year.

Because your assets are limited, you want to get the most bang for your buck. So you decide to put the whole $1,200 into an RRSP, which shelters the income while generating a tax refund for you. Let's say your marginal tax rate is 40 percent, so the tax saving in the first year is worth $480.

You decide that you will do everything possible to increase your savings by at least 10 percent a year. You also decide that, since your resources are limited, you are going to be more aggressive with your investments and aim for an annual return within the RRSP of 10 percent. You choose a time horizon of 25 years. Let's see what happens.

Within the RRSP, the 10 percent projected return over 25 years produces a factor of 270.87 according to the Ongoing Investments 1 table – remember, this assumes you increase your contribution by 10 percent each year. By multiplying your first year contribution of $1,200 by that factor, we get a total RRSP value of $325,044 at the end of that time. But that's not the end of the story. There's the matter of that $480 refund, which we will also project to grow by 10 percent annually. You can spend that if you wish, but since you are short of money for your program, why not plan to reinvest it instead? Again, we'll assume you opt for a more aggressive non-registered portfolio that will generate mainly capital gains. We have to allow for taxes in this case, however, so instead of a 10 percent annual return, we'll use an 8 percent projection. Over 25 years, this gives us a factor of 215.26 for your non-registered account. Multiply that by $480 and we get a total of $103,325.

Add the registered and non-registered portfolios together and the total value is $428,369. That's not bad, considering that you had nothing at the outset and began by putting aside only $100 a month. But it's not the $1 million you were hoping for when you picked up this book.

I have two comments on that. First, remember this is only the liquid portion of your assets. You may have other possessions, such as a home, that will add significantly to your net worth. Second, by extending your time horizon and/or scrimping a little more at the outset, you can bring your liquid assets up to the $1 million level, or close to it.

For example, just by adding five years to your time horizon and leaving all other assumptions the same, you'll increase the total value of your registered and non-registered assets to $819,638. If you also add an additional $25 a month to your first-year savings, the total after 30 years rises to $1,024,548. You're there!

Scenario #2: You've Already Made a Start

In this scenario, we assume that you have already begun the savings/investment process through the use of an RRSP. At this point you (and your spouse if you want to make this a joint calculation) have $25,000 in a registered plan. You also have a little more money to put aside, say $3,600 a year ($300 a month), and you can increase that by 10 percent a year. Your marginal tax rate is 45 percent. You're a little more conservative in your approach, so you use an 8 percent projected annual return inside the RRSP. Outside the plan, allowing for a mix of interest, dividends, and capital gains, you project an after-tax return of 5 percent. Your time horizon is 20 years.

Using these assumptions, we find that the money already in the RRSP will be worth $116,500 at the end of 20 years. Your new RRSP contributions will grow to $401,724. Your non-registered portfolio, built from your RRSP-generated tax refunds, will be worth $138,607. The total works out to $656,831. Here again, the dollars are impressive but they come up short of $1 million if your goal is to accumulate that full amount in liquid assets.

In this case, simply extending the time horizon by five years will do the job. After 25 years, the total value of your registered and non-registered portfolios under this scenario will rise to $1,199,586.

But suppose you don't want to wait that extra five years. Another option is to be more aggressive with your investments while increasing your first year contributions to $4,800 ($400 a month). Instead of being satisfied with an 8 percent return, aim for 10 percent annually inside the RRSP and 6 percent a year after-tax in the non-registered plan. Using those assumptions and a 20-year time frame, we get a total portfolio value of $927,770 – not quite $1 million, but within hailing distance.

Scenario #3: You Have No Savings But a Good Income

In this case, we'll assume you have no liquid assets but you have a good income and you can afford to allocate a high percentage of that money towards your plan. However, your time horizon is relatively short – perhaps only 15 years. This type of situation might be typical of baby boomers in their late 40s or early 50s who have lived well, paid off the mortgage, and sent the kids to college. Now that the responsibilities have been dealt with, they want to accumulate a large nest egg in a hurry.

The starting point is the RRSP contribution. We will assume an annual income of $75,000 or more, which means the person can make the maximum allowable RRSP contribution of $13,500 a year. However, there is no room to increase that by 10 percent annually because of government-imposed limits. So we use the Ongoing Investments 2 table to project the future value of a $13,500 contribution to an RRSP over 15 years. Since the time horizon is limited, we'll choose a more aggressive investment approach and aim for a 10 percent average annual return. The result is an RRSP portfolio value at the end of 15 years of $471,825 ($13,500 × 34.95).

The RRSP contribution will generate a very good tax refund. Using a 45 percent marginal rate, this will be worth $6,075 annually. We will assume this is invested in a non-registered portfolio, with an after-tax return of 6 percent annually. After 15 years, this will add $149,870 to the pot.

So far, however, we have not made any allowance for an increase in the annual savings rate. But with time so short, our baby boomer must step up the pace. So he or she begins by adding another $5,000 to the non-registered portfolio in the first year and increases that by 10 percent annually. Now we refer to the Ongoing Investments 1 table to see what that produces after 15 years, again using a 6 percent after-tax return. The amount is $235,950.

So at the end of the 15 years, our boomer would end up with an RRSP worth $471,825 plus a non-registered portfolio valued at $385,820, for a total of $857,645. Not bad from a standing start, considering the age of the person. With the equity in the home, which we already said was fully paid for, the net worth in this case will be well in excess of our $1 million target.

If this baby boomer wants to aim for $1 million in liquid assets in 15 years, using these base assumptions, he or she would have to add about $8,000 to the non-registered portfolio in the first year, instead of $5,000, and escalate 10 percent annually from there.

As you can see, there are many ways to juggle the numbers, including others we haven't explored here, such as increasing the annual savings by more than 10 percent. Also, in two-income families it will make a big difference whether each of you is aiming to become a millionaire in your own right or you will be content with a jointly generated million – which means you'll be able to get there much faster.

The point is that you cannot make a meaningful plan unless you do some projections first. This gives you some useful targets for tracking purposes and allows you to make adjustments as needed, within the realm of feasibility.

RRSPs or Capital Gains?

While we're on the subject of portfolio projections, there is a growing debate about the wisdom of contributing to RRSPs now that the capital gains inclusion rate has been dropped to 50 percent. The argument has been made that, because withdrawals from an RRSP are fully taxed no matter what their original source, people would be better off to avoid registered plans and invest their after-tax dollars in stocks and equity mutual funds that will generate mainly capital gains. Since this book is about the most effective ways to accumulate $1 million as quickly as possible, we need to address this question.

Let's use a fictional character to examine each option. Jennifer Green works in a middle-management position and has an annual income of $50,000. Her marginal tax rate is 35 percent and she is considering an annual RRSP contribution of $5,000, which is 10 percent of her gross income. She is 35 years old, and is using a time horizon of

25 years. She plans to invest the money aggressively, with a targeted annual return of 10 percent. Let's see what happens.

Making RRSP Contributions and Spending the Refund

Jennifer puts $5,000 into the RRSP every year for the next 25 years. At the end of that time, the RRSP will be worth $540,900. If we discount this by 35 percent for the impact of taxes on subsequent withdrawals (assuming the money comes out gradually and not all at once), we arrive at an after-tax value of $351,585 for Jennifer's RRSP.

Investing in Equities

Instead of putting the $5,000 in an RRSP, Jennifer invests in equity mutual funds or stocks outside a registered plan. Using the same 10 percent average annual rate of return, her non-registered portfolio will grow to the same value as the RRSP after 25 years: $540,900. However, the tax rate is much lower. She pays only on the profits she's made ($415,900), and then at the capital gains rate. Total tax bill, again assuming a 35 percent marginal rate, is $72,783. The after-tax value of the portfolio is therefore $468,117. It's a clear victory for the capital gains strategy.

But wait! What about the tax refund that's generated by the RRSP contribution? We haven't taken that into account. So let's look at a third scenario.

Making the RRSP Contribution and Investing the Refund

If Jennifer invests $5,000 in an RRSP, it will generate a tax refund of $1,750 (at a 35 percent marginal rate). She can spend that money, of course. But the better option is to use it for her non-registered capital gains account (assuming she has maximized her RRSP contribution). This means she would be putting $5,000 a year into a registered plan, plus an additional $1,750 a year into a non-registered portfolio, for a total annual investment of $6,750. In this case, she can put $1,750 a year into a stock portfolio, which will grow to $172,107 in value after 25 years. The capital gain will draw tax of $22,462, leaving a net after-tax value of $149,645. Added to the after-tax value of the RRSP portfolio, the total

comes to $501,230. This is about $33,000 better than skipping the RRSP investment –
but the key is that she must invest the refund.

The shorter the time frame until the RRSP will mature, the less the advantage in using
a registered plan. If we had used only a five-year time horizon in the above examples, the
numbers would have worked out like this:

> After-tax value of $5,000 a year RRSP contribution: $19,841.
> After-tax value of $5,000 invested for capital gains: $29,558.
> After-tax value of $5,000 RRSP contribution with refund invested: $30,863.

The RRSP contribution plus refund investment still works out best, but the margin
of difference is small. There's one other important consideration. We've assumed a
10 percent average annual return in both situations. However, the investments made in
an RRSP are likely to be more conservative in nature, so the return may be somewhat
lower. Conversely, the non-registered capital gains portfolio could suffer a loss, especially
if we're looking at a short time horizon. The bottom line: Although variables may come
into play, all things being equal, the RRSP-plus-invested-refund approach works out best,
and the longer the time frame the greater the differential.

Registered and Non-Registered Portfolios

The recent tax cuts we've enjoyed have had the side effect of reducing the government's
contribution to our retirement savings programs. Every time you make a contribution
to a retirement plan that is "registered" with the Canada Customs and Revenue Agency
(essentially RRSPs and pension plans), you're entitled to an offsetting tax deduction.
The value of this deduction is directly tied to your marginal tax rate. So if you're a high-
bracket taxpayer with a marginal rate of, say, 48 percent, you receive $480 worth of tax
relief for every $1,000 you contribute. If your marginal rate is 30 percent, you get only
$300 worth of tax relief for that same $1,000. Critics of the system have long
complained that this is unfair because it favours high-income earnings and have urged
the government to switch to a tax credit system under which everyone would benefit

equally. To date, however, Ottawa has shown no sign of interest in this idea. So we continue to operate under the long-established rules.

This means that as tax rates drop, the value of an RRSP or pension plan deduction does too. A few years ago, a top-bracket taxpayer might have been looking at a marginal rate of 53 percent, which translated into a tax saving of $530 per $1,000 contribution. With the marginal rate down to 48 percent, $50 worth of that saving is gone. The other side of the coin, of course, is that money withdrawn from registered plans after retirement will be taxed at a lower rate as well (assuming taxes don't rise again in the interim). The people in the best position are those who made their contributions when taxes were at their peak and are only now starting to draw down income.

However, as we saw from the RRSP-versus-capital-gains comparison, registered plans remain the most effective way to build your personal net worth, even with a reduced government subsidy. So your first priority as you construct your $1 million savings/investment plan should be to maximize your RRSP/pension contributions. They deliver the best bang for your buck.

Over time, however, you will probably reach a point when your retirement plan contributions are maximized. At that stage, you will want to look at channelling new savings into a non-registered investment portfolio. This means you'll be running two portfolios side by side: one that is tax sheltered and one that isn't. That requires some careful planning.

I stress this point because I have seen even professional financial planners mess up here. The most blatant case was brought to my attention by a woman, let's call her Mary, who had received a substantial inheritance on the death of her husband. Part of the money was in an RRSP that was transferred into her name and part came in the form of insurance proceeds, which she decided to invest. Not being experienced in money management, Mary hired the services of a well-recommended local professional firm and gave it discretionary control over the placement of the assets. The firm set up two accounts for her, one for the RRSP and the other to invest the insurance money, and she received regular statements. The firm also prepared her tax returns and sent them along for her review and signature. Never having prepared a return herself and not knowing anything about the process, she glanced through it quickly, signed where indicated, and sent it off.

The investments performed reasonably well and Mary was comfortable with the service. In fact, she had absolutely no reason to question anything the company was doing. It was pure coincidence that I happened to have lunch with her one day, just after she had come from a morning meeting with the planner. She had the latest statements in her purse and knew me well enough to ask if I would take a quick glance at them – just in case I had any suggestions that might improve her returns a bit. I don't like second-guessing reputable money managers but I had known Mary and her husband for some years. I could hardly refuse. So, over coffee, I took the statements and glanced over them. Then I looked at them more carefully. I couldn't believe what I was seeing. The planner had indeed set up registered and non-registered portfolios for my friend – and then proceeded to put exactly the same securities in both. The tax-sheltered RRSP and the non-sheltered portfolio were virtual replicas of one another – the only real difference was in the amount contained in each. I was dumbfounded. Clearly, what the planner had done was taken an off-the-shelf investment package that he, or his firm, had prepared for clients who met certain criteria (age, risk tolerance, income needs, etc.) and applied it to both of Mary's portfolios. What was wrong with that? Plenty! By failing to differentiate between the tax-sheltered and non-tax-sheltered securities, I later calculated that the planner was costing my friend more than $2,000 a year in unnecessary taxes!

When you have both a registered and non-registered portfolio, one of the first rules is to maximize the available tax efficiencies. This means placing the most highly taxed securities in the RRSP and the most tax-advantaged securities in the non-registered portfolio. This planner had failed to do that. The non-registered plan held a large quantity of bonds, the interest on which is taxed at the top marginal rate. The RRSP held a chunk of stocks and equity mutual funds, which generate tax-advantaged dividends and capital gains. A little rearranging of exactly the same securities would have put a couple of thousand dollars a year more into Mary's purse – which would have gone a long way towards paying the planner's fee.

Needless to say, Mary quickly moved her business elsewhere. The lesson she learned is the one I want to emphasize now: Make sure that your money is invested in the most tax-efficient way possible, starting with the registered/non-registered distribution. Here are some tips:

Tip #1: Put Interest-Bearing Securities into Your Registered Plan

Since interest is taxed as if it were ordinary income, your goal should be to tax shelter as much of it as possible. This means GICs, Canada Savings and Premium Bonds, regular bonds, bond and mortgage mutual funds, term deposits, short-term notes, Treasury bills, and money market funds should all go into the RRSP where possible.

Tip #2: Hold Tax-Advantaged Securities in Your Non-Registered Portfolio

There are many types of securities that come with a built-in tax advantage. We've already discussed stocks and equity mutual funds, which generate dividends (eligible for the dividend tax credit as long as the company is Canadian) and capital gains. There are others. Royalty income trusts, a relatively new asset class, give you a stake in some type of corporate enterprise that generates income. In some cases, such as energy trusts, part or all of the income is received on what is called a *tax-deferred* basis. That means you pay no tax on the income in the year it is received. However, there is a formula under which your capital gain is increased when you sell by the amount of tax-deferred income you earned. Of course, that may not happen for some years and the reduced capital gains rate makes that penalty much less onerous.

Another example of a tax-advantaged security is the real estate investment trust, or REIT. These plans invest in commercial and industrial properties, which generate rental income. Part of the rental income is tax sheltered by depreciation so that it is received on a tax-deferred basis when distributed to unitholders.

You can also find mutual funds that invest in royalty trusts and REITs, so some of their distributions are tax-deferred. So there are a number of ways to reduce the tax bite on a non-registered portfolio, if it is managed properly.

Tip #3: Switch Assets Around

Contrary to a widely held belief, the assets inside an RRSP are not frozen. They can be moved out of the plan without any tax penalty, as long as they are replaced by something of equal value. The process is called *switching*.

For example, if you have a lot of stocks in your RRSP and would like to move them into a non-registered portfolio, you can do so. You simply arrange to transfer cash or an equivalent value in interest-bearing securities, like bonds, into the RRSP in their place. There are forms to fill out, of course, but it is perfectly legal. Just one word of warning: If the assets you transfer into the RRSP have a capital gain or accrued interest at the time of the switch, you are deemed to have sold them and must declare the gain or interest on that year's tax return.

Stocks in an RRSP?

This leads directly into a long-running debate that will affect your planning process: Should you hold stocks or equity mutual funds in an RRSP or pension plan? The answer is highly equivocal: It depends.

What it depends on is whether the registered plan is your only investment portfolio and is likely to remain so for some time to come. Many people, especially if they do not have an employer pension plan, have trouble simply reaching the maximum contribution limit they are allowed for their RRSPs. Obviously, if you can't max out your RRSP, there shouldn't be any money available for a non-registered investment portfolio. We've already seen that the RRSP is the more effective way to go, even if the non-registered portfolio is invested so as to produce 100 percent capital gains.

In that situation, if you did not have any stocks or equity mutual funds in your RRSP, you would not have any at all. This is not good planning. Whatever the stock market may be doing at this moment, over the long haul it has consistently proven to be the most effective way to build personal wealth. If you eliminate equities from your RRSP because you lose the tax advantages they offer by buying them inside the plan (which is true), then you are cutting yourself off from the most powerful investment option available to you. That makes little sense — and the younger you are, the less sense it makes.

So my position in this ongoing debate is yes, by all means include stocks and/or equity funds in your retirement savings plan. If you reach the point later when you can open a non-registered portfolio as well, you can always switch them out of the RRSP at that time. There's an actual tax advantage in doing it that way, because the capital gains accumulated while the stocks were in the RRSP won't be taxed when they come out of the plan (only the gains that accrue after the switch will be taxable). This is just about the only way I know of to generate an absolutely tax-free capital gain, aside from your principal residence, a family farm, or a small business.

The Principles of Asset Allocation

Every investment plan needs a foundation. Here is where we put it into place. Asset allocation is the process you use to decide how your securities are going to be divided. Only when that is clearly fixed in your mind should you start choosing the actual securities that will make up the portfolio.

This seems so basic that many people overlook it. In fact, asset allocation is generally considered by financial professionals to be the most important single decision you can make in terms of structuring an investment portfolio. Some studies have suggested that, by itself, asset allocation can account for up to 90 percent of a portfolio's return. Frankly, that seems high to me – fill a portfolio with junk and the allocation won't matter much. But assuming you make some intelligent investment decisions, asset allocation will play a critical role in how it all plays out. That's why I'm devoting quite a bit of space to the subject at this point.

There are essentially four stages in the asset allocation process: asset class selection, geographic distribution, style diversification, and risk management. Let's consider each separately.

Asset Class Selection

This is the most basic part of the process. Even if you never move on to the other three stages, you should at least implement an asset class selection before you begin to buy securities.

There are three basic types of assets in every investment portfolio. We have already looked at them earlier in the book, so we will only briefly review them now.

- *Cash.* This consists of currency and highly liquid cash-equivalent securities such as Treasury bills, money market funds, and Canada Savings Bonds. Any asset that can quickly be converted to cash for its full face value qualifies.

- *Fixed income.* These securities pay a rate of return that is either fixed or based on a specific formula. They have a maturity date. If they are sold or cashed in before that date, the result may be a loss or a penalty to the investor. Bonds, mortgages, preferred shares, and GICs fall into this asset class.

- *Growth.* Assets in the growth category add value mainly through capital gains. Stocks and equity mutual funds are the most common examples.

Some assets are hybrids — royalty income trusts, for example, combine some of the features of both the fixed-income and the growth categories. However, because their income distributions are not guaranteed and not predictable, they would usually tend to be slotted in with growth assets.

Now that you know the three asset classes, all you have to do is decide how much of each you want to hold in your portfolio. Easy? Not really. There are several factors to consider, including your age, your time horizon, your tax situation (if it is a non-registered portfolio), the economic climate, and your risk tolerance.

Generally, the higher the percentage of cash and fixed-income securities in your portfolio, the less risky it will be. However, the trade-off is that your profit potential will be reduced as well. The more growth securities you have, the greater the chance that you will achieve above-average returns. But you will also expose yourself to greater losses during periods when the stock market is in decline.

This is what makes the decision difficult. You have to weigh these considerations and decide where you want to place your portfolio on the scale. If you choose to be ultra-conservative, you need to reconcile yourself to the fact that it will probably take quite a bit longer to achieve that first $1 million. If you decide in favour of more growth, you must be ready to accept the ups and downs of a volatile stock market.

I recommend that you start from the position that you will include all three asset classes in your portfolio. I have heard ultra-aggressive investors say, "To heck with that.

Stocks are where the action is and I'm going to put all my money there." Interestingly, I have never heard anyone use that argument during a severe market slump – only when a bull market is in full flight, as it was in the late 1990s. When stocks drop dramatically, as Nasdaq did in 2000, the brave suddenly turn timid.

The real danger in choosing an all-growth portfolio at the outset is psychological. Suppose you had made such a decision at the beginning of 2000 and loaded up with high-flying technology funds? By year-end, the value of your assets might have been down by 30 percent, or even more. Not only would it take a long time to recover from such a heavy loss, but you may well have been left with mental scars that will never heal. I once had a friend who, having lost heavily in the stock market collapse of the 1970s, never invested again in equities for the rest of his life. That's not a healthy, or a wise, approach.

So use all the asset classes. No zeros for any of the three. Now it's a matter of distribution.

Cash is normally allocated the smallest percentage in an investment portfolio because of the low return it generates. So why hold any at all? For two reasons. First, cash is the safest asset you can possess in difficult times. Second, a cash reserve allows you to take advantage of opportunities in the stock and bond markets that may appear. If you don't have any cash, you'll be forced to sell something else, which you may not want to do at that moment.

The minimum cash holding in your portfolio should be 5 percent. The maximum should be 25 percent, and that would only be reached under very unusual circumstances – for example, during a period when short-term interest rates are high and the stock and bond markets are slumping. These conditions do occur from time to time, the early 1990s being the most recent.

The percentage of fixed-income assets will be governed by two main considerations: your risk tolerance level and the outlook for interest rates. Under normal conditions, fixed-income securities carry much less risk than growth securities. So a portfolio that is weighted towards bonds and GICs will be less volatile than one that holds only a small percentage of such assets. As we have previously seen, certain types of fixed-income securities, particularly bonds, have the potential to generate above-average returns during periods when interest rates are falling, so this can be another factor in your allocation decision.

The range of fixed-income securities in a portfolio can vary from as low as 10 percent to as high as 50 percent, depending on the circumstances. Generally, an allocation in the 25 percent range is adequate.

Growth securities should given the lion's share of your allocation. The minimum allocation should be 30 percent, and you would be at that level only during full-blown bear markets or if you are approaching retirement. The maximum growth percentage is 70 percent.

To sum up, here are the recommended asset category ranges:

Cash	5 – 25%
Fixed income	10 – 50%
Growth	30 – 70%

Geographic Distribution

Once you have decided on your initial asset distribution (which may well change over time), the next phase involves looking at the world and determining your geographic asset mix. There are two important factors to keep in mind at this stage: the overall risk/reward balance of your investment portfolio and the outlook for the Canadian dollar.

You may have a natural tendency to favour Canadian securities because they are familiar and because of the foreign content limits imposed on registered plans. However, it is very easy to overdo this, to your detriment.

Many studies have been conducted into what is known as the *efficient frontier*. This is a portfolio analysis technique that seeks to identify the point at which the blend of domestic and foreign content attains maximum reward potential consistent with minimal risk. Although the numbers vary, the results almost always suggest that non-Canadian securities should comprise between 40 and 60 percent of your total mix. If that seems high, remember that Canada represents only about 2 percent of the world's equity markets. We are a bit player on the international stage. We have very few genuine multinational companies (Alcan, Nortel Networks, and Bombardier are among this small, elite group) and most of what we consider to be corporate giants, like the big banks, are small potatoes when measured against foreign competitors in the same field. As well, there are entire industries that are not represented in the Canadian stock market. We have no indigenous auto manufacturer, no retailer of Wal-Mart or Home Depot stature, no entertainment mega-company now that Seagram is gone, no software giant like Microsoft, no world-class pharmaceutical company, and on and on. If you want to participate in the growth of any of these businesses, you have no choice but to look beyond our borders.

You must also give some thought to the future course of the Canadian dollar. This does not mean you should involve yourself in currency speculation – that's a high-stakes poker game that can result in huge losses. But you need to think about whether your investment portfolio should have some built-in protection against the possibility of a continued long-term decline in the value of the loonie.

Let's be realistic about this. The Canadian dollar is a weak currency and has been so for many years. Moreover, there is no indication that anyone in authority in Ottawa is deeply concerned about the problem or willing to do anything about it.

How weak has it been? Take a look at the following numbers, which were obtained from the Bank of Canada Web site (**www.bankofcanada.ca**). They show the value of a U.S. dollar in Canadian dollar terms on November 30 of each year from 1990 to 2000.

CANADIAN DOLLARS NEEDED TO BUY ONE U.S. DOLLAR

YEAR (NOV. 30)	U.S.$ VALUE IN CAN. CURRENCY
1990	$1.1634
1991	1.1307
1992	1.2687
1993	1.3168
1994	1.3656
1995	1.3529

YEAR (NOV. 30)	U.S.$ VALUE IN CAN. CURRENCY
1996	1.3666
1997	1.4133
1998	1.5404
1999	1.4674
2000	1.5429

Source: Bank of Canada (www.bankofcanada.ca).

As you can see, between November 1990 and November 2000, the Canadian dollar was effectively devalued by almost a third against the U.S. greenback. It was a stealthy devaluation, engineered over a lengthy period of time. As a result, public outcry was kept to a minimum until recently. The decline was good news for Canadian exporters, who were able to sell their products at a much more competitive price in international markets – most particularly in the U.S., our largest trading partner by far. But the devaluation was bad news for consumers, who pay higher prices for imported goods, and bad news for travellers, for investors, and for retirees who hope to spend some of their winters in the Sunbelt.

There is no indication that the devaluation process is over; quite the contrary. Even after the Government of Canada cleaned up its financial house by eliminating deficits and running big surpluses, even with the economy in overdrive in the late 1990s and 2000, even with taxes falling, even with energy prices at sky-high levels, the loonie continued to tumble. Liberal Prime Minister Jean Chrétien, who won a third-term majority mandate in November 2000, went on the record as being totally unconcerned about the loonie's decline. His laissez-faire attitude appears to suggest that Ottawa's do-nothing-if-there-isn't-a-crisis stance will continue for the foreseeable future.

The possibility of further devaluation suggests that wise investors should hedge their currency bets in structuring their portfolios. That, of course, speaks directly to the issue of geographic distribution.

There are five dimensions to this question:

- *Canada.* Obviously, some of your securities, perhaps a majority of them, should be in your home country and your home currency.

- *United States.* The number one economic power in the world should be strongly represented in all portfolios.

- *Europe.* Next to the U.S., Europe is the most potent economic unit in the early years of the 21st century, and should be included in your mix.

- *Pacific Rim.* Asia still hasn't fully recovered from its economic crisis of the late 1990s and Japan's continued economic lethargy is frustrating everyone. There is potential for good profits down the road, but the risks are higher in this part of the world.

- *Emerging markets.* The 1990s saw an awakening of investor interest in what used to be known as Third World countries. The theory was that many of these nations were on the brink of explosive growth that would far exceed anything in the developed world. Thus far, however, the promise has been largely unfulfilled from an investor perspective and the risks are very high.

Canadian and Foreign Content Distribution

Step one is to decide what percentage of your assets you will hold in Canada and how much will go to the rest of the world. That determination will depend on a number of factors, but I recommend that you hold at least 40 percent of your assets in Canadian securities, to a maximum of 70 percent. That means your foreign holdings will range from 30 to 60 percent of the total. Don't be concerned about the foreign content limit in registered plans when deciding on the amount of your foreign content; there are many ways to bypass those restrictions.

BASIC GEOGRAPHIC DISTRIBUTION

Canada	40 – 70%
Foreign	30 – 60%

Now it's a matter of deciding how to distribute those foreign assets. Let's consider the options.

United States

The lion's share of your foreign content should be placed here. There are two reasons for this: the massive weight of the U.S. economy and currency hedging considerations. Most of us don't know or care how the loonie performs against the Euro or the yen; we do know and care deeply about what happens vis-à-vis the U.S. dollar.

You can invest in the U.S. in many ways. Stocks and mutual funds are the best known, but you can also buy a range of debt securities (bonds, GICs, etc.) denominated in U.S. dollars, or even just open a U.S. dollar account at your local bank. Your selection of U.S. securities should be guided by your basic asset distribution.

I recommend that at least 50 percent of your foreign assets be placed in the U.S., to a maximum of 70 percent. A point midway between those two numbers is the ideal figure.

Europe

The long-term economic prospects for a united Europe are bright. There have been bumps on the road to economic and monetary union and there will continue to be, but there is no doubt that European businesses as a whole are much stronger today than they were a decade ago. There are now many world-class companies based in Europe that should be represented in your portfolio.

The easiest way to invest in Europe is through mutual funds that specialize in that part of the world. If you prefer, you can choose international funds, which invest in Europe and the Far East but exclude North America.

European holdings should represent between 20 and 30 percent of your total foreign content.

Pacific Rim

Because of the volatility inherent in this part of the world, committing a significant portion of a portfolio to the region is not recommended. Nonetheless, the growth potential cannot be discounted, especially over the long term, so you should have some Pacific Rim representation. This can be done through one or two dedicated Far East funds or by selecting an international fund and letting the manager make the geographic distribution call. The recommended range for this area is 5 to 15 percent.

Emerging Markets

The only effective way to invest in emerging markets is through mutual funds. However, the dedicated emerging markets funds have been so volatile that you may prefer to ignore this area entirely or allow it to be covered through a broader international fund. The recommended range is from zero to 5 percent.

Here is a summary of our overall recommendations for geographic distribution.

OVERALL GEOGRAPHIC DISTRIBUTION

REGION	RANGE	IDEAL
Canada	40 – 70%	50%
U.S.	15 – 42%	30%
Europe	6 – 18%	12.5%
Pacific Rim	1.5 – 9%	5%
Emerging markets	0 – 3%	2.5%

Style Diversification

Even if you stopped your asset allocation process at this point, you would be light-years ahead of most investors, including many experienced ones. But if you want to fine-tune your plan even more, the next step in the process is to consider style diversification.

We've already discussed the different types of management styles. Now it's a matter of making sure they are properly represented in your portfolio. You can apply whatever degree of sophistication you like to this process, but let's keep it very simple for now. All you want to do at this stage is to ensure that two basic management styles are well represented in the equity section of your portfolio: value and growth.

You can do this through a process of individual stock selection; however, that will require a fair amount of analysis on your part, or on the part of your financial advisor. Or you can achieve style diversification by selecting equity mutual funds that adopt each approach.

To reduce the problem to its most basic, let's assume that the entire Canadian equity portion of your portfolio is to be held in just two mutual funds. To implement style diversification in this situation, you want to be sure that one fund is managed according to firm value principles, while the other is run on a growth-oriented basis.

In the case of your value fund, you want to know that the manager bases his or her stock selection on certain fundamental and widely accepted value criteria. One of the best summaries I have seen of these was written by Irwin Michael, the founder and president of the ABC Funds and one of Canada's most respected deep value money managers. They are reprinted here with his permission.

IRWIN MICHAEL'S TEN COMMANDMENTS OF VALUE INVESTING

1. *Low Price to Earnings Multiples.* We search out stocks trading at under 10 times price to earnings multiples, which reduces the risk of overpaying for a security.
2. *Low Cash Flow Multiples.* We look for companies trading at under five times price to cash flow. This also reduces the risk of overpaying and uncovers many "dirt cheap" equities.
3. *Discount to Book/Net Asset Value.* We like to buy stocks trading at a discount to book/net asset value. In many cases, this not only uncovers significantly undervalued stocks but also prime takeover candidates.
4. *Hidden Assets.* Some examples of hidden assets that can be uncovered after a thorough analysis are tax-loss carry forwards, over-funded pension funds, real estate, potential spin-offs, IPOs, and favourable litigation.
5. *Management.* Two types of management could be key in the search for a turnaround candidate: a) Solid, proactive management and b) Poor management, which leaves the company ripe for a proactive acquisition or merger.
6. *Products/Services in Tune with the Times.* This includes expandable, growing markets with good margins. We tend to avoid companies with outdated, shrinking products.
7. *Value Catalyst.* In order to push up the value of a stock, we look for a significant value creator. Some examples of possible value creators are fresh management with new directions, an important sale or purchase of a meaningful asset, an unsolicited takeover bid, or disgruntled and impatient proactive shareholders who may put pressure on management to make changes or sell.
8. *Discounted Valuations Compared to its Peers.* Comparative valuation measures such as price to earnings and cash flow could indicate a take-over by relatively expensive Canadian or foreign competitors looking to expand market presence.

9. *Contrary Opinion and Under-Followed by Investment Analysts.* With little investor exposure, undervalued stocks are "pregnant with possibilities," providing very little buying competition when attempting to accumulate the security. Generally an undervalued and under-followed security will offer terrific capital gains opportunities.

10. *Discipline.* Stay on track and adhere to strict value discipline of low p/es [price/earnings ratios], strong cash flows, and price targets. Do not get sucked into buying the flavour of the day! Combine patience and persistence to attain superior performance. Patience! Patience! Patience!

In short, a value manager looks for stocks in sound businesses that are selling for bargain-basement prices. There are many value-oriented funds available in Canada, with varying nuances. Irwin Michael's ABC Funds fall into what is known as the "deep value" category, along with those of other managers such as Peter Cundill, whose funds are distributed through Mackenzie Financial. The value scale runs all the way to what is known as a GARP style (growth at a reasonable price), which puts a higher degree of emphasis on the growth prospects of a company than a deep value manager like Michael or Cundill would consider appropriate.

Growth managers, by contrast, are less concerned about a company's p/e ratio and balance sheet and more interested in its prospects for expanding the business at a rate faster than that of the economy in general and its competitors in particular. These managers prospered during the late 1990s, when technology stocks were riding high and many growth funds turned in huge gains while value funds languished. But when high-tech stocks tumbled in 2000, growth funds as a group took above-average losses while the more conservatively managed value funds fared much better.

If you were an investment genius and able to predict which style would be in the ascendancy at any given time, you could choose just one fund for our fictional portfolio and switch out of it to one of the other types when conditions so warranted. However, if you don't know intuitively that's extremely difficult, let me be explicit: The chances are that if you try such a strategy, you'll be wrong most of the time. That's why it's better to introduce style diversification into your plan by choosing one top-flight fund of each type.

Many fund companies tell you in their written material or on their Web sites what style each manager uses. You can also find this information in the current edition of *Gordon Pape's Buyer's Guide to Mutual Funds*.

Risk Management

The final piece in our asset allocation puzzle is risk management. This involves a series of decisions that will determine the overall risk/return profile of your portfolio. Many purists will argue that risk management is not a function of asset allocation at all, but something quite different. However, I include it here because I believe it is a basic part of the foundation we are building in this section.

All securities have their own risk/return profile, even those within the same asset class. For example, a U.S. dollar money market fund has to be considered as being higher risk than a Canadian dollar money market fund because it introduces an additional variable: currency fluctuation. Of course, that also means that the reward potential of the U.S. dollar fund is higher since the assets in it will be worth more if the loonie declines.

Risk management involves allocating your assets in accordance with your safety-versus-profits priorities. You already went part way down this path when you decided on your initial asset class selection. Now you're fine-tuning it.

It is very difficult to make generalizations about the risk/return profile of broad asset categories, because there will be many shadings and nuances within each – even some total exceptions to the rule. But this table will give you a general idea. The higher the number of stars in each column (out of five), the higher the asset ranks on the scale. So an asset that receives ***** for safety and * for return is very safe but offers low profit potential.

RISK/RETURN SCALE

ASSET TYPE	SAFETY	REWARD
Canada Savings/Premium Bonds	*****	*
Canadian money market funds, T-bills	*****	*
U.S. $ money market funds	****	**
GICs	*****	**
Mortgage funds	****	*
Mortgage-backed securities	*****	*
Short-term bonds, short-term bond funds	****	*
Mid-term bonds, regular bond funds	***	**
Long-term bonds, long-term bond funds	**	***
Foreign bonds, foreign bond funds	**	**
Large-cap Canadian stocks, large-cap equity funds	***	***
Small-cap Canadian stocks, small-cap equity funds	**	***
Diversified Canadian equity funds	***	***
Large-cap U.S. stocks	***	****
Small-cap U.S. stocks, small-cap equity funds	**	*****
Diversified U.S. equity funds	***	****
International equity funds	***	***
Sector equity funds	*	*****
Index funds	***	***
Balanced funds	***	***
Royalty income trusts	**	***

Again, I must emphasize that there will be wide variations within categories. For example, a sector equity fund that focuses on the financial services industry will normally be less risky but offer lower profit potential than one that specializes in high-tech. Similarly, a conservatively managed value equity fund will offer less prospect for reward, but the safety factor will be much higher than for an aggressively managed growth fund. So use this table for purposes of general guidelines only.

To apply this to the asset allocation plan you have already worked out, simply take each separate element and use a risk management overlay. For example, suppose that the process so far has resulted in a portfolio foundation that looks like this:

SAMPLE PORTFOLIO (BASIC)

ASSET CLASS	ALLOCATION	GEOGRAPHIC DISTRIBUTION	STYLE
Cash	10%	50% Can., 50% U.S.	N/A
Fixed income	30%	60% Can., 40% U.S.	N/A
Growth	60%	50% Can., 30% U.S., 20% Int.	50% Value, 50% Growth

You can now proceed to fine-tune the various asset classes on the basis of the risk/return profile you want to achieve. Let's say your goal is for a portfolio with decent profit potential, but with limited risk. Here's where you might end up:

SAMPLE PORTFOLIO (DETAILED)

TYPE OF SECURITY	ALLOCATION
Canadian money market funds	5%
U.S.$ money market funds	5%
Mid-term bonds	13%
Long-term bonds	5%
Foreign bond funds (U.S.)	12%
Diversified Canadian equity funds (value)	15%
Diversified Canadian equity funds (growth)	15%
Diversified U.S. equity funds (value)	9%
Diversified U.S. equity funds (growth)	4%
Small-cap U.S. equity funds (growth)	5%
Diversified international equity funds (value)	6%
Diversified international equity funds (growth)	6%

For a more aggressive portfolio, you could add some sector funds, change the proportion of growth to value funds, add more long-term bonds, add some Canadian small-cap stocks or funds, and so on.

That's it. Now your foundation is in place and you can begin the process of choosing the specific securities you want to hold in your plan.

A Word about Market Timing

The whole asset allocation process leads to the construction of a diversified investment portfolio. All the asset classes are represented and the parameters are carefully worked out. "But what's the point of the whole exercise," you may ask, "if I'm going to be told at some point to 'Sell everything'?" And, indeed, some stock market gurus do issue warnings of exactly that kind in extreme conditions.

I'm not among them and never have been, for one simple reason: No one can predict consistently and with certainty what the markets are going to do. There are thousands of people out there making informed guesses, some of whom are right more often than others. But I have yet to come across anyone who is right all the time. Every market "expert" trumpets his or her good calls. We hear nothing about the bad ones after the fact.

You don't have to go back any further than 1999 to find a prime example of the problem. As New Year's Eve drew closer, attention was increasingly focused on the Y2K problem. This was a computer glitch that was built into systems years ago, in which years were expressed as two digits rather than four. At midnight on New Year's Eve, the date would roll over from 99 to 00 – presumably leaving the computer completely confused and, perhaps, thinking 1900 was meant, shutting down everything. No one knew how serious Y2K would be, but some of the predictions were dire. Whole books were written on the subject, including some that urged investors to sell all their stocks and hold everything in cash in anticipation of a major worldwide computer meltdown. Some people apparently actually did just that.

Of course, as we all know, Y2K turned out to be one of the great non-events of this generation. Nothing happened. The year 2000 arrived, the computers kept humming, and the world went about its business. The only disaster was in the portfolios of those who had sold all their stocks during the previous summer. They missed out entirely on one of the strongest market rallies of the decade.

I've seen this sort of thing happen time and again. Forecasts of a market crash fail to materialize or, when they do, the crash is followed within a few months by a big rally. If you sold everything and were out of the market when the crash occurred, chances are you were still out of the market at the time of the rally, sitting on the sidelines trying to decide when to go back in.

The other main problem with market timing is a psychological one. We all have a strong tendency to base our future outlook on past experience. When this is applied to the world of money, it creates a phenomenon I call rear-view mirror investing. An example of this thinking: High-tech stocks were hot in 1998 and 1999, so they will likely continue to make big gains in 2000. Of course, anyone who followed that line of reasoning took a beating in the markets. The right approach in that case would have been to say something like: "This can't go on forever. I'd better put my money elsewhere." But that's all too easy in hindsight. When the markets are going wild and investors are paying absurd prices, the natural inclination is to jump on the bandwagon.

If you're going to indulge in any sort of market timing, I suggest you do so through a process of portfolio rebalancing. Don't sell out of any asset class, just reduce its weighting somewhat if you feel the short-term prospects don't look good. There are many ways to do that. For example, if you think the stock market is about to come under pressure, you could simply reduce the weighting of your growth equity funds and add to your value funds, which should perform better in those conditions. Or, if you wanted to take more decisive action, you might reduce your total equity position by 10 percentage points and put it into cash. There are many ways to adjust your portfolio to the conditions of the day without completely restructuring it or, worst of all, selling everything.

Investing with Borrowed Money

There will almost certainly come a time when you will be tempted to use other people's money to enhance your investment returns. Some financial planners made *leveraging*, as it is called, a major part of their business when stock markets were riding high in the late 1990s. The concept was given added credibility by some authors who wrote books extolling the virtues of using borrowed money to build a personal fortune. In fact, I was directly criticized in one such book as being old-fashioned and too conservative because of my resistance to the idea of borrowing against one's home to buy stocks or mutual funds.

I plead guilty, and I am unrepentant. I wonder how comfortable people who took that advice felt when stock markets were being battered in 2000 — especially if they had loaded up on high-tech issues.

However, that does not mean that I am adamantly opposed to borrowing to invest under every circumstance. There are times when it makes sense to include the use of other people's money in your planning. But you should do everything possible to minimize the risk involved. And you should be sure that you have the right psychological makeup to go down this road.

Leveraging Scenarios

There is no doubt that, properly used, leveraging can be a powerful tool and can significantly increase the returns on a portfolio. Consider this situation: You have $25,000 to invest. You select a portfolio of mutual funds. Over a year, it increases in value by 15 percent. Your marginal tax rate is 45 percent but because the profits in the portfolio include some dividends and capital gains you pay tax on the income of $3,750 at an average rate of 30 percent. You are left with an after-tax portfolio value of $27,625, which represents a net after-tax gain of 10.5 percent. Here's what it looks like:

Your personal capital	$25,000
Gain at 15%	3,750
Gross value of portfolio	28,750
Less taxes on gain	– 1,125
Net value of portfolio	27,625
Your profit	10.5%

Now let's suppose that you borrowed another $25,000 to invest in that first year, using the portfolio as security. The interest rate you are changed is 8 percent. Since the loan is for investment purposes, the interest is tax deductible, so your effective interest rate is 5.5 percent. Here's the result:

Your personal capital	$25,000
Loan	25,000
Total invested	50,000
Gain at 15%	7,500
Gross value of portfolio	57,500
Less taxes on gain	– 2,250
Less net interest cost	– 1,375
After-tax value of portfolio	53,875
Loan principal repayment	– 25,000
Net value of portfolio	28,875
Your profit	15.5%

The after-tax value of the portfolio in this case would be $55,250, less your net interest expense of $1,375, for a total of $53,875. If you repaid the loan at that point, you would be left with $28,875, for a net after-tax gain on your original investment of 15.5 percent. By using leveraging, you added five percentage points to your profit. Or, put another way, your net after-tax return was almost 48 percent higher thanks to your leveraging strategy. Extend this example out over many years and we're talking a lot of money. It's examples like this (usually using much bigger figures) that get people excited and may persuade them to mortgage their homes to invest.

But there's a dark side to this equation. What if the markets turn against you? Just as leveraging will magnify your profits when the indexes rise, so will the strategy inflate your losses if things turn sour. Let's look at exactly the same two scenarios, only this time we will assume a 15 percent decline in portfolio value rather than a gain. First, the result if the portfolio is unleveraged.

Your personal capital	$25,000
Loss at 15%	3,750
Gross value of portfolio	21,250
Less taxes	0
Net value of portfolio	21,250
Your loss	15.0%

The only good news in this picture is that you don't have to pay any taxes and that any capital losses you incurred can be written off against taxable capital gains.

Now let's look at a losing leveraged scenario.

Your personal capital	$25,000
Loan	25,000
Total invested	50,000
Loss at 15%	− 7,500
Gross value of portfolio	42,500
Less taxes	0
Less net interest cost	− 1,375
After-tax value of portfolio	41,125
Loan principal repayment	− 25,000
Net value of portfolio	16,125
Your loss	35.5%

Whoa! As you can see, this is getting pretty heavy. Your relatively modest loss of 15 percent has been transformed into a huge drop of 35.5 percent through the use of leveraging. By doubling your invested capital, you doubled the size of your gross loss. Of course, you still had to repay the loan in full, so your original $25,000 bore the full brunt of the hit.

So far, we've worked with fairly modest numbers. But now I want to extend this into the kind of real-world situation that some unfortunate people encountered in 2000. As the stock markets soared through most of the 1990s, some financial advisors became increasingly aggressive in recommending that their clients borrow heavily to invest, often against the equity in their homes. Most firmly believed this to be sound advice – over the long term, leveraged investments of this type would pay off in a big way.

Clients simply had to roll with the inevitable market corrections that would come along from time to time. It must also be said, however, that there was often a large degree of self-interest in such recommendations. Most financial advisors make their money from fees and/or commissions. In either case, the larger the portfolio, the more income it generates for the advisor. The use of leveraging increases the size of a portfolio significantly, with a resulting higher payout to the advisor.

As a result, some people were persuaded to borrow heavily against their homes, perhaps hundreds of thousands of dollars. And the bulk of that money went into stocks or equity mutual funds, often growth funds that were riding high at the time. While the markets were churning out big gains, the strategy looked terrific and those who stuck to it through most of the decade did well. But let's look at the situation of someone who came to this party late, say in the dying days of 1999 or the first 2 months of 2000. Let's deal with a couple who were persuaded to borrow $200,000 against the equity in their home, which was added to $100,000 they already had invested in a non-registered portfolio. Over the subsequent 12 months, they saw the value of their portfolio decline by 25 percent – and in terms of what actually happened to some markets, like Nasdaq, that's letting them off lightly. We'll keep all the other factors the same as in the previous examples. Let's look at where they stood at the end of one year.

Personal capital	$100,000
Home equity loan	200,000
Total invested	300,000
Loss at 25%	– 75,000
Gross value of portfolio	225,000
Less taxes	0
Less net interest cost	– 11,000
After-tax value of portfolio	214,000
Loan principal outstanding	– 200,000
Net value of portfolio	14,000
Your loss	86.0%

I want you to look at these numbers very carefully. They may save you from a financial disaster at some point in your life. After just one year, using a true-to-life scenario, the original stake of this couple has been virtually wiped out. The portfolio still has enough to repay the home equity loan, but once that is done there will be only $14,000 in capital remaining from the $100,000 they had at the outset.

At this point the financial advisor will urge them to stay the course, reminding them that they were told at the time they made the original decision that they had to adopt a time horizon of at least five years. And the advisor will be right to make such a recommendation. But consider the psychological state of the couple at this point. They are likely to be shell-shocked. They have just suffered a loss of a magnitude they have probably never before experienced. Moreover, they had to pay out $11,000 in after-tax interest charges to service the loan. Their faith in the advisor's advice is likely to be at least shaken, if not shattered. The advisor can throw all kinds of numbers at them to show that in another four years they'll regain all their losses and more. But will they be prepared to take that risk in the face of what has just happened? Or will they want to cut their losses and run? What would your reaction be?

Now perhaps you understand why I am so cautious about the use of leveraging. I can tumble the numbers as well as anyone. I know the potential power of the strategy. It's the psychology I'm worried about. When stock markets are running strong, too many people allow greed to overcome prudence and expose themselves to risks they are simply not mentally equipped to handle. It's easy to tell yourself, "I'll just tough it out" when a market crash is hypothetical. It's quite different when the money has actually been lost and your spouse's tears are falling into the eggs as you both wonder if you could lose the house.

This is not to say you should never, ever use leveraging. After all, we use a form of leveraging when we take on a mortgage in order to buy a house. I am saying, however, that as an investment strategy it needs to be approached with great caution and with a clear understanding of the risks involved.

Reducing the Risk of Leveraging

One of the ways to reduce the risk is to keep the proportion of leveraged money to your personal capital relatively small. If you are using the strategy for the first time, limit yourself to a loan of no more than 25 percent of the value of your own capital, which will allow you to get a better feel for the process. Never put yourself in a position where the amount of borrowed money exceeds your own personal stake.

There are two specific situations in which the risks involved in leveraging can be significantly reduced. Let's consider them.

RRSP Loans

My favourite risk-reduction approach is the RRSP loan – money borrowed to top up your RRSP contribution. These loans are now available both for short and long terms. I prefer the short-term variety because it reduces the risk factor to almost zero.

RRSP leveraging works because the government subsidizes your return on investment, making it almost impossible to lose money if the loan is repaid quickly. There is one negative: interest on RRSP loans is not tax-deductible. However, that is a small price to pay for the other advantages.

Using leveraging to make your maximum RRSP contribution works best if you can repay the loan within one year, two at the most. After that, the benefits of the strategy start to erode and the risk factor increases. Let's look at an example.

We'll use the illustration of a woman who is entitled to make a maximum RRSP contribution of $8,000 for the current tax year but has only saved $3,000. She's wondering whether to contribute just $3,000 or to borrow an extra $5,000, which would allow her to make the maximum $8,000 deductible contribution. Let's assume her marginal tax rate is 45 percent, that she can invest the money in her RRSP at a conservative 6 percent, and that the loan is repayable in 12 monthly instalments at an interest rate of 8 percent (RRSP loans are offered at prime rate or close to it).

Here are her options:

	NO RRSP LOAN	WITH RRSP LOAN
Contribution	$3,000	$8,000
Tax refund @ 45%	1,350	3,600
Interest income for one year @ 6%	180	480
Gross benefit	1,530	4,080
Less cost of loan @ 8%	0	– 351
Net benefit	1,530	3,729

As you can see, her net gain in one year is more than twice as much by borrowing the $5,000. And this assumes she make no prepayment against the principal over the year. If she uses her $3,600 tax refund to pay it down as soon as the money arrives, her actual borrowing costs will be much less.

Let's assume that instead of doing that, she repays the loan out of her regular income and invests the refund outside her registered plan. We'll assume she buys a balanced mutual fund for her non-registered portfolio and generates an after-tax return of 8 percent. Here are the comparative numbers after the first 12 months. We'll look at only the one contribution here. The original value of the non-registered portfolio using the RRSP loan has been adjusted to subtract the interest cost.

	NO RRSP LOAN	WITH RRSP LOAN
Value of RRSP	$3,180	$8,480
Value of non-registered portfolio	1,652	3,509
Subtotal	4,832	11,989
Loan repayment	0	5,000
Net gain in one year	4,832	6,989

You can see why this use of leveraging is almost risk-free. The woman in this example would have to invest her money in such a way that she lost $2,158 or more in the first year in order to end up a net loser as a result of having borrowed. That's not impossible, but given the numbers we are working with, she would either have to be overly aggressive (never a good idea in an RRSP) or very unlucky. This also assumes she wouldn't make the same mistake and suffer a proportionate loss without the RRSP loan. In short, if she sticks to very conservative investments in her RRSP and doesn't indulge in wild speculation outside her plan, she's virtually guaranteed to come out a winner.

Moreover, the RRSP has an additional $5,000 in it that will continue to generate tax-sheltered income for years to come.

Segregated Funds

The other way to greatly reduce the risk inherent in leveraging is to use the borrowed money to invest in segregated (seg) funds. These are the insurance industry's equivalent of mutual funds but, as I explained earlier, they come with an assortment of features that aren't offered on conventional funds. The most important of these for leveraging purposes is the guarantee of principal. There are two types of guarantee: a death benefit guarantee that applies if you die, and a maturity guarantee that normally becomes effective after 10 years. In some cases, the guarantee is set at 75 percent of the value of the total amount you invest; in others it is 100 percent. You want the 100 percent guarantee, especially if you are using leveraging.

The guarantee effectively protects your capital. This means that, whatever happens, your principal will be preserved and the money to repay the loan will be there at the end of the day. Even if you have no profits at all over that time (unlikely), at least you can be secure in knowing you won't lose the family homestead — assuming, of course, that the insurance company that provides the guarantee remains solvent.

Of course, having to wait 10 years before the maturity guarantee cuts in won't make you happy if you suffer big reverses at the outset. But the security of knowing that you will eventually be made financially whole again may prevent you from panicking and locking in a big loss.

As I explained in Step Four, you'll pay a price for that peace of mind in the form of higher annual management fees. Consider them as insurance premiums and they'll be less painful.

If you are going to use leveraging to invest in segregated funds, you may as well take an aggressive approach. There isn't much point in paying good money to insure a bond or even a balanced fund. Select a portfolio of top-quality equity mutual funds and aim for above-average returns. Why not, since the insurance company is assuming the risk on your behalf.

It's Time for the Last Step

We've accomplished a lot. You've learned a great deal about yourself. You should by now have decided what route you want to take to your first million. You've started the process of arming yourself with the necessary knowledge. And now you should have the foundation of a plan and know how to achieve it.

Think of this process as a vacation trip. The car is packed. You've carefully studied the road maps. You've called ahead for reservations. Now all that remains is to call the family out of the house, lock the door, and get in and start driving.

That's where we're going next. We're going to start driving.

Step 6

Step **6**

Make It Happen

The time has come for action, for making a start. Exactly what your start will consist of depends on which path to a million you have chosen.

Creating Your Million

If you are planning to create your wealth through the use of your personal talents and inner genius, you have come to the point where you have to stop thinking and start acting. You can no longer afford to let doubts inhibit you. Recently, I was talking with a friend who was having an inner debate with himself on exactly this point. He felt he had a lot to offer in terms of specialized knowledge and was thinking about writing a book on the subject. His wife and friends were encouraging him to do so. But he was unsure. He had never written anything more challenging than a university term paper. He found expressing himself in print to be difficult and painstaking. He knew his subject well and he believed some of the work he had done was unique and would be of broad interest. But he wondered if he could effectively put that knowledge on paper and, even if he did, whether anyone would publish it. He was in a real dilemma.

I suggested that he was being stymied by the size and scope of the project and suggested that he break it down into bite-size chunks. Start by simply jotting down notes in outline form of what the book might cover, I said. Don't worry about the quality of the prose or whether it all comes out in a logical order. No one but you will ever see it. Since you know the subject so well, it shouldn't take more than half a day to do this.

When you finish the notes, look them over carefully. If you still think there's enough material for a book, and that it will offer a different perspective on your specialty, try writing one chapter. Set aside an hour or two each day to work on it and see how long it takes. If you're satisfied with the result, write a second chapter and then a third. Then stop, go back and edit what you've written, and show the result to two or three people whose opinion you respect and whom you can count on to give you an honest appraisal. If at the end of this, you are even mildly encouraged, find the names of some publishers who specialize in books of this type. Send them your outline and the three chapters, along with a copy of your resumé that details why you are especially qualified to write on the topic. See if you can elicit any interest. Obviously, encouraging words from a publishing house, even if not accompanied by a formal contract and an advance cheque, would be a strong motivator to continue.

Even failing that, the experience of actually writing three chapters may be enough to encourage you to proceed with more. Or it may tell you that your doubts were well founded and that this isn't really how you should be spending your time. You then have two choices – you can either abandon the idea or, if you still firmly believe it has merit, find a professional writer who will work with you to craft your ideas into a presentable form.

Whatever happens, I told my friend, you'll resolve the issue. By taking action you'll know within a reasonable period of time whether this is something that you really want to do and whether it has a realistic prospect for success. If not, then you can move on to something else, knowing that you've made the effort and answered your inner question to your satisfaction.

It doesn't matter whether your goal is to write a book or to start a business or to go on the stage. The same advice applies. Start the process and get the momentum going.

If setting up your own business is the plan, as it will be in many cases, this doesn't mean that you necessarily have to quit your job and wager everything you have on the ultimate success of your project. Many people prefer to put their toe in the water first. I incorporated my own business several years before I decided it was capable of sustaining our family if I were to make it my full-time occupation. Much depends on the nature of what you want to do, of course, but look at your options carefully.

Lining Up Support

At this point, if you are considering starting your own operation, you should have a business plan in front of you. It should have been reviewed several times and you should feel comfortable with it. Your first step in implementing it must be to line up the support that the plan calls for, unless you believe that you can do it all yourself.

There are three types of support that a fledgling business may require: money, staff, and customers.

Financial Backing

The first requirement is money. You'll need some to get going. If you don't have the resources yourself, it will have to come from outside. There are two ways to raise the needed cash: by obtaining loans or by selling an interest in your venture to one or more investors.

The borrowing route is fairly straightforward. You can go to a financial institution for a loan, in which case be prepared to jump through a lot of hoops. They'll want you to put up collateral or they will want to be assured of your income level. If you don't have any acceptable collateral and you're planning to quit your job, the chances of you obtaining a loan in this way are slim. There are some government programs designed to assist small businesses with loans but they have rigid standards. You may not qualify.

That means you may be tempted to fall back on friends and relatives for financial assistance. A word of warning here. The fastest way to lose friends is to borrow money from them and then not repay it when you say you will. And your mother-in-law may love you dearly, but she may not be thrilled with the idea of putting money into a venture she thinks is somewhat harebrained to begin with. In short, obtaining a business loan may not be easy. Don't underestimate the potential problems.

Alternatively, you may be able to persuade some people to invest money in your venture in exchange for shares in the company. This is more complicated than obtaining a loan, however. It means you have to set up some kind of formal structure that allows for such investment (a corporation or partnership, for example), with all the costs that are involved in doing that. And you'll need to work out detailed agreements with your partners/investors as to ownership and responsibility.

If your venture needs money, you have to go one route or the other (or a combination of both), however. So you should begin exploring the possibilities available to you.

Staff

Whether you will require support staff from the outset will depend on the scope of your enterprise. It may be possible to go it alone initially, with perhaps some spare-time assistance from your spouse. But if more help is required, you will need to find the right people and work out appropriate compensation.

The best rule here is: Don't hire any help you don't absolutely need. Keep your costs and your obligations to a minimum. If you can get by with part time, don't hire full time. If you think that you need two employees, start with one and see what happens. Many fledgling businesses have run into immediate problems because they took on too much staff overhead from the outset.

If you need to hire, start with people you know who are qualified for the job. These may include friends, relatives, or co-workers. But don't hire anyone simply on the basis of friendship or kinship. That's almost certain to create problems. If the person is not knowledgeable and experienced in the work you need done, don't take her on, even if she's your twin sister.

In cases when you have to go to the job market and hire a stranger, ask for references and check them — all of them. I know of many situations when a person gave a terrific interview but a few phone calls quickly revealed some serious potential problems. Better to find these out before you make the hire, not later.

Orders

Your business can't succeed without money coming in the door, no matter what it is. You may offer a unique and exciting product, but if no one buys it you're not going to be producing it for very long. Ideally, when you launch you will already be sure of some guaranteed orders. These will provide a foundation on which to build — and will also impress potential lenders or investors.

You may need to use your network of contacts to generate this initial business. Perhaps the first order will come from a company you previously worked for — always a good sign. However you go about it, you should know before you start that there will be at least some money coming in during the first few months, even if it won't cover all the bills.

Saving Your Million

Most readers of this book will probably choose the savings/investment route to a million, simply because it is the easiest and involves minimal risk. You don't have to give up your job, depend on other people's money, or undergo all the hassles and headaches that come with creating wealth through entrepreneurship. Creating wealth is certainly more challenging and potentially more rewarding. But it can involve significant lifestyle disruption, which the saving/investing path does not – presuming it's done properly.

So let's focus on how to put your investment plan into action. By now you have the framework and you should know what your objectives are and the time line you will use to achieve them. Now what?

Choosing Winning Mutual Funds

We'll start with mutual funds, which is where most people begin once they have moved beyond the GIC/CSB phase. Based on the asset allocation plan you have worked out in Step Five, the goal is to select an appropriate number of high-quality funds that are likely to generate above-average returns for you over several years.

Before we discuss the selection criteria, a cautionary word: Don't expect all your funds to be winners every year. Some funds may come in with below-average returns on occasion, and losses are quite probable at some stage as well. What we're trying to achieve is a balanced portfolio of well-managed funds with a good risk/return profile that will provide a decent return while allowing you to rest comfortably at night. That said, here is the process for choosing top-quality funds.

Step #1: Check Out the Track Record

Whenever you see a performance claim in a mutual fund advertisement or brochure, you'll find a line in small print that reads something like this: "Past performance does not necessarily reflect future results." How true! The investing world is littered with the wrecks of funds that did well for a year or two and then tanked. Just because a fund turned in a good return last year does not mean it will repeat the performance this year – in fact, it probably won't. The manager may have changed, the economic climate may be different, or the portfolio may be overweighted to a sector that collapses, as technology did in 2000 – anything can happen.

Moreover, historic performance numbers may mask a fund's internal weaknesses. For example, one sensational year can pull up the three- and five-year averages to make it look like the fund is a world-beater. In fact, the rest of the time it may have been in the doldrums. It happens frequently.

You will also find situations in which it appears that some funds within a given category are performing much better than their peers. Naturally, people are attracted to them because of the numbers but it may simply be a case of comparing apples and oranges. Dividend income funds are notorious in this regard. Some are nothing more than blue-chip stock funds, which means they'll turn in some great-looking numbers when stock markets are strong. Others follow the dividend mandate more closely, investing a large part of their money in preferred shares. Since preferreds are less volatile than common stocks, they won't rise (or fall) as much when markets are volatile. As a result, they may end up looking like underachievers if you do nothing more than compare historic returns.

In other cases, you may find the returns have been skewed by the reporting process. A few companies don't charge management fees directly to the funds; rather, they are charged to the clients separately. As a consequence, the results that are published in the media appear to be higher than they should be because most of the competitors are deducting management charges first, before they calculate performance. The result is another apples-to-oranges comparison.

So why bother at all? you may ask. If the past performance numbers are so flawed, why use them in the fund selection process? Because, wisely used, they're better than nothing. It's like studying the bloodline of a racehorse. Those with the best breeding don't always win the race, but they have an advantage that should not be ignored.

Think of a fund's track record as a guideline. If it hasn't performed well in the past, why should you think it's going to do better? If you can't find a good reason, pass. Conversely, a consistent record of solid returns in both good and bad economic times suggests the managers have known what they were doing up to now. Maybe next year they'll stumble. But that's the chance you take.

In considering a fund's track record, there are a number of factors to take into account. The first is the average annual compound rate of return over a period of time. These numbers tell you what return you could have expected from an investment made several years ago, assuming you reinvested all dividends, interest, and capital gains.

This information is easy to find. All the newspapers and Web sites that publish performance numbers include 3-year, 5-year, and 10-year results, so you can see how any given fund has performed over time.

The differences can be dramatic, even within the same fund group. *The Globe and Mail* report published in December 2000 showed that among Canadian equity funds, the average annual compound rate of return over 10 years ranged from a low of 2.5 percent (Industrial Growth Fund) to a high of 24.7 percent (AIC Advantage Fund). That means that a $10,000 investment made at the beginning of December 1990 in the Industrial Growth Fund would have been worth only $12,800.84 a decade later. That same investment in the AIC fund would have grown to $90,921.07. See why it's so important to find a quality fund?

Even in the less volatile bond funds you'll find a wide divergence. The best 10-year average was 11.4 percent (Altamira Bond); the worst was 5.3 percent (Trans-Canada Bond). Over a decade, that translates into a $10,000 investment being worth $29,434.18 if the money was placed in the Altamira fund, versus just $16,760.37 in the Trans-Canada fund.

The next thing to look at is the simple rate of return over the past year. These figures tell you how the fund is doing at present. You shouldn't place too much emphasis on them, however, because they can be distorted by specific events. For example, the crash of the high-tech market in 2000 left most science and technology funds pretty battered by year-end, in many cases with losses in the double digits. But because they had scored such huge gains during the halcyon years of the late 1990s, their three-year records still looked respectable.

So don't be overly influenced by short-term results. The record over several years is more significant.

Now that you've looked at the raw numbers for the funds in which you're interested, compare them with the industry averages. These figures are shown at the end of each fund section in the tables published by the financial papers. Here's where you get out your red pencil. Cross off your list any funds that have consistently done worse than the average, in both the short and long term. Circle those that have consistently done better – these are your prime prospects. Put a question mark beside those showing a long-term average or below-average performance, but which have been above average over the past one to three years. These are your secondary prospects.

Once you've developed a short list based on historic performance, put it to a completely different test. Calculate what I call the Average Quartile Ranking (AQR).

Here's how it works. Find an Internet site, such as Globefund, that provides quartile rankings for every fund. The quartile ranking shows you how a fund performed against its peer group in a specific time frame, say one year, by dividing the funds into four groups. If it was in the first quartile, that means it was among the top 25 percent in its category. Second quartile means it was above average but not in the top league. Third quartile is below average but not terrible. Fourth quartile is pretty bad. By adding the quartile rankings and dividing by the number of periods under review, we get the AQR for the time frame you're looking at.

For example, a fund that was in the first quartile for every period would receive an AQR of 1.00 – a perfect score. One that finished in the bottom quartile every year would end up with a rating of 4.00. It's not complicated – you can calculate it yourself for any fund in which you are interested.

For example, a fund that showed a quartile ranking of 1, 3, 2, 1, 2 over the past five years would have an AQR of 1.80 for that period (nine divided by five). That's a very good result – anything under 2.00 tells you the fund has been in the top half of its class most of the time during the period being measured. On the other hand, a fund with a pattern of 1, 4, 3, 4, 3 would have an AQR of 3.00, which is not very good. Yet many people may be drawn to it because during the most recent year it finished in the top quartile. The rest of the time it was a lousy performer, however, which the AQR reveals.

Applying this overlay to the list of funds you have chosen based on raw historical data will enable you to screen out several of the mediocre performers. Now you can move ahead.

Step #2: Consider the Future Prospects

Now that you have done some analysis of the history of the funds you're considering, you should give some thought to their future prospects. Of course that's not easy and there are no guarantees. But you should never make an investment without first looking ahead.

I often ask audiences at my seminars whether they would prefer to put their money into a fund that has a good chance to gain 15 percent in the first year or one that could lose 15 percent in that period. A few (surprisingly) choose the one that is likely to lose 15 percent, perhaps on the theory that it will eventually rebound. But that's fuzzy thinking; a fund that loses 15 percent in a year must gain 18 percent in the next 12 months just to get back to break-even. Your choice should always be the fund with the best chance of a good one-year gain. That builds in a cushion against future losses.

This is not to say that your fund purchase decisions should always be decided on short-term prospects — far from it. Of course, you should be looking ahead several years and selecting funds that you believe will stand up over the long haul. But if the short-term prospects for a fund you like appear to be weak, hold off on that commitment.

For example, as the year 2001 began, technology funds were in disarray. Nasdaq had fallen more than 50 percent from its highs and many high-tech stocks had lost 70 or 80 percent of their value. No one doubted that high-tech would eventually recover. But who could say when that might be? Given that climate, an investor might well decide to postpone putting money into a science and technology fund until the situation clarified. Why risk the prospect of a short-term decline of 15 or 20 percent? Putting the cash to work elsewhere, even in a money market fund, would be a prudent move in the circumstances. When it appears the technology slump has bottomed out, you can make a switch.

Key indicators, which are closely watched by economists, can also offer some useful investing clues. If the numbers are indicating a slowing economy, falling corporate profits, rising unemployment, and a decline in the growth rate, the chances are that central banks will begin to ease interest rates. That would be good news for bond funds and dividend funds, as well as for funds that specialize in bank stocks. Conversely, a rising inflation rating and runaway growth, such as we saw in the late 1990s, would be a signal that interest rates are likely to rise: bad news for bond and dividend funds.

Although you're investing for the long term, it doesn't make sense to put a lot of money into a fund that is likely to struggle for the next year or two because of the current economic conditions. So if interest rates are on the rise, for example, a long-term bond fund, even a well-managed one, shouldn't be an immediate choice. It will probably sustain some serious losses before things turn around.

Step #3: Choose a Good Management Team

The fund manager is the person who calls the shots. He or she makes the investment decisions that will determine the fate of your money. You should therefore make every effort to learn something about the person or team to whom you're entrusting your capital. As in every other profession, there are good managers, mediocre managers, and bad managers.

Of course, no one comes out and publicly says a manager is bad – not unless they want to incur the risk of a libel suit. So you have to use your own judgment and sometimes read between the lines.

Good managers are somewhat easier to identify. The stars are often written about and quoted in the media and sometimes win major awards. However, many top-notch managers labour in relative obscurity. Few people, for example, could name a single manager in organizations like Phillips, Hager & North, Perigee, GBC, or Standard Life, yet their funds perform consistently well, year after year. In situations such as that, you have to look at the overall team and the track record of the company in ensuring that quality leaders are always in place.

It's also important to determine whether a manager's approach is consistent with your investment philosophy. For example, look at the Vancouver-based Sagit Funds, which are managed by Raoul Tsakok. In some years they do very well, posting impressive returns. In other years, the losses can be in double-digit territory. Investors who aren't comfortable with this kind of volatility would probably wish to avoid putting money into these funds as a result.

At the other end of the scale, you'll find managers who are very conservative in their approach, such as those who run the Templeton funds. Investors who are seeking above-average returns may find the cautious, value-driven style used here to be too tame for their liking.

Step #4: Look at the Fund Family

Never buy a mutual fund in isolation. Look also at the total family and determine its strengths and weaknesses. There may come a time when you want to switch part or all of your assets to another fund within the organization, or to add other funds from the company to your portfolio. So you want to know a good deal about the other options available to you and how strong they are.

Start by examining the product range. Does the organization offer funds in all the categories that interest you, or is it limited to only a few choices? This is especially important to know if you're planning to build your portfolio using only one or two fund families.

Next, find out how good the other funds are. Some fund companies are strong almost across the board. For example, all the funds offered by the little-known Toronto-based firm of McLean Budden have been very good performers for many years. Other companies may have only a few standouts in an otherwise mediocre line-up. Global Strategy, which was absorbed into AGF in 2000, fell into that category.

While you're at it, look for areas of weakness within a company. Some organizations are very strong in equity funds, for example, but have a poor record when it comes to fixed income. In other cases, a company may offer several good Canadian funds while displaying a pronounced weakness internationally. Phillips, Hager & North, one of the most respected firms in the business, suffered from that problem for years, although they have moved recently to try to remedy the situation.

A major plus is a mutual fund company that provides style options. If you can choose a good value fund and a good growth fund from the same company, it makes the decision-making process easier. Several organizations now offer this kind of style diversification, including Synergy (which started it all), Mackenzie, C.I., and AIM, which added the Trimark funds to their roster in 2000.

Tax considerations may also come into play in your fund family selection if you are investing outside a registered plan. Several companies offer "umbrella" funds, which allow you to switch from one "class" to another without incurring capital gains tax liability. (Normally a switch from one fund to another is deemed to be a sale by the Canada Customs and Revenue Agency and therefore taxable if there has been a gain.) Among the firms that provide for this sort of tax-deferred switching are C.I., Mackenzie, AGF, AIM, Clarington, and Synergy.

Step #5: Consider the Costs

You should always be aware of the costs involved in buying units in any mutual fund. But you may be surprised to learn that, while the impact of high costs can be significant, as we previously discussed, I do not consider this to be a major factor in the purchase decision. In fact, I believe the cost issue has been blown out of proportion by the media.

There are two parts to the cost equation, which we looked at earlier. One is the commission structure. Many people still believe they should focus only on so-called "no-load" funds, even though in doing so they cut themselves off from some of the top performers in the business. These days, limiting your options in that way does not make a lot of sense.

Using a back-end load option (also known as deferred sales charge) means you pay no commission up-front – just the same as with a no-load fund. The difference is that you will be assessed a charge if you cash in before a certain period of time has elapsed (typically seven years). However, if you switch to another fund within the same family, no deferred sales charge is normally assessed, although your financial advisor may charge a switching fee of up to 2 percent.

As far as front-end loads are concerned (commission paid at the time of purchase), some financial advisors now offer these funds at zero cost. They do so because they want to "build their book" – add to their assets under management. There's a strong incentive to do that in the form of "trailer fees," which are paid annually by the fund companies. Typically, these fees amount to 0.5 percent of the value of the assets in an advisor's "book." That may not seem like a lot until you do some math and realize that it amounts to $5,000 a year in revenue for every $1 million under management. That can add up pretty quickly.

Even if you have to pay a front-end load, it shouldn't be more than 2 or 3 percent. If the fund is a proven above-average performer and you're buying for the long term, that's a small price to pay.

Be wary of price gouging, however. I recently received an e-mail from a man who wanted to set up a registered education savings plan for his two children. He wanted to buy AGF funds and was told by a broker he would have to pay a 5 percent front-end load. Not only that, the broker said he was "giving him a break" – his normal charge was 6 percent. The investor wondered if this was a typical cost and asked whether he should go to Altamira and use their no-load funds instead.

This is an example of a broker who was getting too greedy. It's true that the top front-end commission that AGF allows is 6 percent, but few people pay that. In fact, any front-end charge over 3 percent is excessive these days. As well, all AGF funds offer a back-end load option. Since the investor was planning to hold for the long term, that made a lot more sense in his case – and, incidentally, would not have cost the broker anything since he would get a commission from AGF anyway.

In this situation, the cost did matter – but only because the broker was attempting to take advantage of an inexperienced investor. If you know the facts before you buy, you should never be exposed to this sort of thing.

The other main element of fund cost is the management expense ratio (MER). I noted earlier that there has been a growing chorus of complaint about the high MERs of Canadian mutual funds compared to those sold in the U.S., some of which is justified. However, the reality is that we do not have legal access to U.S.-based funds that are not registered for sale in this country. Unless that changes, we must work with what we have.

Some investors have become so obsessed with MERs that they will only consider buying units in funds that have below-average annual costs. That's a short-sighted approach that effectively eliminates many fine funds from consideration. There are many excellent low-MER funds – just because they're cheap does not mean they're bad. There are also many high-MER funds that are chronic underperformers. So this is not a case of "you get what you pay for." A high MER doesn't mean the fund is any better than one with a low MER. It may just be less efficiently managed.

When all is said and done, the test is how much is left in your pocket after the fees and expenses are deducted. Over the past decade, for example, the Investors Summa Fund has turned in results that are well above average, even though its MER is high for the Canadian equity category. In fact, it outperformed the TD Canadian Stock Fund by a wide margin, even though the TD fund had a much lower MER.

The lesson should be obvious. By all means, check out the MER and know what you're paying. But a high MER is not a reason in itself to reject a fund. The other factors we've discussed are far more important to its long-term success – and yours.

How to Buy Stocks

If you're just starting out on the investment track, I strongly recommend that you stick with mutual funds for the combination of professional management and diversification that they offer. But the siren call of the stock market will undoubtedly tempt you at some point, especially when those markets are riding high. At the peak of the high-tech boom in the late 1990s, the allure of big profits and the excitement of day trading were impossible for many people to resist. Some did indeed make a fortune. Most lost, in some cases heavily.

The Internet bubble is yet another reminder of the danger of getting swept away in a market frenzy. It was hardly the first time such a thing has happened. Japan, for example, is still struggling to recover from the collapse of its hyper-valued Nikkei Index more than a decade after the event.

If you decide to venture into the turbulent waters of the stock market as you implement your savings/investment program, at least give yourself a reasonable chance to succeed. That means following some fundamental rules and not being overly greedy if things work out well. Here are some essential guidelines to stock market investing. If you follow them, you should at least stay out of deep trouble and you may end up doing very well for yourself.

Rule #1: Be Disciplined

If there is one single virtue that a stock market investor must have, it is self-discipline. Without it, you haven't a hope of success.

You need discipline in constructing your portfolio. It must be as diversified as possible, so as to spread your risk across a number of companies and industry groups. But it must not become so unwieldy you can't easily keep track of the companies you own and how they're performing. A well-constructed portfolio of 10 to 15 stocks is probably about right.

You need discipline in your stock selection. You'll be bombarded with advice from all sides, some of which will be difficult to ignore. Even though you carefully lay out your investment philosophy to your broker, he or she will almost certainly be on the phone to you with recommendations that don't fit. You'll hear hot tips at cocktail parties. You'll read articles in the financial press about stocks that sound good. You'll receive glowing research reports about attractive issues. You'll get enthusiastic calls about exciting new IPOs. You'll quickly discover that your major problem will be ignoring these tips and sticking with your game plan.

You'll need discipline in selling. Buying stocks is easy. Selling is always a wrench. If the stock has moved up, you'll be reluctant to let it go because it may move still higher. If it has dropped in value, you'll be reluctant to sell because it means locking in a loss. There never seems to be a right time to sell. Sooner or later, however, if you want to secure your profits, you have to sell.

To be disciplined, you must have a well-defined philosophy and goals. Write these down at the outset and review them periodically. Don't buy stocks that don't fit the philosophy. Ask yourself whether the portfolio you've put together meets your goals and, if not, where and how you got off track. And make sure your objectives are still valid – all things human change. If you decide to switch direction, fine. Just be sure you know why you're doing so and how you plan to proceed.

Rule #2: Buy Quality

As with anything else — cars, paintings, clothes — true quality will eventually show its value. You're not going to hold shares in hundreds of companies, so every stock you purchase should be selected with quality in mind. That means the company should be a proven leader in its field, should have a reputation for excellent management, should consistently show good earnings, should be innovative, and should have a good public image. If a company doesn't fit the bill, don't buy it, no matter how good a story someone tells you.

Rule #3: Buy Stocks in the Lower End of Their Recent Trading Range

You're not only looking for quality; you're looking for quality at bargain prices. Many people who would haggle endlessly over a car price or negotiate tenaciously on a house deal will go out and pay top dollar for their stocks. We saw that mistake repeated again and again during the high-tech frenzy.

Money manager Francis Chou was one of those who refused to be swept along, and the words he wrote in his 1999 annual report should be burned into your memory: "Let's not play a fool's game by thinking that a stock can be bought at 100 times revenues and then proceed to hope, against hope, that someone who is carried away by emotion, and is unaware of the risk involved, will buy it at 200 times revenues the following week. When the urge hits to make such a leap, take a cold shower until the inclination passes."

Remember, the stock market has sales, just like any other business. That's when you should do your shopping.

Rule #4: Buy Stocks That Pay Dividends

There are two ways to make money from your stocks: dividends and capital gains. Capital gains are usually the number one priority for stock investors. But a steady dividend flow will ensure a continuing return on your investment and, if your stocks are Canadian and held outside a retirement plan, will entitle you to claim the dividend tax credit.

You'll hear a lot of conflicting arguments on this point. Many investment counsellors will advise you to forget about dividends, especially if you're younger, and concentrate on stocks with the greatest growth potential. High dividends and strong growth potential usually don't come together in the same package, they'll point out.

They're wrong. It's true that stocks with high dividend yields will usually be those of large, well-established companies, such as banks and utilities. Normally, their share prices will tend to appreciate in value as the market rises, but not as much as some of the more volatile high-flyers. But there are many, many exceptions. For example, bank stocks were badly beaten up when interest rates were pushed up in 1999–2000. The dividend yields rose (the banks were still making great profits and cutting dividends was never an issue). But the potential for future capital gains grew as the share prices sank. Sure enough, when interest rates levelled off, the bank stocks bounced back. At the end of 2000, the Financial Services sub-index of the Toronto Stock Exchange showed a 47 percent gain for the year. So much for the theory that dividends and capital gains are always mutually exclusive.

Rule #5: Buy Stocks of Companies with Low Debt

I'm an old-school conservative when it comes to buying stocks. I don't like companies with a lot of debt. Many experts would dispute this particular bias, pointing out that some companies have used debt successfully to increase the asset base many times over. That's true – but many of those same companies subsequently crashed in flames.

Laidlaw Corporation is one example. The company skilfully deployed borrowed money to help build a transportation network across North America that at one point made it a powerful force in school bus services, ambulances, trucking, and municipal public transit. The firm even used its seemingly limitless credit lines to purchase the venerable Greyhound Bus Lines. But the huge debt load and some bad management decisions eventually caught up with Laidlaw. The shares, which had risen as high as $23.50 in 1998, were trading in the 12¢ range at the end of 2000, and the company experienced the ignominy of being delisted by the New York Stock Exchange because of its penny-stock status.

There are some blue-chip companies, such as utilities, that, by their nature, will carry a high debt load. You can make an exception in these cases because the companies are conservatively managed and government regulated. The chances of them going under because of an overextended debt load are remote, although as we have seen in California, it can happen when privatization programs are poorly devised. As a general rule, avoid high-debt enterprises.

How do you know when a company's debt is out of line? A standard measure is a company's debt/equity ratio. This is arrived at by dividing the total long-term debt by the current market value of the company's common stock (calculated by multiplying the number of outstanding shares by the market price). A good research report will contain this information; otherwise, ask your broker for it. A debt/equity ratio of less than 1 is good; under 0.5 is excellent.

Rule #6: Buy Stocks of Companies with Positive Cash Flow

This is a lesson from the dot-com collapse. Many of the Internet firms that went down in 2000 had great concepts but not enough money coming in the door. As a result, they went through their cash reserves faster than the money could be replaced, in the process creating a new test of financial strength known as the *cash burn rate*. In the early days of the Internet bubble, that wasn't a problem – dot-com companies just sold more stock to eager investors to raise money whenever it was needed. But when the bubble burst and investors fled to the sidelines, cash burn became a serious issue. When the money ran out, the doors were closed – it was as simple as that.

So find out about a company's cash flow (which is not the same thing as profitability) before you put any money into it. If the cash is flowing out the door faster than it is coming in, be very wary.

Rule #7: Buy Stocks That Are Widely Traded

Every once in a while you'll come across a stock that looks good but has only a limited number of shares outstanding. It may trade only a few hundred shares a day, and may go for days at a time with no action at all. These are called "thinly traded" stocks and they can be dangerous. They're subject to sharp price movements, up and down. And you may have difficulty getting your price when you want to sell because of a lack of buyers (this is known as a liquidity problem). In general, avoid these thin issues and concentrate on stocks that are widely held and traded.

Rule #8: Buy in the Secondary Market

If you deal with a full-service broker, every so often you may get a call with the offer of a hot new issue. (New issues are always "hot" — can you imagine a broker telling you it's a loser but you should buy anyway?) There are two problems with initial public offerings (IPOs). The first is hype. Often these issues are talked up in the investment community, to the point that demand for the shares exceeds supply and the issuer can bring out the stock at a top price. They may shoot up from there, which sometimes happens. More often they sink back after the initial excitement and you can pick them up more cheaply on the open market.

The second concern is conflict of interest. Brokerage houses are sometimes involved in underwriting the stock that your advisor is recommending to you. That doesn't necessarily mean the stock is bad, but the brokerage firm does have a vested interest in seeing the IPO do well. If your broker recommends a new stock, ask whether his or her firm is involved in the issue in any way. If so, be extra cautious.

I usually advise waiting until the stock has traded for at least a week in the secondary market before considering it. That way you get a feel for what investors really think of its chances.

Rule #9: Avoid Stories with No Substance

The brokerage community is rife with wonderful stories about great little companies that have a terrific concept and are going to develop into sure-fire winners. Of course, they don't have much revenue yet and profits are a long way off in the future. But the prospects are terrific and the stock is cheap.

I have heard so many of these tales over the years that I have lost count. I have even invested in a few and usually ended up losing money. But I have to confess that, even with all this experience behind me, I can still be swayed by a convincing story. If it can happen to me, it can certainly happen to you. So the best advice I can offer is, if you're ever tempted to invest in a company like this, go easy. Commit only a small amount of money. That way, if you lose it won't hurt too badly. Of course, if the stock soars you'll think this was lousy advice. But it probably won't.

Rule #10: Avoid Manias

It's very easy to get caught up in a stock-market buying frenzy. Sometimes you even make money, as investors did who sold out of Bre-X before it was revealed that the fabulous gold mine it had supposedly found in the jungles of Indonesia was nothing more than an elaborate hoax.

But most manias end badly, and it is the people who got on board at the end who end up being hurt worst. Think of these phenomena as gigantic pyramid scams. If you get in at the beginning, indeed if you originate the scheme, you can get rich (of course, you may also go to jail). But as more people are drawn in, the danger mounts until the whole scheme collapses under its own weight. That's what happened with the Internet bubble, the Japanese stock run-up, the emerging markets craze of the early 1990s, the runaway stock market of the late 1920s, and on back into history. Keep in mind that if something appears to be ridiculously expensive, it is. Sooner or later, its true value will reassert itself. You don't want to be the person who owns it when that happens.

Stick with stocks that meet most or all of these criteria and you'll be able to construct a portfolio that will provide you with income, moderate growth, and tax benefits, with a minimum of risk — at least by stock market standards.

Tips for Successful Portfolio Management

Managing an investment portfolio is something akin to maintaining a car. If it's going to work well, it needs periodic attention and the occasional tune-up. Just as you wouldn't open your hood to look at the engine every day, you don't need to check out the performance of each security you own every morning in the financial pages. If you do, you're becoming obsessed with your money – not a healthy sign!

But just as you take in the car for regular oil changes, you should make it a point to review your portfolio at least once every three months. See if it is performing according to your expectations and decide whether adjustments are needed. A few hours spent in this way will significantly increase your profit potential and reduce your risk of serious loss.

Here are some guidelines to help you in this process.

Guideline #1: Check Your Financial Statements Thoroughly

Make sure your financial statements are correct and complete. See that everything you own is properly listed – on several occasions I have discovered the mysterious disappearance of assets worth thousands of dollars into limbo because of an incorrect data entry.

Also, be sure that you have been credited with all interest and dividends that are due to you. Sometimes money that should be yours will inadvertently be credited to another account – I've seen it happen. If your assets are in a registered plan, check your foreign content percentage. Make sure you are taking advantage of the diversification offered by foreign investing, but that you have not gone over the limit.

Review the performance of each security that you own. If the statement is well designed, you should see both the original purchase price and the current market price side by side, so you can tell at a glance how well the particular investment is performing. If it's not up to standard, find out why, particularly if it's a stock. There may have been some recent news that has long-term negative implications for the company.

At all times in the review process, ask yourself: Would I buy this today, at the current price? If the answer is no, then it may be time for a change.

Guideline #2: Know When to Sell

Whenever you buy a security, you should establish a target point for selling it, both on the upside and the downside. That doesn't mean you must automatically dump it when it reaches that level. But reaching a target should be a signal for a thorough review. If you conclude that it's time to move on, you must make a move.

Selling when a security has moved up in value is psychologically easy, because you have the satisfaction of a profit. There are also ways to hedge your bets if you think it may go higher still. One is a "stop loss" order, which a broker will execute if the security (usually a stock in this case) falls back to a pre-determined level. The problem with that idea is that stop-loss orders are often worthless in a rapidly falling market, when panic selling is taking place and buyers have fled.

I prefer a "half-profits" approach. This involves selling half your holdings to lock in that portion of your profits, while holding on to the rest of the shares. A variation of that is the "zero cost" approach, in which you sell enough shares to recover your entire original investment. The stock remaining is, in effect, free and represents clear profit.

I used exactly that technique when I purchased shares in the high-tech company Research in Motion in the late 1990s. My original purchase price was $7 each, and I bought 300 shares. When the market price passed $21, I sold 100 shares, thereby recovering my capital. That meant that no matter what the stock did from that point, I wouldn't lose any money – even if it went to zero, which some high-tech stocks eventually did. Not in this case, however. The stock continued to rise. I sold a second 100 shares at $120, which was 17 times what I had paid for them. At that point, I guaranteed myself a profit of $12,000 on a total initial investment of $2,100. That was locked in. As of this writing, I still own the final 100 shares. Whatever happens to them, I have come out of this transaction with a huge gain because I wasn't overly greedy and did some timely selling.

You should also considering selling if a security achieves your upside target and its momentum appears to be slowing or it is actually starting to slip back. Often a stock will run ahead of itself and be pushed to unrealistic levels by investor enthusiasm – as we saw in the high-tech boom. Then, like a rocket, it will reach its apex and turn back towards Earth. That's a good time to take your marbles and go home.

You should sell part of your position when a security reaches the point where it is grossly overweighted in your portfolio. That situation was fairly common in the late '90s, when stocks like Nortel Networks and mutual funds that specialize in science and technology ran up wildly in price. In one of my newsletters, the *Internet Wealth Builder,* we developed a Blue Chip Portfolio that held shares in BCE Inc. The stock quadrupled in value in just two years, to the point where it accounted for 35 percent of the total portfolio. That was putting too many eggs in one basket, so we reduced our holdings by half to get things into better balance and pocketed a big gain in the process.

Finally, sell a stock when there is unexpected bad news. This is a rule that is not always applied as diligently as it should be, usually with unhappy consequences. After all, it is human nature to believe that a problem is temporary, that it will be fixed, and that the stock price will recover. Unfortunately, it frequently doesn't work out that way. Bad news seems to beget more bad news, as was the case in recent years with companies like Laidlaw, Geac, Moore Corp., Loewen Group, Xerox, and many others. Of course, I'm not talking about minor hiccups here, such as a short-term profit warning or a stock falling a few cents below analysts' expectations on earnings per share. It's the major setbacks that are of concern, such as a surprise dividend cut, a dramatic change in company policy, or an environmental disaster. In such cases, you're usually better off to take your losses and get out. Always remember: Better a small loss now than a big loss later.

Of course, you should never sell a security outside a registered plan without considering the tax implications. You may be about to trigger a capital gain (or loss) and you should be aware of that so that you can prepare for the filing of your next return. There won't be any tax withheld on a capital gain, so if you sell for a profit, put some of the proceeds aside in a special account so that the money will be available when the Canada Customs and Revenue Agency claims its share.

Guideline #3: Learn from Your Mistakes

Nobody gets it right all the time. You will make mistakes and invest in losers. Everyone does, and you aren't immune. Accept that as a given going in. It will make you more realistic and temper your disappointment when you do lose.

When that happens, learn from the experience. The natural inclination will be to turn away, to try to forget about the bad call as quickly as possible because it's painful.

Overcome that tendency. Analyze the mistake and understand why it happened. Perhaps there was nothing you could have done to prevent it – how could any ordinary investor have known that the FBI was going to swoop in on the Pennsylvania headquarters of YBM Magnex on suspicion of Russian mafia connections, causing the stock to crash and, eventually, to be delisted? But in other cases, maybe you could have foreseen the problem. Perhaps you even had an inclination to sell but didn't act on it until it was too late. Maybe it was a security you invested in because of bad advice from someone. You'll know better than to listen to that person next time. That's the kind of lesson you need to take away from such experiences. However hurtful it may be, if it stops you from making the mistake again it will have been worth it.

Guideline #4: Measure Your Progress Realistically

There will be some years when your investments perform astoundingly well. There will be other years when they do poorly. That's all par for the course. You shouldn't allow yourself to become too ebullient during the good times or despondent during the bad periods.

What you do need to establish is a realistic means for measuring your progress. How can you tell if you are doing well or doing poorly over the long haul?

One way is to do what the pros do – compare your results against established benchmarks. For example, you might look at the combined performance of all your Canadian stocks and equity mutual funds in a year and compare the result to the performance of the TSE 300 Index. If you did better than the Index, you did well – even if you lost money. That would simply mean the Index lost more that year and that your portfolio management worked to protect your capital.

For U.S. stocks and equity funds, the S&P 500 Index is a solid benchmark, as is the Wilshire 5000. For your bonds or bond funds, use the Scotia Capital Markets Universe Bond Index. For your tech stocks, use the Nasdaq Composite. No matter what you invest in, there is a credible benchmark available against which you can assess your performance.

If all that seems to complicated, then use a more simple approach. At the beginning of each year, establish a target range for the rate of return you anticipate over the next 12 months. Base this on the assets in your portfolio, your risk level, and the general state of the markets. For example, you may set a target of 8 to 10 percent for the coming 12 months. At the end of that time, see how you did. If you fell short, try to determine why. Was it the general market, or were your picks not as good as they should have been?

I stress again, be realistic. If, over time, your portfolio produces an average annual return of 10 percent or better, you're doing very well. If you're coming in below 6 percent, take another look at your holdings. You can do better than that.

Finding Good Advisors

I told this story in one of my earlier books but I like it so much I want to retell it here in case you missed it. I first came across it in a newsletter published by the U.S. brokerage firm of Rosenthal & Company.

The scene is London in 1524 – a time when a poorly educated population was easily misled by the hocus-pocus of soothsayers and astrologers. For some reason, these false visionaries collectively decided that the Thames was about to overflow its banks in a great flood that would devastate a large section of the city. This prophecy was spread among an increasingly terrified populace, with the predicted ravages of the roiling waters growing more frightening with each retelling. The date for this terrible disaster was fixed as February 1, 1524.

As you might expect, people began to flee the city as the date for the Great Flood grew nearer. Accounts from the time tell of roads jammed with refugees and carts piled high with family possessions. Many of those who stayed behind took the precaution of having a boat available – just in case.

Finally, the terrible day came. Those who remained in the city watched the Thames closely for the first signs of rising water. But nothing happened. The placid river continued to flow at its normal pace, totally oblivious to the doleful forecasts of its wrath. Sheepishly, the townspeople who had fled to the hills began to trickle back, and, in time, normal life resumed.

Now, you would think that the reaction of ordinary Londoners would have been to toss the prophets of doom into the same river they had said would wreak such havoc. But the astrologers managed to wriggle off the hook by claiming they had rechecked their calculations and found that they were, in fact, correct. It was just their timing that was slightly off – the Great Flood would take place in 1624, not 1524. A small error, but of course understandable when one is interpreting the universal movements of the stars. Now, for our next prediction …

I like that story because it says so much about relying on other people to guide your decisions. It's not just good advice that you want. It's good advice *at the right time*. It's not much help to know that a Great Flood is going to occur or that the stock market is going to drop. Both of those things will happen sometime; you need to know *when*. No one's perfect, but the best advisors are those who can at least make educated guesses that aren't 100 years off the mark.

Which brings me to the main point of this section. Every investor needs some good, trusted advisors – people who, as Alexander Pope said, will not only provide guidance but will also share your investing philosophy and who may even, in time, become friends.

What advisors do you need? Here's a list of possibilities. You shouldn't require the services of all of them, but you may need more than one.

Financial Planners

Financial planners can provide assistance in a variety of ways, from minimizing your taxes to setting up and managing an investment portfolio. The best of them can combine most or all of these services into one package, which can save you both time and expense. However, before you entrust all your financial requirements to one person, be sure that he or she is fully qualified in every area that concerns you. Many planners specialize in one specific field, such as estate planning. They may offer other services as well, but those may be limited. For example, their investment sales license may allow them to deal only in mutual funds, which means you would have to go elsewhere if you wanted to trade in stocks or bonds as well. In other cases, the advisor may be able to sell only products offered by a specific company, which means his or her advice will be limited to those offerings.

As with all professions, there are good and bad financial planners. The business is unregulated in most provinces, so you have to use common sense and sound judgment when selecting someone to work with.

Occasionally, you will read stories in the media about planners who bilked their clients out of large amounts of money. Unfortunately, such things occasionally happen – no profession has a monopoly on honesty. But such incidents are rare. Most planners are decent, hard-working business people who know their field and who recognize that the best way to build long-term client relationships is to provide sound, conservative financial guidance.

I often get questions about how to go about choosing a good financial advisor. Here are two suggestions:

First, talk to friends and relatives. Ask if they use an advisor. If so, do they recommend the person, and how strongly? This should be your primary source of information.

If this course doesn't prove fruitful, check out the Web site of the Canadian Association of Financial Planners (**www.cafp.org**). They have a facility that provides you with the names of their members in your area who meet your criteria in terms of fields of expertise, method of payment, and so on. Arrange interviews with three or four of them. At the interviews, discuss your portfolio and your needs, ask what services they would provide, ask about their investment approach, discuss their fees, and see if you are on the same wavelength with the person. Then ask them to send a written proposal for your consideration, including client references. Check out the references, evaluate the responses you get, and make your decision.

Some planners charge by the hour for their services, while others are compensated by the commissions they receive when you purchase financial products through them. You will also find a growing number of planners who charge fees based on assets under management.

A few points to remember:

1. Some planners believe strongly in the use of leveraging (borrowing money) to build personal wealth. Ask prospective candidates for their views on this before you sign on.

2. Many planners will try to persuade you to commit all your assets to them. Resist these entreaties. Tell the planner you will allocate perhaps a quarter of your investments to his or her care. You will decide about the rest later, on the basis of performance.

3. You will find some financial planners who will recommend no-load funds if they are appropriate. The majority of those who earn their income by commissions will not do so, however. Ask about the policy of the person(s) you are considering.

Tax Consultants

Tax advising is a role that can be filled by an accountant, a financial planner, or a tax lawyer. I do not recommend relying on a tax preparation firm, as most of them are staffed by people with minimal training.

Even though you may want to seek professional help, I suggest that you devote some time to learning about the tax system, developing your own tax-saving strategies, and preparing your own return. You're the best person to look after your own interests; no one else cares about your money as much as you do.

However, it's a good idea to have a qualified expert review your plan and check your tax return once it's completed. He or she may come up with some wrinkles you hadn't thought of – which may both save you some money and give you new tax-saving ideas.

In choosing your advisor on taxes, look for three assets. First, he or she should have a thorough knowledge of the tax regulations. You'd be amazed how many so-called "experts" don't have it. Perhaps that's not so surprising considering the complexity of our tax system, but if you start finding you know more than your tax advisor does in certain areas, it's time to consider looking for a new expert.

The second asset you want is practical knowledge of how the Canada Customs and Revenue Agency (CCRA) works. You need someone who can say with authority, "The regulations are ambiguous on that point, but in practice CCRA will accept the claim if...." Accurate advice of that sort can save you thousands of dollars.

Finally, you're looking for honesty. Most of us really don't want to cheat on our taxes. We simply want to organize our financial affairs in such a way as to legally pay as little as possible. So unless you're willing to run the risk of an audit, you don't want a tax advisor who's going to be constantly encouraging you to push the envelope to the limit. In any event, such people are increasingly hard to find now that the CCRA has brought in regulations that will punish not only overly aggressive taxpayers who get caught, but their advisors as well.

Brokers

Many people think of brokers purely in terms of stocks. The reality is that they're a source for the full range of investment vehicles, including bonds, mortgage-backed securities, mutual funds, tax shelters, and options. Some financial planners now also offer this full range of products and services, but not all.

There are basically two types of brokers: full service and discount. The latter includes the Internet brokerage houses that have appeared in recent years, such as E*TRADE. There is no doubt that discount brokers are less expensive for most transactions. They will charge lower commissions for stock purchases and for load mutual funds. However, if you buy a no-load mutual fund through a discount broker, you'll pay a fee either at the time of purchase or when you sell. If you want to save money, buy no-load funds directly from the sponsoring company.

Because of the cost savings, many investors have turned to discount brokers in recent years, and I am constantly asked to recommend the best firm. The situation is so fluid that I prefer not to do that; however, an excellent source for such information is the annual On-Line Brokerage Report published by Quicken.ca. You can find it at **www.quicken.ca/eng/stocks/brokers/ranking/intro**.

Before you decide to go the discount broker route, however, let me caution you that this is something of a you-get-what-you-pay-for situation. Discount brokers are essentially order takers. They will process your buy or sell order over the phone or online, execute the transaction, and send you a confirmation. Don't expect them to provide advice about your decision, to alert you to IPOs (if you're interested in them), or to handle more sophisticated transactions. That said, the intense competition has forced discount brokerage firms to upgrade their services. Most now provide at least a minimum level of research, and in some cases more than that. Some provide high-quality online portfolio management tools, capable of complex tracking functions and calculations. So cost should not be the sole criterion for choosing a discount broker. Find out what else he or she can do for you before making a decision.

Why choose a more expensive full-service broker if the discounters are offering so much?

Because in my experience, a *good* broker (and I stress the adjective) is perhaps the most valuable financial partner you can have. A good broker will recommend securities that are well suited to your needs. He or she will hold your hand (figuratively) during tough markets and perhaps dissuade you from ill-advised panic selling. A good broker will tell you when to sell and will be a sounding board for your ideas. (One broker endeared himself to me early in my investing career when he refused to buy a stock I wanted and told me that if gambling was my passion I should go to Vegas. The stock subsequently tanked.) A good broker will provide you with solid research materials (I have one who e-mails his company's latest research reports every morning), who can intelligently discuss the state of the market, and who understands the importance of timing (remember the Thames flood). I firmly believe that to operate in the financial world without a trusted, full-service broker or financial planner to advise you is akin to flying blind. If you choose to proceed without one, you had better be very sure of your investment ability.

Think Like a Millionaire

If you are going to be a millionaire, you have to start thinking like one. In some cases, that will require a change in mindset, although hopefully not a radical one. There is nothing inherently mysterious about the way most millionaires think. In fact, you may find some of their thought processes to be rather mundane. That's because they are. Yes, there are some who are born to wealth and therefore have a tendency to take their good fortune for granted, as if it were some inherent right. They can often be insufferable. But they're the minority. Most of today's millionaires are just ordinary people who have acquired wealth through their talent, or by saving and investing wisely, or by a stroke of luck such as winning a lottery. They tend to come from middle-income backgrounds and they don't stand out in a crowd. The next millionaire you meet probably doesn't live in Beverly Hills or drive a Rolls. In fact, you probably won't even suspect he or she is a millionaire. That's one of the characteristics of the way most modern millionaires think: They don't flaunt it. There's a certain amount of self-preservation in that, of course – the wealthy don't want to make themselves targets for criminals. But there's also a recognition that the wealthy are no longer some kind of noble class. We've come a long way from the days when the lord of the manor was a world apart from the peasants who tilled the land.

That is not to say the wealthy aren't privileged. Of course they are. How could it be different in a world where 80 percent of the population live in substandard housing, half suffer from malnutrition, and only one person in 100 owns a computer? But privilege should not be synonymous with pomposity. The boor who berates waiters or complains about standing in line or tells a street beggar to get a job needs a wake-up call. Such people should be made to sit at a desk and write 1,000 times this statistic that was sent to me by a friend on New Year's Day of 2001: "If you have money in the bank, in your wallet, or even spare change in a dish, you are among the top 8 percent of the world's wealthy." Sobering thought, isn't it?

With that in mind, here are some of the most important character traits a millionaire should have in this 21st century.

Humility

Millionaires are incredibly fortunate people. Yes, you may have worked your butt off and made great sacrifices to get there. And yes, you should take personal satisfaction from your achievement. But keep your ego in check. If you start to become overly impressed with your status, ask yourself this question: Could I have done this if I had been born to an undernourished mother in Sudan or in a yurt on the wind-swept plains of Mongolia? That's about as fast a lesson in humility as you'll get.

Realism

Never forget that wealth is fleeting. You will be allowed to enjoy it for only so long. Hopefully, it will be for the rest of your natural life, but if you are careless with your money you could fritter it away without even being aware of it, until one morning, you wake up to discover your car has been repossessed and the bank is about to sell your house out from under you. It has happened and it will happen again. Most wealthy people understand this risk. That's why they are careful with their money; the image of the bored millionaire lighting a cigar with a hundred dollar bill is a stereotype that should be relegated to the trash can.

Enthusiasm

If wealth doesn't enhance your love of life, what good is it? Use your money. Have some fun. Do some of the things you have always dreamed about. Ever since I began my working career, I dreamed of one day owning a home by the sea where I could look up from my typewriter (those were the days before computers) and recharge my mind watching the waves roll in. It took more than 30 years, but we finally achieved that goal when we bought a winter home on the shore of Estero Bay in southwest Florida. The joy that we experience as we watch the dolphins swim by the seawall, laugh at the pelicans as they plummet like dive bombers in search of a fish dinner, and marvel at the great flocks of white ibis that fill the sky at sunset as they return to their nesting island make the years of work and sacrifice more than worthwhile.

That kind of renewed zest for living should be an integral part of your millionaire experience. As I have repeatedly said, money is only a means to an end, not an end in itself. Don't lose sight of that.

Responsibility

Although you should enjoy your wealth, you should not assume that the only purpose you now have in life is to find pleasure wherever it is to be had. Just because you're rich doesn't give you a right to be irresponsible. On the contrary, it imposes responsibility upon you. Because you are a success, your family and friends will tend to look upon you as a role model. The image you convey will be one they will try to emulate – and how you will be remembered. What do you want that to be? As a person who attained wealth and used it to buy cocaine or to break up a family unit? As a miser who became obsessed with money to the exclusion of all else? As a spendthrift? Or as someone who used wealth to enhance the life of his or her family, to make possible things that might not otherwise have been such as a college education, to assist the less fortunate in the community? Does this sound Pollyannaish? Perhaps it is. But doesn't it also sound like a satisfying way to live and a fine legacy to leave behind? I certainly think so.

Climb the Hill

There's a small ravine near our home where I regularly take the dog for a walk. At one point in our twice-daily journey, the trail runs up a steep little hill that rises out of a valley created by a creek. In the winter, the path often becomes icy. Getting up it can be extremely difficult, especially if you try to take it slowly. Your boots won't grip, and you slip and start to slide backwards.

One cold morning, when the temperature was below freezing, I discovered how to beat the hill. I didn't try to go up cautiously. Instead, I approached it at a brisk pace and the momentum kept me going all the way to the top.

That's what you need to establish now – momentum. You need to put your plan into motion and get it moving forward at an ever accelerating pace.

Remember, planning is important but action is essential. You must now make the moves required to take your plan off the written page. That doesn't mean the planning phase is over; in fact it never is. There will always be some adjustments needed along the way. But you have to make a start and now is the time to do it. Delay is defeat. You will *not* be defeated in this quest. You *will* achieve your goal. *You* will be a millionaire.

It is not a dream. It is not impossible. All it takes is for you to make it a reality.

Start climbing that hill!

appendix A

Net Worth Calculator

Your net worth is the total value of all your assets less any outstanding liabilities. Knowing your current net worth is a necessary step towards accumulating $1 million. It gives you a financial snapshot of your present situation and helps you set priorities for debt reduction and investment. Review your net worth position annually to see if you're on track to achieve your goal within the allotted time frame.

You may wish to make some photocopies of the worksheet that follows before you start so you can update your position in the future. The numbers to include on the asset side should represent the value of each item if it were sold today – not what you originally paid.

Here are some additional pointers to help you.

- *Registered assets.* Include here the current value of any holdings you have in registered plans at their market value today.

- *Non-registered liquid assets.* This category consists of investments that can normally be converted to cash reasonably easily, although not always at their face value. Use current market values in all cases. Use updated bank statements, brokerage reports, and mutual fund statements as your information sources.

- *Non-registered non-liquid assets.* In this group, list the current value of any assets that are not easily convertible to cash. Real estate is included here because the sale of property can sometimes take several months. Show the full current market value of any property you own; outstanding mortgages will be deducted in the Liabilities section. Limited partnerships are also listed here, as there is usually no ready market for such units if you need to sell. Business interests should include the value of your ownership position in any company not publicly traded. Vehicles, collectibles, furnishings, and the like should be listed on the basis of *how much they could be sold for today if you needed to raise cash.*

- *Liabilities.* List the current amounts outstanding on all loans. This will help establish priorities for the debt reduction part of your retirement plan.

If you're married, show the total value of the assets and liabilities of both you and your spouse in all cases.

NET WORTH CALCULATOR

DATE:	ASSETS
TYPE	**CURRENT VALUE**

Registered

RRSPs	_____
Employer pension plans	_____
Deferred profit-sharing plans	_____
RRIFs	_____
Subtotal #1	_____

Non-Registered (liquid)

Cash and equivalent

Savings/chequing accounts	_____
Short-term deposits	_____
Savings certificates	_____
Canada Savings Bonds	_____
Treasury bills	_____
Money market funds	_____
Foreign currencies	_____
Other	_____
Subtotal #2	_____

Income

Bonds	_____
Mortgages	_____
Income mutual funds	_____
Mortgage-backed securities	_____
Guaranteed investment certificates (GICs)	_____
Preferred shares	_____
Royalty trusts and REITs	_____
Other	_____
Subtotal #3	_____

Growth

Stocks _____

Equity mutual funds (Canadian) _____

Equity mutual funds (international) _____

Gold and precious metals funds _____

Other _____

Subtotal #4 _____

Subtotal # 5 (Add subtotals #2, #3, and #4) _____

Non-Registered (non-liquid)

Principal residence _____

Recreational property _____

Income property _____

Limited partnerships _____

Business interests _____

Vehicles _____

Boats _____

Collectibles _____

Furnishings/appliances _____

Jewellery _____

Silver _____

Clothing _____

Other _____

Subtotal #6 _____

Total Assets

(Add subtotals #1, #5, and #6) _____

LIABILITIES

Short-Term Loans (non-deductible)

Credit card balances _____

Personal lines of credit _____

Demand loans _____

Instalment loans _____

RRSP loans _____

Other _____

Subtotal #7 _____

Short-Term Loans (deductible)

Student loans _____

Margin accounts _____

Investment loans _____

Business loans _____

Deductible PLC loans _____

Other _____

Subtotal #8 _____

Long-Term Loans (non-deductible)

Mortgage (principal residence) _____

Mortgage (recreational property) _____

Other _____

Subtotal #9 _____

Long-Term Loans (deductible)

Mortgage (income property) _____

Limited partnership loans _____

Other _____

Subtotal #10 _____

Total Liabilities

(Add subtotals #7 through #10) _____

Net Worth

(Subtract total liabilities from total assets) _____

appendix B

Future Value of Investments

Future Value of Present Investments

The tables that follow can be used to project the future value of current investments that you own, both inside and outside a registered plan.

Before you begin, you must decide on which nominal rate of return you wish to use. This is the projected average annual rate of return on your money, before taxes or inflation. For investments held outside a registered plan (RRSP, etc.), you should then make an adjustment to reflect the taxes that will be assessed. For example, if you are projecting a 6 percent nominal return that you expect will be received mainly as interest, you may want to use a 3 percent projection since interest income will be taxed at your marginal rate. However, if you are projecting an 8 percent nominal return that you expect will be mostly in the form of capital gains, you may decide to use a 6 percent projection, reflecting the lower tax rate on capital gains. Of course, income earned inside a registered plan is exempt from tax until it is withdrawn. If you want to make a further allowance for inflation to project actual purchasing power, deduct another two percentage points from your nominal rate.

Do a separate projection for your registered and non-registered investments, using the time frame that is most appropriate to your situation.

For example, if you currently have $10,000 in an RRSP and you use a 20-year time frame with an 8 percent annual return, your RRSP will be worth $46,600 at the end of that time ($10,000 × 4.66). Note that this calculation does not take into account any future contributions.

FUTURE VALUE OF PRESENT INVESTMENTS

	FUTURE VALUE OF $1 AT					
Years	3%	4%	5%	6%	8%	10%
5	1.16	1.22	1.28	1.34	1.47	1.61
10	1.34	1.48	1.63	1.79	2.16	2.59
15	1.56	1.80	2.08	2.40	3.17	4.18
20	1.81	2.19	2.65	3.21	4.66	6.73
25	2.09	2.67	3.39	4.29	6.85	10.83
30	2.43	3.24	4.32	5.74	10.06	17.45
35	2.81	3.95	5.52	7.69	14.79	28.10
40	3.26	4.80	7.04	10.29	21.72	45.26

Future Value of Ongoing Investments

The next table allows you to project the future value of your ongoing savings, using various rates of return. See the previous section for guidance on how to choose a rate of return that's appropriate for you.

This table is constructed on the assumption that the amount you put aside for savings and investing will increase by 10 percent each year and that the deposits are made at the start of each year. I suggest you do a separate calculation for registered and non-registered investments.

FUTURE VALUE OF ONGOING INVESTMENTS 1

	FUTURE VALUE OF $1 PER YEAR, INCREASING BY 10% ANNUALLY, AT					
Years	3%	4%	5%	6%	8%	10%
5	6.64	6.83	7.02	7.22	7.62	8.05
10	18.39	19.30	20.26	21.28	23.48	25.94
15	38.54	41.19	44.06	47.19	54.27	62.66
20	72.41	78.63	85.56	93.29	111.59	116.20
25	128.62	98.35	156.42	173.39	215.26	270.87
30	221.04	246.24	275.68	310.21	398.88	523.48
35	372.10	418.71	474.31	541.03	719.12	983.59
40	617.96	701.28	802.60	926.80	1,270.88	1,810.37

The next table projects the future value of annual contributions, but does not include any annual escalations.

FUTURE VALUE OF ONGOING INVESTMENTS 2

	FUTURE VALUE OF $1 PER YEAR, ASSUMING NO ANNUAL INCREMENT, AT					
Years	3%	4%	5%	6%	8%	10%
5	5.47	5.63	5.80	5.98	6.34	6.72
10	11.81	12.49	13.21	13.97	15.65	17.53
15	19.16	20.82	22.66	24.67	29.32	34.95
20	27.68	30.97	34.72	38.99	49.42	63.00
25	37.55	43.31	50.11	58.16	78.95	108.18
30	49.00	58.33	69.76	83.80	122.35	180.94
35	62.28	76.60	94.84	118.12	186.10	298.13
40	77.66	98.83	126.84	164.05	279.78	486.85

Index